Scottish Philosophy after the Enlightenment

Edinburgh Studies in Scottish Philosophy

Series Editor: James A. Harris, University of St Andrews

Scottish Philosophy Through the Ages

This new series will cover the full range of Scottish philosophy over five centuries – from the medieval period through the Reformation and Enlightenment periods, to the nineteenth and early twentieth centuries.

The series will publish innovative studies on major figures and themes. It also aims to stimulate new work in less intensively studied areas, by a new generation of philosophers and intellectual historians. The books will combine historical sensitivity and philosophical substance which will serve to cast new light on the rich intellectual inheritance of Scottish philosophy.

Editorial Advisory Board
Angela Coventry, University of Portland, Oregon
Fonna Forman, University of California, San Diego
Alison McIntyre, Wellesley College
Alexander Broadie, University of Glasgow
Remy Debes, University of Memphis
John Haldane, University of St Andrews and Baylor University, Texas

Books available
Adam Smith and Rousseau: Ethics, Politics, Economics, edited by Maria Pia Paganelli, Dennis C. Rasmussen and Craig Smith
Thomas Reid and the Problem of Secondary Qualities, Christopher A. Shrock
Hume's Sceptical Enlightenment, Ryu Susato
Imagination in Hume's Philosophy: The Canvas of the Mind, Timothy M. Costelloe
Essays on Hume, Smith and the Scottish Enlightenment, Christopher J. Berry
Adam Ferguson and the Idea of Civil Society: Moral Science in the Scottish Enlightenment, Craig Smith
Hume's Scepticism: Pyrrhonian and Academic, Peter S. Fosl
Scottish Philosophy after the Enlightenment, Gordon Graham

Books forthcoming
Eighteenth-Century Scottish Aesthetics: Not Just a Matter of Taste, Rachel Zuckert
Thomas Reid and the Defence of Duty, James Foster

www.edinburghuniversitypress.com/series/essp

Scottish Philosophy after the Enlightenment

Gordon Graham

EDINBURGH
University Press

Edinburgh University Press is one of the leading university presses in the UK. We publish academic books and journals in our selected subject areas across the humanities and social sciences, combining cutting-edge scholarship with high editorial and production values to produce academic works of lasting importance. For more information visit our website: edinburghuniversitypress.com

© Gordon Graham, 2022, 2024

Edinburgh University Press Ltd
The Tun – Holyrood Road
12(2f) Jackson's Entry
Edinburgh EH8 8PJ

First published in hardback by Edinburgh University Press 2022

Typeset in 11/13 Adobe Sabon by
IDSUK (DataConnection) Ltd, and
printed and bound by CPI Group (UK) Ltd,
Croydon, CR Y Y

A CIP record for this book is available from the British Library

ISBN 978 1 3995 0090 6 (hardback)
ISBN 978 1 3995 0091 3 (paperback)
ISBN 978 1 3995 0092 0 (webready PDF)
ISBN 978 1 3995 0093 7 (epub)

The right of Gordon Graham to be identified as the author of this work has been asserted in accordance with the Copyright, Designs and Patents Act 1988, and the Copyright and Related Rights Regulations 2003 (SI No. 2498).

Contents

Preface and Acknowledgements   vi
Series Editor's Introduction   viii
A Note on Women in Scottish Philosophy: Mrs Oliphant   ix
A Chronology of Scottish Philosophy after the Enlightenment   xv

1. An Autobiographical Prologue   1
2. Sir William Hamilton and the Revitalisation of Scottish Philosophy   20
3. James Frederick Ferrier and the Course of Scottish Philosophy   48
4. Psychology and Moral Philosophy: Alexander Bain   75
5. Thomas Carlyle and the Philosophy of Rhetoric   95
6. Hegelianism and its Critics   113
7. Scottish Philosophy's Progress   128
8. Religion, Evolution and Scottish Philosophy   147
9. The Gifford Lectures and the Re-affirmation of Theism: Alexander Campbell Fraser   167
10. The Culmination of Scottish Philosophy: A. S. Pringle-Pattison   188
11. John Macmurray and the Self as Agent   206

Bibliography   231
Index   241

Preface and Acknowledgements

This book is the result of several years of reading and reflection in an area of the history of philosophy that has generally gone almost entirely unexplored. For this reason, it cannot address an established readership – since no such readership exists. Accordingly, it seemed best to present the results of my reading and reflection in a series of free-standing essays, each with a distinctive focus that may catch the newcomer's attention. Written on the reasonable assumption that readers interested in philosophy are likely to know little or nothing of the period, the style is sometimes rather elementary. While each essay is meant to be independent of the rest, they all touch on larger and recurring themes, even those that are focused on a single philosopher. Inevitably, the relative independence of each essay means that the same material recurs in several different chapters. I have tried to avoid straightforward repetition, and noted interconnections between chapters here and there. But the nature of the subject matter puts a limit on how far this is possible. The opening essay is autobiographical and relates the story of how I came to study nineteenth-century Scottish philosophy in the first place. In telling it, I hope very much that I have avoided any self-indulgent element. The second essay, on Sir William Hamilton, is a substantially revised amalgamation of two previously published essays. An earlier version of the essay on religion and evolution appeared in the *Journal of Scottish Philosophy*. A version of the chapter on Thomas Carlyle was circulated in the 'Occasional Papers' of the Carlyle Society. Chapter 9 reuses a small amount of material from my contribution on the Gifford Lectures to the three-volume *History of Scottish Theology* edited by David Fergusson and Mark W. Elliot. The remaining material is new, and several of the essays, especially Chapters 8, 9 and 10, are an attempt to make good what I now see to be important omissions from *Scottish Philosophy in the Nineteenth and Twentieth Centuries* (Oxford University Press, 2015).

The book might be called an 'act of piety', in the proper and best sense. That is to say, it is the acknowledgement of a debt owed, and a tribute due, to historical forebears who are at risk of being neglected. In this connection it is a matter of particular satisfaction to me that Henry Calderwood, Alexander Campbell Fraser, Thomas Chalmers and Andrew Seth Pringle-Pattison all lived a few streets away from where I live now.

I gladly acknowledge the interest and support that this initially unpromising project received from my good friend David A. S. Fergusson, formerly Professor of Divinity at the University of Edinburgh, and now Regius Professor of Divinity at the University of Cambridge. I am grateful to my daughter Kirsty for assistance with the bibliography, and to my daughter Lindsay for compiling the index.

Series Editor's Introduction

Philosophy has been taught and written in Scotland since the fifteenth century. The purpose of this series is to publish new scholarly work on any and every aspect of the history of Scottish philosophising, from John Mair to John Macmurray. Scotland's most celebrated philosophical achievements remain those produced by Hume, Smith, Reid and their contemporaries in the eighteenth century. It is, however, no longer possible to believe that the Scottish Enlightenment had no indigenous roots. Nor is it possible to believe that there was no significant philosophy produced in Scotland once the Enlightenment was over.

There is no single set of intellectual concerns distinctive of and unique to philosophy as it has been taught and written in Scotland. Historical study of Scottish philosophy must be, to a significant extent, study of the changing nature of philosophy itself. It should be open to the idea that the preoccupations and methods of philosophers today may not be those of philosophers in the past. It should also concern itself with philosophical connections and intellectual affinities between Scotland, England, Ireland and the rest of Europe, and, where appropriate, between Scotland and America.

James Harris

A Note on Women in Scottish Philosophy: Mrs Oliphant

The history of Scottish philosophy contains virtually no reference to women. The explanation is not far to seek. Scottish philosophy over several centuries was almost exclusively university based, and women could not attend universities. It was not until late in the nineteenth century that this changed. In 1876 St Andrews became the first university in Britain to allow women to be students, though initially this was for the LLA (Lady Literate in Arts diploma) rather than the MA (Master of Arts degree). In 1889 the Universities (Scotland) Act finally made it possible to admit women on the same basis as men. The first women permitted to take a degree graduated in 1892, but the first woman to teach philosophy in a Scottish university was not appointed until very much later.

Surprisingly perhaps, despite this exclusion, women occasionally contributed to philosophical debate as writers. Deborah Boyle has uncovered two notable cases. Elizabeth Hamilton's *Memoirs of Modern Philosophers*, published in 1800, can be read as a philosophical criticism of Godwin, and Lady Mary Shepherd's two books – *An Essay upon the Relation of Cause and Effect* (1824) and *Essays on the Perception of an External Universe* (1827) – engaging as they do with Hume and Reid, among others, are unmistakably philosophical works.[1] However, as Leslie Stephen once remarked, it is a mistake to suppose that the eighteenth century ended with the year 1800. So while Hamilton (1758–1816) and Shepherd (1777–1847) lived into the nineteenth century, they were Enlightenment rather than post-Enlightenment thinkers. I

---

[1] See *Lady Mary Shepherd: Selected Writings*, edited with an introduction by Deborah Boyle, Imprint Academic, 2018.

am not aware of any nineteenth-century women comparable to Hamilton and Shepherd who engaged directly in the philosophical debates with which the essays in this book are concerned.

There is, however, one partial and important exception – Margaret Oliphant. Margaret Wilson, always known on her publications as 'Mrs Oliphant', was born in East Lothian in 1828. She left Scotland at the age of thirteen, and though she married a Scottish cousin – Frank Oliphant – and visited Scotland on many subsequent occasions, she was never resident there again. While she lived the larger part of her life in Windsor and was very widely travelled, she nonetheless retained a keen interest in things Scottish, and in many respects exhibited a distinctively Scottish outlook throughout her life. Her career as a writer began before she was married, with the publication of her first novel in 1849. In 1851, on a visit to Edinburgh with her mother, she attended a literary event and met William Blackwood, brother of John Blackwood, publisher of *Blackwood's Edinburgh Magazine*.[2] This meeting began a connection with both the magazine and the publishing house that lasted to the end of Oliphant's life.

In 1859, at the age of thirty-one, and pregnant with her fourth child (one having died), she was widowed. As a consequence, for almost forty years she was under relentless pressure to earn money through writing, to provide for an extended family in the slightly extravagant lifestyle for which she had a taste. Under this necessity, Oliphant proved capable of writing with astonishing speed and fluency, and produced publications on a scale so prolific and across so many genres as almost to beggar belief. By the time of her death she had authored several works of history, three travel guides, five substantial biographies involving original research, the volume on Dress in Macmillan's *Art at Home* series, and, most amazingly, 100 novels, many of them of a literary quality equal to or better than those of her contemporary Mrs Gaskill (who wrote eight). Her five popular 'Carlingford' novels are comparable to Anthony Trollope's Barsetshire series.

---

[2] From its creation in 1817 until 1905, this publication was entitled *Blackwood's Edinburgh Magazine*, and thereafter, until it ceased publication in 1980, simply *Blackwood's Magazine*. But even in the earlier years it was often referred to by the simpler title, which I will use for convenience.

In addition to all this, for over four decades Mrs Oliphant was a regular contributor to '*Maga*', the insiders' name for *Blackwood's Magazine*, and wrote dozens of lengthy articles on a vast range of subjects. Only two of these essays are directly related to philosophy, though each of them runs to almost thirty two-columned pages. 'The Philosopher' (January 1869) is about Berkeley, and 'The Sceptic' (June 1869) is about Hume. Both are contributions to her series of articles 'Historical Sketches of the Reign of George II' and they are primarily biographical. In the first, Mrs Oliphant includes this disclaimer: 'The present writer has no pretensions to touch the history of philosophy as a philosopher should. It is with the eyes of the outside spectator, or, as the subject of this sketch expresses it, the vulgar, that we regard its strange, long-continued, unproductive toil' (Oliphant 1869a: 3). The essay on Hume ranges across the full extent of Hume's life and writings, with a particular focus on the end of Part One of the *Treatise*, where Hume, faced with deep metaphysical perplexity, turns to dining and backgammon as a solution. For Oliphant, unlike most philosophers, the 'problem' in which she is explicitly interested is not how to make this transition coherent, but how to understand it psychologically. How can Hume's cheerful personality, taste for companionship, and gift for friendship be squared with 'the darkness in which his being was shrouded' by the sceptical conclusions he had reached? She concludes that Hume's contentedness is a consequence of his 'incapacity to understand the heights and depths of the soul, his indifference to his race, and the contempt for it that is involved in all his philosophy' (Oliphant 1869b: 690). But, she adds, 'we forget how superficial are his affections' because '[n]ever Christian fronted death more bravely, nor with a more peaceful calm' (691). She sees a parallel here with Hume's misleading physical appearance, quoting at length the description in which Lord Charlemont remarks on the impossibility of discovering 'the smallest trace of the faculties of his mind in the unmeaning features of his visage' (680).

Mrs Oliphant is markedly more sympathetic to Berkeley than to Hume, and this colours her attitude to their philosophical views. Moreover, it is evident that both these lengthy essays are highly dependent on secondary works, especially on G. H. Lewes's *Biographical History of Philosophy* (1846) and, in the case of Hume, on the somewhat gloomy biography published by Hill Burton (also in 1846). Still, it is no less clear that Mrs Oliphant is not parroting other people's opinions. She has a good understanding of the philosophical positions she discusses, as well as a strong sense of philosophy's importance. 'By general consent', she says, 'the title of a great philosopher has been allowed to represent the highest eminence to which the human mind can attain ... There is no intellectual occupation to which the common mind yields such unvarying reverence ... it is a kind of instinct in humanity (as appears) to respect philosophy' (Oliphant 1869a: 1). But she is more interested, we might say, in mentality than in mind, and in the thinker rather than the thought. Her insight in these matters is what makes her an accomplished novelist of some distinction, and it shows itself no less importantly in her biographies. That is where her value for the study of nineteenth-century Scottish philosophy is to be found.

Blackwood's was a major publisher of philosophy in Scotland. Between 1838 and 1847 a long series of influential philosophical articles by J. F. Ferrier appeared in *Blackwood's Magazine*, including the essays constituting his *Introduction to the Philosophy of Consciousness*, 240 pages in his *Collected Works*, and, posthumously, Sir William Hamilton's *Lectures on Metaphysics and Logic*. Among many other philosophy books, Blackwood's published Andrew Seth's *Scottish Philosophy*, John Tulloch's *Modern Theories of Philosophy and Religion*, Robert Flint's Baird Lectures on *Theism*, J. F. Ferrier's *Collected Works*, James Seth's *Study of Ethical Principles* and Alexander Campbell Fraser's Gifford Lectures on *The Philosophy of Theism*. Beginning in 1881, the series *Blackwood's Philosophical Classics* was launched, prompted, the general preface says, by 'a growing interest in Philosophy' which it declared to be 'one of the marked features of the present age'. The General Editor was William Knight at St Andrews and most of the volumes were written by Scottish professors, including John Caird, Robert Flint, Alexander Campbell Fraser and John Veitch.

Oliphant's connection with and work for Blackwood's thus made her wholly familiar with the world of philosophy and religion in nineteenth-century Scotland. This became especially apparent when, towards the end of her life, John Blackwood commissioned her to write the history of his family's business. Two volumes of *The Annals of a Publishing House: William Blackwood and his Sons* appeared in 1897. This represented two years' work on a vast quantity of correspondence. The volumes she completed recount the history of the firm from the birth of the first William Blackwood in 1776 to the death of Major William Blackwood in 1861, though she did not live to see their publication. She corrected the proofs of these two volumes on what turned out to be her deathbed.[3]

A few years previous to this, Blackwood's had also commissioned her to write a *Memoir of the Life of John Tulloch*, whom she had known well. This was published in 1888 and was one of several major biographies that throw light on the intellectual issues of the times. The first was *The Life of Edward Irving, Minister of the National Scotch Church London* (1862), which some critics think to be her finest work. After the memoir of John Tulloch she undertook a life of Thomas Chalmers, published by Methuen in 1893. All these volumes exhibit a remarkable facility for concentrated research, together with a striking degree of imaginative sympathetic insight into both the cultural context and the intellectual motivations of some of its most influential figures. Together with the *Annals*, these books provide an invaluable background against which to explore the philosophical, religious and educational questions that were of central concern to the Scottish philosophers of the nineteenth century. Mrs Oliphant's essays on Berkeley and Hume are still worth reading, but her most valuable contribution to the topics in this book is to be found in the *Annals* and the three biographies.

In this respect, and for the purposes of this book, her books are on a par with David Masson's two collections of essays – *Edinburgh Sketches and Memories* (1892) and *Memories of Two Cities* (1911). Masson was a student at Aberdeen and then Edinburgh at the time of Sir William Hamilton and Thomas Chalmers. After sixteen years as Professor of English Literature at University College London, he was appointed Professor of English and Rhetoric in Edinburgh, a position he held for over thirty years. He was a friend of Alexander Bain, Thomas Carlyle, John Stuart Mill and James Hutchison Stirling, among others, and George Davie makes extensive use of Masson's recollections and reflections in *The Democratic Intellect*. I have drawn on them to great advantage as well, and in the context of this note, it is appropriate to add that Masson was one of the leading protagonists for the admission of women to universities, and a supporter of the suffragette movement of which his wife and daughter were a part.

---

[3] The third projected volume was completed by someone else several years later.

One other significant woman author should be mentioned. *James Hutchison Stirling: His Life and Work*, published in 1912, is a biography written by his daughter, Amelia Hutchison Stirling. Amelia Stirling, to my knowledge, never published any academic work of her own, but the biography of her father reveals a natural aptitude for philosophical thinking. Her book is full of insight as well as information, and given her evident devotion to her father, it is remarkably free of any element of hagiography.

While there are, then, no women among the philosophers discussed in the essays that follow, the books by Oliphant, together with Stirling's biography of her father, greatly enrich the narrative by revealing intellectual and personal connections between diverse figures from the history of philosophy who might otherwise seem far apart. These include Alexander Bain, Thomas Carlyle, Thomas Chalmers, Ralph Waldo Emerson, Alexander Campbell Fraser, John Stuart Mill, James Hutchison Stirling and John Tulloch. The purpose of this note is to make apparent a debt that would otherwise remain hidden.

A Chronology of Scottish Philosophy after the Enlightenment

1796 Death of Thomas Reid
1802 First issue of the *Edinburgh Review* edited by Francis Jeffrey
1803 Death of James Beattie
1810 Appointment of Thomas Brown as Professor of Moral Philosophy at Edinburgh in conjunction with Dugald Stewart
1817 First issue of *Blackwood's Edinburgh Magazine*, a rival to the *Edinburgh Review*
1820 Death of Thomas Brown and posthumous publication of his *Lectures on the Philosophy of the Mind*; John Wilson (Christopher North) appointed Brown's successor in the Edinburgh Chair of Moral Philosophy in preference to Sir William Hamilton
1823 Thomas Chalmers appointed Professor of Moral Philosophy at St Andrews
1829–30 Publication of Hamilton's 'Philosophy of the Unconditioned' and 'Philosophy of Perception' in the *Edinburgh Review*
1836 Publication of Thomas Carlyle's *Sartor Resartus*; Sir William Hamilton appointed to the Chair of Logic and Metaphysics at the University of Edinburgh
1838–9 Publication of J. F. Ferrier's *Introduction to the Philosophy of Consciousness* in *Blackwood's Magazine*
1843 The 'Disruption', when the 'Free Church' led by Thomas Chalmers split from the Church of Scotland
1845 J. F. Ferrier appointed Professor of Moral Philosophy at St Andrews

1846	Publication of *Reid's Collected Works*, edited by Sir William Hamilton; opening of New College Edinburgh as an alternative 'Free' university
1852	Patrick MacDougall, Professor at New College, appointed to the Edinburgh Chair of Moral Philosophy in preference to Ferrier
1854	Publication of Ferrier's *Institutes of Metaphysic*
1855	John Tulloch appointed Principal of St Mary's College, St Andrews
1856	Death of Sir William Hamilton; A. C. Fraser, Professor at New College, appointed Hamilton's successor as Professor of Logic and Metaphysics in preference to Ferrier; pamphlet 'war' between Ferrier's supporters and his opponents led by John Cairns
1858	Parliament passes the reforming Universities of Scotland Act
1860	Alexander Bain appointed Regius Professor of Logic at the merger of King's and Marischal into the University of Aberdeen
1864	Death of Ferrier; Robert Flint succeeds him as Professor of Moral Philosophy at St Andrews in preference to T. H. Green
1865	Publication of J. H. Stirling's *The Secret of Hegel*; publication of J. S. Mill's *Examination of Sir William Hamilton*
1866	Edward Caird appointed Professor of Moral Philosophy at Glasgow; Thomas Carlyle elected Lord Rector of Edinburgh University; John Stuart Mill elected Lord Rector of St Andrews University
1868	Henry Calderwood appointed Professor of Moral Philosophy at Edinburgh in preference to J. H. Stirling and Robert Flint
1875	Publication of James McCosh's *The Scottish Philosophy*
1876	Alexander Bain establishes the journal *Mind* under the editorship of George Croom Robertson
1877	Publication of Edward Caird's *A Critical Account of the Philosophy of Kant*
1881	Death of Thomas Carlyle; *Blackwood's Philosophical Classics for English Readers* book series launched with William Knight, Professor of Moral Philosophy at St Andrews, as General Editor

1883	Publication of the Idealist 'Young Turks' agenda, *Essays in Philosophical Criticism*, edited by Andrew Seth and R. B. Haldane
1885	Publication of Andrew Seth's *Scottish Philosophy*; Adam Gifford's bequest establishes the Gifford Lectures at Aberdeen, Edinburgh, Glasgow and St Andrews
1888	Publication of Selby-Bigg's new edition of Hume's *Treatise*
1889	J. H. Stirling gives the first Gifford Lectures at Edinburgh on *Philosophy and Theology*
1891	Appointment of Andrew Seth to the Edinburgh Chair of Logic and Metaphysics in succession to Fraser; appointment of Henry Jones as Professor of Logic and Metaphysics at St Andrews in succession to Seth
1893	Edward Caird elected Master of Balliol College, Oxford and succeeded at Glasgow by Henry Jones
1894–6	Alexander Campbell Fraser's Gifford Lectures on the *Philosophy of Theism* at the University of Edinburgh
1901	Scots Philosophical Club established
1901–2	William James delivers his Edinburgh Gifford Lectures on *The Varieties of Religious Experience*
1903	Death of Alexander Bain; posthumous publication of his *Autobiography* the following year
1908	Death of Edward Caird
1912–13	Andrew Seth Pringle-Pattison's Gifford Lectures at Aberdeen on *The Idea of God in the Light of Recent Philosophy* (published 1917)
1950	Scots Philosophical Club establishes *The Philosophical Quarterly*
1953–4	John Macmurray's Gifford Lectures in Glasgow on *The Form of the Personal*
1961	Publication of George Davie's *The Democratic Intellect*

I

An Autobiographical Prologue

I

In 1968, at the age of nineteen, I left my native Ireland to become an undergraduate at the University of St Andrews. I knew very little about Scotland, and almost nothing about its universities. I had expected to attend Trinity College Dublin, but circumstances called for a change of plan. I chose St Andrews only because a history teacher I liked was a St Andrews graduate. For this reason, I applied to study History, with English, but discovered when I arrived that admission was to a Faculty, not a subject. This required me to take a year-long course in either 'Logic and Metaphysics' or 'Moral Philosophy', and the choice had to be made in those few minutes with an 'Adviser' that each entering student was allocated. 'Logic and Metaphysics' meant absolutely nothing to me. 'Moral Philosophy' was almost equally opaque, but I thought I had some understanding of the term 'moral', so I chose that. Within six weeks, happily, I had discovered that Moral Philosophy was the perfect subject for me. Consequently, I switched my attention and allegiance, took only one course in History, none at all in English, and in the end went on to devote no less than five decades to studying and teaching philosophy.

At the time, students could not study 'Philosophy' at St Andrews. There was no such honours degree, so having discovered this new intellectual enthusiasm, I had to take *joint* honours – 'Logic and Metaphysics & Moral Philosophy'. The two halves of this degree proceeded quite independently, with odd consequences occasionally. For instance, I studied Books 2 and 3 of Hume's *Treatise* a year before I studied Book 1. The division even found physical expression. Edgecliffe, a matching pair of fine Victorian houses on the Scores overlooking St Andrews Bay, housed two departments with separate entrances and separate classrooms. None of this struck me as strange, since I knew no different, but I was taught almost exclusively by Oxford-trained philosophers to whom, clearly, the division seemed absurd. Accordingly, there were occasional meetings when Bernard Mayo, the Professor of Moral Philosophy, solicited the support of students in his efforts to merge the two subjects and departments into one. Nothing came of this, though such a merger had taken place in Edinburgh some years before. But the exercise served to generate a sense that the study of philosophy in Scotland was, or at any rate had been, different from elsewhere. This left me wondering why it should be so, and whether it mattered.

The courses of study themselves threw no light on the question. I cannot remember the expression 'Scottish philosophy' ever being used. We studied Hume, but never Hutcheson or Reid, and there were only occasional mentions of Smith's 'impartial spectator'. George Davie was still teaching philosophy at Edinburgh then, but there was never any mention of 'the democratic intellect'. One event stands out. Bernard Mayo, who had not long come to St Andrews from the University of Birmingham, devoted his inaugural lecture to a nineteenth-century predecessor, J. F. Ferrier. His choice of subject, I seem to remember, was regarded as eccentric, and I never heard Ferrier mentioned again. The lecture was printed and distributed, but it was not published. Almost forty years later I reread it, realised how interesting and insightful it was, and published it in the *Journal of Scottish Philosophy* of which by then I was editor.

There was nothing in the syllabus of either department that could be called 'history of philosophy'. Texts were studied without any special reference to provenance or context. Hume, for instance, was treated as an important contributor to current debates in epistemology and metaethics, Hobbes, Locke and Rousseau to political philosophy, and Descartes to the philosophy of mind. The impression was given that, though authors as ancient as Plato and Aristotle were still worth reading, great strides in philosophy had recently been made by Moore, Russell, Ayer, Austin, Ryle and their contemporaries. Alongside Austin's *Sense and Sensibilia* and Ryle's *Concept of Mind*, we were required to read Hare's *Language of Morals*. The book struck me as impossibly dull, so I seized with relish on Alasdair MacIntyre's *Short History of Ethics*, and even more so on his (then) new collection of essays *Against the Self-Images of the Age*.

From both these books I learned that moral philosophy had a long history, and considerable cultural significance. This was in contrast to the ahistorical, strictly academic character that 'linguistic' philosophy presented. Still, I cannot say that I felt any dissatisfaction with the philosophical style into which I was being inducted. On the contrary, I relished its conceptual precision and argumentative rigour, and when in my final year I studied Wittgenstein, his *de novo* treatment of philosophical problems did not detract at all from a powerful sense of the subject's importance. Indeed, the tone of Wittgenstein's *Philosophical Investigations* greatly intensified my belief that philosophy really mattered, though it was very many years later (2015) before I published a book about Wittgenstein that had the aim of articulating this importance.

When I moved to Durham University for graduate study in political philosophy, I encountered another figure of whom I had hitherto known nothing – Michael Oakeshott. I found his magnum opus, *Experience and its Modes*, rather impenetrable, but Oakeshott's beautiful prose, especially in his introduction to Hobbes's *Leviathan*, together with what might be called his method of 'reasoning by insinuation', proved compelling. The 'British Idealists', my undergraduate studies had led me to believe, were metaphysicians whose uncontrollably inflated ideas had been conclusively 'refuted' by G. E. Moore's famous essay. Reading Oakeshott, alongside R. G. Collingwood's fierce attacks on the 'Oxford Realists' of his day, remedied this misconception, and hugely widened my philosophical horizons. The MA course at Durham also required me to study Hegel. Finding his *Lectures on the Philosophy of History* the most accessible of the texts with which we were presented, I began to think seriously about philosophy's relationship to history. But I was not inclined, in the end, to follow either Hegel or Collingwood. A few years later, one of the first papers I published (in the journal *History and Theory*, appropriately) was entitled 'Can There Be History of Philosophy?'. It gave a negative answer to its own question. Properly understood, the argument ran, philosophical questions are perennial, and for that reason have no history. In Oakeshott's terminology, philosophy and history are distinct 'modes' of thought. Any conflation of the two inevitably leads to confusion between what people at a particular time have thought about philosophical questions, and what – at any time – they ought to think about them. This is a view to which I still subscribe, though I have arrived at a rather more nuanced version of it.

In 1975 I returned to teach moral philosophy at St Andrews and my lectureship gave me no occasion to explore its history more fully. Nor did it lead me to any greater knowledge of Scotland's philosophical tradition. Just once I heard a talk about 'Reid on Smelling', and once I attended a short conference on Adam Smith's 'theory of moral sentiments'. Debate continued over the desirability of merging the two departments at St Andrews, and was intensified with the financial cuts that were a consequence of the Thatcher government's economic policies. I resisted any merger, chiefly on the grounds that it would inevitably mean contraction. But I had also come to think that moral philosophy should be conceived broadly, to include the philosophy of art, politics and religion, as well as ethics, and that so conceived it had an intellectual integrity, as well as cultural relevance beyond the intellectual confines of the academy.

My growing conviction on this matter arose in part because of curricular changes. In common with the other ancient Scottish universities, St Andrews had abandoned the centuries-long practice of requiring all students in Arts to take a philosophy class. It was a requirement from which I personally had benefited hugely, but the philosophers were unanimously against it, since the teaching of 'conscripts' so often proved unsatisfactory for both teachers and students. With the end of 'conscription', however, initiatives were needed to maintain the number of students taking philosophy classes. In St Andrews, the Moral Philosophy Department responded by offering a wider range of first-year courses – Moral Problems, Philosophy of Art, Political Theory, Philosophy of History, Philosophy of Religion. I took my turn at teaching all of these, and had to work up a lot of new lecture material, especially in aesthetics. In the course of doing so, I discovered that before the influence of 'linguistic philosophy' took hold, this wide range of subject matter had been relatively commonplace for moral philosophy as taught in the Scottish universities. It seemed, then, that in our innovations there was also an element of reviving the past. More importantly, it worked. Student numbers in moral philosophy were sustained at higher levels than the other ancient Scottish universities had generally experienced.

If I became aware of an older way of teaching moral philosophy, however, I did nothing to investigate it. I remained ignorant of those teachers of moral philosophy (in this broad sense) who had truly inspired the students they taught – Dugald Stewart, Sir William

Hamilton, James Ferrier, Alexander Campbell Fraser and Sir Henry Jones, for instance. In 1990 or thereabouts, I took over as Secretary of the Scots Philosophical Club (now Association) – the organisation of professional philosophers in Scotland. Four years later, this led me to organise a conference in Glasgow marking the tricentenary of the birth of Francis Hutcheson. The conference attracted philosophers and intellectual historians from across the world, but very few of the philosophers in Scotland turned up. A little later, I proposed that the Club should mark its approaching centenary by commissioning a new history of Scottish philosophy. That was when I first learned of James McCosh's volume on *The Scottish Philosophy* published in 1875 – though I didn't seek it out as something worth reading. The proposal, described for a short while as commissioning 'a new McCosh', failed to attract much support and was dropped. In 2001, the centenary celebration itself included two guest lectures. One was on an aspect of the history of Scottish philosophy, the other a contribution to a topic of contemporary interest. I do not recall any connecting link being made between the two. For most of those who attended, I suspect, the historical talk was not of any great philosophical interest, and for the few historians of philosophy this was just what was to be expected.

II

A serious desire and determination to know more about the Scottish philosophical tradition was first occasioned six years before that, in 1995, when I was appointed to the Regius Chair of Moral Philosophy at Aberdeen. Even I knew that philosophy at Aberdeen could claim an important figure in the history of philosophy – Thomas Reid – as its most distinguished alumnus. While my knowledge of Reid was minimal, I was nevertheless very surprised to find that Aberdeen University's heavily promoted research centre in the humanities – the 'Thomas Reid Institute' – was connected with Reid in name only. Neither the Director nor the Deputy Director had any interest in Reid, still less any expertise in his philosophy, and the Institute's special interdisciplinary postgraduate programme N.E.R.V.E.[1] did not include any philosophy. More strikingly, nothing had been done, or was planned, to exploit (or even catalogue)

---

[1] I have forgotten what this acronym stood for.

the Reid manuscripts that were a uniquely valuable possession of the university's Special Collections. Apart from a short-lived attempt in the mid-1980s, the Aberdeen Philosophy Department itself had made no serious effort to give special attention to, or advance, the study of its most distinguished philosopher.

It seemed evident to me that as the holder of the Regius Chair (which had been unoccupied for thirteen years) I had an obligation to remedy this. I resolved to make Reid and philosophy in Scotland the subject of my inaugural lecture. In order to dispel my more general ignorance, I read George Davie's *The Democratic Intellect*. In an essay entitled 'The Discovery of Ferrier', Davie says it was Torgny Segerstedt's book *The Problem of Knowledge in Scottish Philosophy*, published in 1935, that 'first awakened me to the dramatic as well as the intellectual interest of Scottish philosophy' (Davie 1991: 87). I could say precisely the same about *The Democratic Intellect*. From a scholarly perspective, the book has many flaws, yet it has remained in print since first publication, and is now widely regarded as a 'classic'. I found it inspirational because Davie led me from Reid to Ferrier, from the eighteenth to the nineteenth century, and thus to a narrative that seemed, uniquely, to span and integrate close on two centuries of philosophical thinking. Thanks to this book, it was Ferrier's relationship to Reid and the philosophy of Common Sense that eventually provided me with a topic for my inaugural, finally delivered, as these things sometimes are, almost three years after my appointment.

Though Ferrier was virtually unknown even to historians of philosophy, I discovered that in his own day he was a philosopher of European renown. Were there others like this? While I found the nineteenth century intriguing, for the purposes of raising the profile of Scottish philosophy, it seemed wisest to focus first on Reid and the eighteenth century. With the invaluable help and expertise of colleagues at Aberdeen, 'The Reid Project' was established. It had three immediate purposes: to arrange and fund the proper cataloguing of the Reid manuscripts; to resurrect the journal *Reid Studies* that had had a fleeting, single-issue existence a decade earlier; and to organise a regular International Reid Symposium that would bring Reid to the attention of philosophers worldwide. The Project succeeded, partly because it coincided with other developments – notably the appearance of several volumes in the new Edinburgh University Press edition of *Reid's Collected Works* and the Liberty Fund's *Natural Law and Enlightenment Classics* series that reissued many newly edited key texts from the period. Eventually the Reid Project built a solid foundation for an expanded Centre for the Study of Scottish Philosophy (CSSP), established in 2004 with some financial assistance from the Carnegie Trust for the Universities of Scotland.

In 2005, I was offered the position of Henry Luce III Professor of Philosophy and the Arts at Princeton Theological Seminary. I hesitated to accept it lest the fledgling CSSP wither away before it had accomplished anything. The Seminary, however, offered some financial support if I was willing to transfer the CSSP's operations to Princeton. The appropriateness of this proposal rested on an incontestable historical connection between Scotland and Princeton,[2] most evident in the fact that John Witherspoon in the eighteenth century and James McCosh in the nineteenth were Scottish graduates schooled in philosophy, and both hugely influential in the history of the College of New Jersey, which spawned the Seminary in 1812, and became Princeton University in 1896. Accepting the position I had been offered opened up new avenues of thought for me, as I gradually discovered still more extensive connections between the intellectual and educational ideals of Scotland, Princeton and the other early American colleges. Accordingly, from 2006 to 2018, Princeton Theological Seminary was the editorial home of the *Journal of Scottish Philosophy*, which had replaced *Reid Studies* in 2004, and the location of no fewer than twenty conferences and meetings on topics in Scottish philosophy, drawing participants from North America and Europe, and occasionally Asia, Australia and South America. It was in Princeton that the Oxford University Press *History of Scottish Philosophy* was launched (still to be completed), and over the years many more volumes were added to the *Library of Scottish Philosophy*, including selections from Brown, Kames, Lady Mary Shepherd and Scottish Philosophy in America.

III

My interest in 'Scottish philosophy' had arisen after twenty years engaged in fashioning a certain conception of moral philosophy in my own mind. I wanted to honour the conceptual clarity and

---

[2] I have written about this at greater length in 'Scotland and Princeton', Chapter 9 of *Schools of Faith: Essays on Theology, Ethics and Education*, ed. David Fergusson and Bruce McCormack, London, T&T Clark, 2019.

argumentative rigour of the analytical style in which I had, so to speak, been raised, while at the same time persisting with the normative questions relating to ethics, politics, art and religion that had attracted me to moral philosophy in the first place. The combination of critical rigour and cultural significance promised, I thought, to secure the relevance that I was certain moral philosophy ought to have for ethical, political and religious thought beyond the academy. Logical positivism and its British equivalents had tended to deny this, a tendency strikingly exemplified in A. J. Ayer's *Logic, Truth and Language*, a much-celebrated book when I was an undergraduate. The positivists corralled Hume into their service, or better perhaps, raised him up as their patron saint. They discounted, or at any rate overlooked, the full range of Hume's interests and writings on history, art and politics, and my discovery of Reid, his neglected contemporaries and successors (Adam Ferguson being a notable example of the first, and Ferrier of the second) introduced me to an intellectual debate in which Hume was just one voice – a highly significant voice, certainly, but not necessarily the *most* significant. Hume's application of empiricism, as Alexander Broadie once memorably expressed it, was the speck of sand in the pearl. The pearl itself was the product of the reactions he had prompted.

Kant's awakening from dogmatic slumbers was the most famous of these, and one with which I was familiar. It was when an Aberdeen colleague pointed me to Andrew Seth's Balfour Lectures on *Scottish Philosophy* that I came to see Hume in his native context for the first time. Seth's lectures are subtitled 'A Comparison of the Scottish and German Answers to Hume'. For the most part, by 'Scottish' Seth means Reid, and by 'German' he means Kant. His comparison is very illuminating, and rises above any partisanship in its contention that, though ultimately a failure, Kant's response constitutes a much higher order of philosophy than Reid's. My attention was especially caught by an opening remark in the lectures: 'the thread of national tradition, it is tolerably well known, has been but loosely held of late by many of our best Scottish students of philosophy.' This sentence prompted several thoughts. First, Seth seemed to take for granted that there was, or had been, a 'national tradition' in philosophy. Second, since he was lecturing in 1882, his expression 'of late' suggested a tradition that had lasted more than eighty years beyond Reid's death. Third, 'tolerably well known' implied that the decline or demise of the 'national tradition' had been a subject of discussion. In short, Seth was lecturing within a self-conscious post-Enlightenment intellectual context, but a context of which philosophy in twenty-first-century Scotland knew nothing. Why not?

Added to this was the interesting phenomenon of Seth himself. Though thoroughly versed in German philosophy (as his second set of Balfour Lectures confirms), he was a personal embodiment of the intellectual tradition to which he referred. Having been a student at Edinburgh, he went to Germany for two years of advanced study. In due course, he became Professor of Logic and Metaphysics at St Andrews, moving five years later to the corresponding position in Edinburgh. There he succeeded his much-admired teacher, Alexander Campbell Fraser, to whom he dedicated his Scottish philosophy lectures. Fraser, I recalled from reading Davie's *Democratic Intellect*, competed with Ferrier in 1856 for the Chair that Sir William Hamilton had occupied for twenty years. The competition for his successor generated a fierce argument about what could and could not count as Scottish philosophy, made fiercer, Davie claimed, by divisions resulting from the 'Disruption' of the Church of Scotland in 1843. There followed something of a pamphlet war. John Cairns, a minister of the Church of Scotland, had published a pamphlet arguing that Ferrier, then Professor of Moral Philosophy at St Andrews, was unsuitable for appointment since he had abandoned the philosophy best fitted to Scotland in favour of an alien import from Germany. Ferrier responded (after the election) with an animated defence of his philosophy as 'Scottish', even though it departed radically from Reid (for whom he had scant respect). Twelve years later, a similarly animated debate broke out over appointment to the Chair of Moral Philosophy, when James Hutchison Stirling, the great protagonist of Hegel, was passed over in favour of the relatively little-known Henry Calderwood.

Elements of the same debate were subsequently the subject of published exchanges between John Veitch at Glasgow, Hamilton's amanuensis, and David Ritchie at St Andrews, one of the group Seth describes as 'our best Scottish students of philosophy' (a group from which Seth had come to distance himself). In all these instances, the accusation was that the Scottish philosophical tradition was being abandoned in favour of Idealism. Ferrier was accused of Hegelian leanings (which he emphatically denied); Stirling was rejected in part because the Electors thought that lectures on Hegel would be unsuitable for Scottish students (a view shared by J. S. Mill); Veitch attacked Hegelianism in the name of Scottish philosophy, while Ritchie, as a protégé of Edward Caird, Professor of Moral Philosophy at Glasgow, was identified as an especially talented proponent of a new direction for philosophy in Scotland.

From the point of view of those who opposed Ferrier in the 1850s, Stirling in the 1860s, and then Caird in the 1880s, philosophy in Scotland had a cultural role and an educational function that required it to have a distinctive style – the analytical, empirical and normative style of thinking specially well exemplified in Thomas Reid, but also found in Adam Smith, Adam Ferguson and Dugald Stewart. In 1875, with the publication of *The Scottish Philosophy: Biographical, Expository, Critical, from Hutcheson to Hamilton*, James McCosh became its most self-conscious and articulate exponent. McCosh had been a philosophy student at Glasgow and Edinburgh. After a time as a Church of Scotland minister, and a participant in the Disruption, he was appointed the founding Professor of Logic and Metaphysics at Queen's University Belfast, a position he modelled closely on the historical Scottish equivalents. In 1868 he moved from Belfast to be President of the College of New Jersey (now Princeton University), exactly 100 years after another minister of the Kirk, John Witherspoon, had given the curriculum at Princeton its unmistakably Scottish stamp.

McCosh's book, it turned out, was not unique in its concern to identify and explicate something called 'Scottish philosophy'. As noted earlier, in the next decade, Andrew Seth's *Scottish Philosophy* appeared. Then, at the turn of the century, Henry Laurie published *Scottish Philosophy in its National Development* (1902), and even later T. E. Jessop produced an extensive *Bibliography of Scottish Philosophy* (1938).

Despite repeated references to 'the Scottish School of Common Sense', eighteenth- and nineteenth-century Scottish philosophers did not constitute a 'school', I discovered. Often, their differences were very deep, and in some cases expressed with great vehemence by modern standards. Reid's principal philosophical ambition was to answer Hume. His respectful tone, however, was not replicated in Hamilton's denunciation of Brown, or Stirling's contemptuous dismissal of Bain. Ferrier's fierce attack on Reid and Common Sense almost amounted to abuse, while at the same time insisting on the 'Scottish' character of his own philosophical endeavours. The journal *Mind*, founded by Alexander Bain, published exchanges between Jones and Seth that were not much less vigorous in style. There were, consequently, no doctrines, or even methods, that all those to whom the label 'Scottish philosopher' had been applied could be said to have shared. So where, then, was an encompassing 'tradition' to be found? The conclusion I came to was that all these different voices were unified by participation in a protracted philosophical conversation that paid a distinctive kind of attention to mind, morality, religion and politics (and in the eighteenth century 'taste'). This conversation gained its singularity by being based largely, though not exclusively, in Scotland's four universities (five before 1860). Consequently, those who participated, however much they disagreed, rarely lost sight of the pedagogical ideal that had long underlain the university professoriate to which most of them belonged. It was this ideal that ultimately gave point to the philosophical 'researches' that they undertook.

So deeply in sympathy did I find myself with this 'research agenda', almost by osmosis it also became my own. I embraced 'Scottish philosophy' in the way that philosophers have been, or become, Platonists, Aristotelians, Thomists, Hegelians and the like. All these 'schools' lend special significance to a set of texts and a range of ideas. Of course, this preference easily degenerates into philosophical dogmatism, or else collapses into antiquarianism. Philosophy's antipathy to the first hardly needs to be affirmed. The danger of collapsing into the second – more likely to be called 'contextualism' than 'antiquarianism' – is less easily recognised, and hence less easily resisted. Indeed, there are notable and distinguished philosophers who have asserted its desirability. During my undergraduate and graduate education, R. G. Collingwood and Alasdair MacIntyre, who both take this line, were rightly read with respect and care. Both were philosophers I found far more congenial than I did Ryle, Austin or Hare, whose stars were at that time still in the ascendant. Nevertheless, I came to think that the ultimate implication of their more historically sensitive approach was the demise of philosophy properly so called.

At the same time, I also came to see the paucity, and falsity, of conceptions of philosophy that ignore its past and that, in the spirit of logical positivism (and of Hume and Mill, of course), suppose philosophy should begin *de novo*, believing it can only make 'progress' if it does. As a result, I began to read texts from the 'history' of philosophy with renewed interest. Rejecting the 'Oxford Realists' condemned by Collingwood, however, need not drive us into the arms of 'Cambridge Contextualists'. I was searching for a middle way here, and found it well expressed in a sentence with which Andrew Seth Pringle-Pattison began his first set of Gifford Lectures. 'Although I do not intend these lectures to be primarily historical, a certain amount of historical orientation is indispensable, if only to enable us to understand how [a philosophical] question takes for us today the form it does' (Seth Pringle-Pattison 1917: 2). Philosophy's continuing intellectual and cultural relevance means that its questions are perpetually for 'today'. However, by the very same token, we need some appreciation of how they have been framed in times past. In practice, this way of pursuing philosophical questions involves holding in tension two competing tendencies. On the one hand, we must be faithful to the philosophical authors and texts that we inherit, and be careful not to project our own interests and concerns on to them. On the other hand, we must study them for their philosophical fruitfulness, and not for the insight they might offer us with respect to the peculiarities of the times and places in which they were composed.

IV

How is this balancing act to be accomplished? In an article intriguingly titled 'Blue-Eyed Philosophers Born on Wednesdays', Sarah Hutton writes:

> Anglo-American history of philosophy focusses on those canonical figures which are now regarded as major philosophers, and on those aspects of their thought believed to have direct relevance today. This excludes from the purview of the history of philosophy non-canonical figures, themes which no longer command attention, the context (both philosophical and social) in which philosophers philosophized, and what they, in their time, considered relevant and important . . . The Anglo-American model of the history of philosophy has not served so-called 'minor' figures well. Although a few more 'minor' figures have been admitted for scrutiny . . . elsewhere their fate has been to be relegated to the history of ideas, or to oblivion, from which they are only likely to be rescued if they are perceived to be relevant to one of the 'great' philosophers. (Hutton 2015: 8)

Hutton's article is subtitled 'An Essay on Women and History of Philosophy' and her principal interest is in the general relegation of women philosophers to the role of 'minor' figures whose significance relies entirely on their connection with the canonical 'greats'. The historiographical point she makes, however, has much wider application. It is easy to find philosophers, male as well as female, whose publications were held in their own day to be significant contributions to philosophical debates of the first importance, but who, at best, have long been relegated to footnotes in the history of philosophy, or, more frequently, consigned to oblivion.

The lesson to be drawn is that what interests us now, philosophically speaking, is not an infallible or even an especially reliable guide to what is intellectually significant within a wider historical perspective. On the other hand, alongside this salutary lesson we must acknowledge the no less evident truth that previous periods can be mistaken about the identification of 'major' and 'minor' figures in their own time. The history of music provides many examples of this. In 1827, for instance, the Leipzig music press Probst refused to publish new compositions by the relatively unknown Franz Schubert because they had secured the rights to the complete works of Friedrich Kalkbrenner. Schubert, of course, proved to be among the greatest composers of all time, while Kalkbrenner's compositions very soon ceased to attract the attention of either audiences or performers (see Frost 2017: 142). There are equivalents to Kalkbrenner in philosophy. Few philosophers have been more highly regarded in their own day than Sir William Hamilton, lauded in both Scotland and the United States, yet it took just a few decades for his reputation to decline to the point (it seems) of no return.

The test of time, in other words, is sometimes a very pertinent one, and previous ages have been no less susceptible to what we might call 'the prejudice of the present' than we are. How is this consideration to be squared with Hutton's equally important reservation about the history of philosophy? One solution, it is plausible to think, lies in seeking a larger historical perspective within which to place the works and authors whose significance we are seeking to appreciate. We can best assess the intellectual significance of a philosopher, in other words, by locating him or her within an intellectual trajectory that transcends any of the more particular contexts that it includes. To do so helps us counter the tendency to take any such context at its own estimation. At the same time, in line with Hutton's observation, we must resist the quasi-Hegelian assumption that all such trajectories ultimately find their culmination or conclusion in the present. Bearing both these considerations in mind, we can hope to avoid any a priori attribution of canonical status, whether contemporaneous or with hindsight.

Approached in this way, a philosopher may prove to be a 'great' figure within a given intellectual trajectory, but of little or no significance within another. The key, of course, lies in identifying the right trajectory. All the essays in this volume are intended to illustrate the value of 'Scottish philosophy' as an intellectual trajectory that casts fresh light on the Scottish professors of philosophy in the nineteenth century. It is worth noting their professional status. In 'The Professionalization of British Philosophy', Stuart Brown charts the demise of the 'amateur' and the rise of professional journals and institutions as a notable feature of British philosophy in the later decades of the nineteenth century. These changes affected Scotland as well as other parts of the UK, but in Scotland, philosophy had been professionalised for many centuries. With very occasional exceptions, philosophy was the preserve of those employed to teach it, and even the most important exception – Hume – sought a university post, unsuccessfully. This role as teacher made a difference to the relationship of philosophy to its past. From *The Life of Henry Calderwood* I discovered that in the nineteenth century there was an acknowledged difference in the way Scottish and English (meaning primarily Oxford) students were taught philosophy and its history. While students at Oxford were expected to master the history of philosophy (and especially ancient philosophy) before venturing on to the exploration of philosophical problems themselves, the Scottish 'method' did things the other way round. Students were encouraged first to grapple with the problems, and then to turn to the history of philosophy as a means of deepening and enlarging their understanding of those problems.

V

The task of persisting with this tension between philosophy and its history, and making it a fruitful one, became the animating spirit in my pursuit of the Scottish philosophical tradition, and led me to lecture, publish and review books on all the major philosophers of the Scottish Enlightenment. However, after a time, I started to give greater attention to Scottish philosophy in the nineteenth century.

An important incentive in this direction was an invitation from the *Stanford Encyclopedia of Philosophy* to contribute the entry on 'Scottish Philosophy in the Nineteenth Century', soon followed by an invitation to write on the same subject for the *Cambridge Companion to the Scottish Enlightenment*. Subsequently I was asked to contribute an essay on Sir William Hamilton to the *Oxford Handbook of British Philosophy in the Nineteenth Century*. Meantime, I had initiated a multi-volume *History of Scottish Philosophy* with Oxford University Press, and undertaken to edit the volume on *Scottish Philosophy in the Nineteenth and Twentieth Centuries*. The general lack of relevant expertise made suitable contributors quite hard to find, with the result that I was obliged to write several of the chapters myself. In this way it came about that I was reading more and more in the unexplored territory of nineteenth-century Scottish philosophy, and given the vast literature published, and continuing to appear, on the philosophers of the Scottish Enlightenment, it seemed obvious that I could more usefully focus my own efforts on Scottish philosophy after the Enlightenment.

This proved to be an area in which original research was easy to do, partly because, in addition to a great many philosophical publications of considerable interest, there were biographies and autobiographies of almost all the notable philosophers of the period. These more personal sources illuminated my reading of the philosophical writings, but they also gave me a much deeper insight into the intellectual climate of the time. The world of Scottish philosophy in the nineteenth and into the twentieth centuries was not in any way isolated from the wider world of ideas, but it was unusually integrated because it was based almost entirely in the universities. Thomas Brown, Sir William Hamilton, James Ferrier, Alexander Bain, John Veitch, Alexander Campbell Fraser, Henry Calderwood, Andrew Seth Pringle-Pattison, Edward Caird and Henry Jones, all of whom make repeated appearances in the essays that follow, were educated in Scottish universities, and went on to hold university Chairs of philosophy. There are exceptions to this general rule, but it is striking that most of them sought the philosophical recognition that was bestowed by a university appointment. A notable example is James Hutchison Stirling, a Glasgow graduate who became a doctor and practised medicine for some years before returning to philosophy. The book that he then published, *The Secret of Hegel*, was very widely read, but Stirling saw that appointment to a university Chair was key to being a fully acknowledged participant in Scottish philosophical debate. And so, like Hume, he applied (unsuccessfully) for such a position, first in Glasgow and then in Edinburgh. Similarly, Thomas Carlyle, who also appears in this book, made application, again unsuccessfully, for the Chair of Moral Philosophy at St Andrews. John Tulloch, Principal of St Mary's College in the University of St Andrews, is also an exception of sorts, since he held a Chair of Theology, not philosophy, though the cast of his mind was decidedly philosophical. The most important exception might be said to be John Stuart Mill. Mill never held a university teaching position (though he was elected Rector of St Andrews University), and was not even resident in Scotland. Yet he was an important presence for most of the Scottish philosophers. His *System of Logic* was used as a textbook in both Aberdeen and St Andrews, his devastating *Examination* was regarded as ending Hamilton's influence, and through his connections with Alexander Bain his empirical psychology and utilitarian ethics were prominent topics of debate.

Perhaps the most notable feature of this institutional base is the role and influence it gave to philosophy within Scottish society as a whole. When Henry Jones succeeded his teacher and mentor Edward Caird in the Chair of Moral Philosophy at Glasgow, while continuing to write and publish, he devoted himself especially to teaching since this, he believed, counted for more than any other of his (many) valuable activities. He attributed the influence of the teacher to the special educational context of the Scottish university. This contrasted sharply with most other British universities, as his biographer related.

> Year after year [Jones] met some two hundred students, drawn for the most part from Scottish homes . . . They were in various ways an audience of rather special quality. Nearly all of them were destined for professional life, in the schools or churches or courts of Scotland, or in medical practice, or in some sort of public service, or in industry or commerce. From their number would be drawn a large proportion of the leaders of national life in the succeeding generation. They were, for the most part, of very modest means, and had to make their way in the world by hard work, and in a country where university honours are prized. And they came, most of them, from a metaphysically minded race – not indeed trained in the science, but inured to such discussion by the disputatious habits of their elders

and by the argumentative discourses of the Scottish pulpit. As a rule, they reached the moral philosophy class only in their third year of university residence. (Hetherington 1924: 72)

The Moral Philosophy class at Glasgow was the largest in Scotland. Henry Calderwood, Professor of Moral Philosophy at Edinburgh, had a class of 140 similarly constituted. Both of these were considerably larger than philosophy classes at Aberdeen or St Andrews. Yet their character and role was much the same. They also produced new generations of philosophy teachers. In his *Biographia Philosophica*, Alexander Campbell Fraser records Edinburgh's success in this regard.

> The young metaphysicians formed themselves into a society for weekly discussion, and the class-room, aided latterly by this 'Philosophical Society,' has sent not a few professors and books of philosophy into the world, in the latter decades of the nineteenth century. It has given two professors of philosophy to Edinburgh, two to Glasgow, three to Aberdeen, two to St Andrews; one to Oxford and another to Cambridge; besides a still larger number to American universities, and to colleges in India and Japan and Australia. (Fraser 1904: 206)

A further important dimension to the broader cultural role of philosophy was the widespread interest it attracted beyond the universities. When James Hutchison Stirling gave the first set of Gifford Lectures at the University of Edinburgh,

> the application for tickets was so great that, even though the largest class room in the university was chosen for the lectures, it was found impossible to meet it . . . In spite of the large audience, which continued to attend the lectures on Saturday mornings, there were many who wished to attend but were, for various reasons, unable to do so . . . and in response to a request, Stirling afterwards re-delivered the lectures in the evenings. (A. H. Stirling 1912: 313)

Some years before, Robert Flint, then Professor of Moral Philosophy at St Andrews, had delivered his Baird Lectures on 'Theism' in Edinburgh, Glasgow and St Andrews and had attracted 'an attendance on the part of the public, especially in Edinburgh . . . greater than that of any course within the memory of those who were present' (MacMillan 1914: 324).

Some of these 'nineteenth-century' philosophers lived into the twentieth century, and in a few cases their most important work was published after 1900. By the third decade of the new century, however, partly because of the long-term effects of World War I, the Scottish universities and the world in which they operated had begun to change radically. They gradually lost their distinctive character, and this loss was effectively completed with the huge expansion of British universities in the 1960s and the creation of a nationwide, centrally funded, system of 'higher education'. Without a unifying institutional base, there was very little left that could sustain a continuing tradition of Scottish philosophy. With the rise of interest in the Scottish Enlightenment (a term first coined in 1904), the philosophers of the eighteenth century, especially Hume, attracted renewed attention. It was in the second half of the nineteenth century, however, after the university reforms of 1858, that Scottish philosophy was at its most vibrant. Yet interest in the philosophers who made it so had died away almost completely. As a result, there were neither the people nor the texts that would keep the tradition alive.

An interesting test case for this contention is to be found in John Macmurray, Professor of Moral Philosophy at Edinburgh from 1945 to 1958. Macmurray is the last of the philosophers included by Alexander Broadie in his *History of Scottish Philosophy*. Though also identified by others as a 'Scottish philosopher', this identification is debatable. Accordingly, I have devoted the final essay to Macmurray's rather different relationship to Scottish philosophy, focusing primarily on the Gifford Lectures he delivered in the University of Glasgow in 1953–4, but giving some attention also to his 1951 contribution on the philosophy of language to the newly established *Philosophical Quarterly*.

Very few of the philosophers with whom the essays in this book are concerned would have been inclined to identify themselves as contributors to an unfolding tradition of 'Scottish philosophy'. Hamilton and Veitch, Alexander Campbell Fraser and Seth Pringle-Pattison are possible exceptions. Consequently, the burden of proof falls on the essays themselves to show that this is a fruitful way of regarding them. It is also part of the book's ambition to stimulate renewed interest in Scottish philosophers who were highly regarded in their own day and wrote widely discussed books that ran into several editions. Many of them gave Gifford Lectures that drew large audiences and attracted widespread attention. Scarcely any attention is paid to them now, but is this something to lament, or try to rectify? It must always be borne in mind, after all, that dispassionate investigation may uncover 'justly' as well as 'unjustly' neglected figures. Besides, it simply is the case that each passing century produces only a tiny number of 'major' philosophers.

Hume and Smith (and possibly, though not certainly, Reid) are to be identified as such in the eighteenth century. Are there any nineteenth-century equivalents? Among English language philosophers, only John Stuart Mill seems a plausible candidate. Even Mill, though, could scarcely be listed in the first rank of philosophers, on a par with Hume or Kant, say. In any case, out of all his copious writing, it is chiefly his moral and political philosophy that has proved to be of continuing interest. The Scottish philosophers who appear in the essays that follow were all held in very high repute in their own day, yet very few, if any, are likely to attain even Mill's modest position in the philosophical pantheon. Nevertheless, as I hope the essays in this book demonstrate, there is considerable value to be derived from reading their works and exploring their debates. This is especially the case with respect to some fundamental and recurring philosophical problems, since these are the constant themes in those debates. The relation of mind to reality, the nature of morality, and the rival claims of empiricism and rationalism are issues that do not go away. For that reason, revisiting a sophisticated body of philosophical literature about them that has become largely unknown offers the prospect of genuinely fresh illumination.

It is the mark of philosophy that everything worth saying about the topics with which it is concerned is more likely to generate debate than agreement. The result, in sharp contrast to some other academic disciplines, is that nothing is ever finally settled or logically secured. This is a subject to which I return from time to time in the essays that follow. For the moment, though, it is enough to observe that the best hope for those who devote themselves to philosophical thinking is that their teaching and publication, whatever its lifespan, will engage the talent and enthusiasm of successive generations. This is precisely what marked the Scottish philosophical tradition over a very long period, and what it is the purpose of these essays to illustrate – and to revitalise, perhaps.

2

Sir William Hamilton and the Revitalisation of Scottish Philosophy

I

It is widely agreed that eighteenth-century Scotland was remarkable for its philosophical fertility. From the early years of the century almost to its close, a line of notable philosophers engaged each other in debate on many of the main topics of philosophy, and in the course of it wrote books that have remained important texts in the history of the subject. The philosophers were not alone. They were simply the most prominent group within a larger community of intellectuals engaged in social, historical, literary and scientific inquiry.

For the most part, this intellectual activity took place in three locations, and centred on four small university colleges – two in Aberdeen, one in Edinburgh and another in Glasgow. (Scotland's most ancient university – St Andrews – seems to have played little part in this intellectual ferment.) For most of the century, the University of Edinburgh was renowned for its medical sciences, while Aberdeen and Glasgow were especially notable for their philosophical prowess. In Aberdeen George Turnbull and George Campbell at Marischal College, and then Alexander Gerard and Thomas Reid at King's, set philosophical inquiry in new directions. In Glasgow, Francis Hutcheson assumed the Chair of Moral Philosophy in 1726. His student Adam Smith later occupied the same Chair, in which he was succeeded by Aberdeen's Thomas Reid. Though Hutcheson was venerated as the 'Father' of this remarkable line, it was Reid who came to be identified as the founder of a distinctive philosophical school – 'the Scottish School of Common Sense'. The name was derived from Reid's *Inquiry into the Human Mind upon the Principles of Common Sense*, completed while he was still at Aberdeen.

Another key contributor to this philosophical ferment was David Hume. Though he never held a university post, despite applications to Glasgow and Edinburgh, Hume provided the single most important stimulus to the philosophical debates of the period. Just as on the continent of Europe he awakened Immanuel Kant from his 'dogmatic slumbers', so in his native land the sceptical conclusions of his *Treatise of Human Nature* became a challenge to the holders of university Chairs, and the esteem in which Reid's *Inquiry* was held resulted primarily from the belief that it contained a conclusive answer to Hume. More than a century after the publication of Reid's *Inquiry*, Henry Calderwood, in his inaugural lecture in the Chair of Moral Philosophy at the University of Edinburgh in 1868, could still see himself engaged in a distinctively Scottish philosophy, and he put the philosophical differences between Hume and Reid at its heart.

> It is the glory of our own land to be distinguished pre-eminently for its philosophy ... [and] Scottish Philosophy may be said to owe its origin to conflict. It sprang up under the necessity which the nation felt for delivering itself from the disorder and uncertainty which a philosophical scepticism showed itself competent to bring about with the materials afforded to it by an empirical philosophy. The dangers which threatened were, on the one hand, an intellectual scepticism; on the other, a utilitarian system of morals: on the one hand, the loss of the real in the phenomenal; on the other, the loss of an immutable morality in a higher or lower type of utility. (W. L. Calderwood and Woodside 1900: 167)

With Reid's demise in 1796, philosophical leadership passed from Glasgow to Edinburgh, where Dugald Stewart held the Chair of Moral Philosophy. Stewart's personal learning and international prestige sustained the 'School' but added nothing innovative to it. His successor Thomas Brown found more to praise in Hume than Reid, of whom he was highly critical. But though a popular lecturer, he did little to displace the pre-eminence of 'Common Sense', which became a rather dull philosophical orthodoxy across the Scottish universities. As a student of moral philosophy at Marischal College in 1839, Alexander Bain found that the substance of the course taught by Dr Glennie, the Professor of Moral Philosophy and Logic, 'had long been fixed, so that the student had to take down, word for word, the notes already in the possession of former students for many years back' (Bain 1904: 71–2). A few years later, as Assistant to the Professor, Bain discovered that Glennie actually read some of his lectures directly from the pages of Reid.

A similar situation prevailed at the University of Glasgow. No one of the stature of Hutcheson, Smith or Reid arose to take their place, and philosophy fell into a period of relative intellectual decline. 'The dry instruction of the class-room', James McCosh recalls, was 'solid, but not inspiring. The course of instruction was substantial, but very narrow, and the professors were bitterly opposed to enlarging it' (McCosh and Sloane 1896: 27). Yet out of these inauspicious circumstances, almost from nowhere, another intellectual giant appeared to emerge – William Hamilton.

II

Sir William Hamilton was born in Glasgow, where his father was Regius Professor of Anatomy and Botany at the University (and Thomas Reid's family physician). He attended schools in both Scotland and England, before matriculating at the University of Glasgow in 1803. Hamilton took classes in Logic with Professor George Jardine, noted more for his student-centred educational methods than for any contribution he made to philosophy. Reid's successor in the Chair of Moral Philosophy, Professor James Mylne, was more inclined to the French sensationalist school, but in the course of almost forty years in the Chair he published nothing, so that Reid's 'Common Sense School' retained its intellectual dominance. Hamilton rapidly made a powerful impression. Being so intellectually gifted (as well as strikingly handsome), by the votes of his fellow students, he was awarded honours in both classes. It was as an undergraduate that he began to collect the books that came to comprise his outstanding personal library of almost 10,000 volumes.

In the year after his graduation from Glasgow, Hamilton took up the study of medicine, and though he soon abandoned the idea of a medical career, his knowledge of physiology later stood him in good stead in his exchanges with phrenologists. The following year (1807), his outstanding academic record at Glasgow enabled him to follow in the footsteps of Adam Smith (among others) by winning a Snell Exhibitioner at Balliol College, Oxford. These scholarships, founded in 1677 and reserved for Scottish students, were intended to enable gifted Glasgow graduates to continue their studies at a more advanced level. At Oxford the study of Aristotle was in the ascendant, and Hamilton's philosophical work thereafter was strongly influenced by his knowledge and admiration of Aristotle. Once again he shone academically. He graduated with a first class arts degree in 1811, having chosen to be examined on an unprecedented number of texts. In place of his earlier medical ambitions, he took up the study of law and became a member of the Scottish bar in 1813. In 1816 his legal investigations enabled him to claim the baronetcy of the ancient family of Hamilton of Preston. This had been in abeyance since the death of Sir Robert Hamilton of Preston in 1701. Hamilton became the 9th Baronet and was thereafter always referred to as Sir William.

In 1817 and 1820 Hamilton made two key visits to Germany. He became fluent in German and read extensively, thus becoming the first Scottish (and British) philosopher of any consequence to engage with the immensely influential German philosophical movement that Kant had inaugurated. This third strand in his intellectual formation gave Hamilton a unique orientation. His assimilation of the Common Sense tradition in Glasgow left him with an enduring admiration for Thomas Reid. His study of Aristotle at Oxford resulted in a great facility in logic, and a deep belief in its importance. His two visits to Germany gave him unrivalled textual knowledge of Kant's philosophy as well as Schelling's (though not of Hegel's, it seems). This combination of disparate elements proved a powerful source of new intellectual energy for philosophy in Scotland, while at the same time drawing widespread attention to Hamilton's writings in England and on the continent of Europe. In due course, this new energy gained Hamilton immense intellectual authority in the universities of Canada and the United States, where the texts by Reid and Stewart had come to seem stale.

Hamilton's enthusiasm for philosophy greatly exceeded his interest in the law. Accordingly, when the Chair of Moral Philosophy in the University of Edinburgh was rendered vacant by the unexpected death of Thomas Brown in 1820, he applied for it. Though his application was unsuccessful, a year later he was appointed to the Chair of Civil History. This was a peculiar position. No students were required to attend his lectures (on history and literature), and the salary (which relied on a local beer tax) was discontinued after a time. Unsurprisingly Hamilton relinquished the Chair, but he continued his intellectual work, and between 1829 and 1836 he published a series of fourteen essays in the *Edinburgh Review*. Three of them were devoted to exclusively philosophical topics – 'Cousin and the Philosophy of the Unconditioned', 'Brown and the Philosophy of Perception' and 'Logic'. It was these essays, especially the first two, that constituted the basis of a successful application for the Chair of Logic and Metaphysics at Edinburgh, to which he was appointed in 1836. Hamilton held the Chair for the next twenty years, and his lectures attracted significant numbers of students, and exercised an enormous intellectual influence over generations of Scottish intellectuals including several future professors of philosophy in the Scottish universities. John Veitch, who attended the lectures and subsequently became Professor of Logic, first at St Andrews and then at Glasgow, tells us that over his first two sessions as Professor, Hamilton spent night after night writing lectures on psychology, metaphysics and logic, and to extraordinary effect. 'Nothing like them had been known or felt before in Scotland or a Scottish university. These lectures were for twenty years the most powerful factor in the philosophical thought of Scotland' (Veitch 1882: 13). Veitch's assessment is echoed by Alexander Campbell Fraser, Hamilton's successor in the Chair. Fraser attended Hamilton's lectures as a private student in 1838, and joined the group of students invited to meet at Hamilton's house.

> Never, I suppose, were the ultimate questions about meaning and the universe, which constitute metaphysics, approached in a Scottish university in a more disinterested and earnest temper than by the band of students ... inspired by the directing intelligence of one who unfolded before our wondering eyes the ancient, medieval, and modern world of thought ... I owe more to Hamilton than to any other intellectual influence. He moved us all to think out questions for ourselves ... Hamilton was perhaps the most learned Scot that ever lived. (Fraser 1904: 57–62)

James McCosh, who also attended Hamilton's lectures, notes that 'every year a larger or less number [of students] ... rejoiced to find that he awakened independent thought within them, and were ready to acknowledge ever afterwards that they owed more to him than to ... all the other professors under whom they studied' (McCosh 1875: 428).

In addition to his teaching, Hamilton worked for many years on a copiously annotated edition of the *Collected Works of*

Thomas Reid. This finally appeared in 1846, and Reid's texts were accompanied by over 300 pages of 'supplementary dissertations'. The *Edinburgh Review* essays were republished (with additions) in 1852-3 under the title *Discussions on Philosophy and Literature, Education and University Reform*. By this time, however, a paralytic stroke had seriously crippled him. Fortunately, it left his mind unimpaired, and with the help of his wife he completed nine volumes of the *Collected Works of Dugald Stewart*, published in 1854-5, though the accompanying *Memoir* of Stewart was never finished. With the help of assistants, he was able to continue teaching until very shortly before his death in 1856. In 1859 the first of four volumes of lectures appeared, edited by his two greatest philosophical admirers, Henry Mansel, Waynflete Professor of Metaphysical Philosophy at Oxford, and John Veitch, Professor of Logic and Rhetoric at Glasgow. In the introduction Mansel and Veitch repeat the plaudits of Fraser and McCosh, declaring that in Hamilton 'speculative accomplishments [and] profound philosophical learning . . . were conjoined in an equal degree by no other man of his time' (Hamilton 2001: ix). That same year Mansel published *The Limits of Religious Thought*, the text of his Bampton Lectures delivered in Oxford a year earlier. These were essentially an elaboration of Hamilton's philosophy in defence of religion, and the Christian faith in particular. Ten years later in 1869, Veitch published a full-scale biography of Hamilton. It included a lengthy, and laudatory, appendix by Noah Porter, President of Yale University, who records the astonishing impact that Hamilton's *Edinburgh Review* articles had on philosophy in the United States, where he came to be regarded as 'the greatest writer and teacher among living Englishmen [*sic*!]' (Veitch 1869: 424). As late as 1870, John Clark Murray published an *Outline of Sir William Hamilton's Philosophy* which was intended, and for some years served, as the standard philosophical text for the universities of Canada.

The outstanding academic prestige and genuine intellectual admiration William Hamilton enjoyed during his lifetime persisted for some years after his death. Veitch's volume on Hamilton in the *Blackwood's Philosophical Classics* series appeared in 1882, and since preceding volumes in the series had included Descartes, Berkeley and Kant, this itself is evidence of the esteem in which he was held. By the turn of the new century his star was no longer in the ascendant, though William James was still holding him in high esteem when he delivered his Gifford Lectures at Edinburgh in 1901.

> The glories of the philosophic chair of this university were deeply impressed on my imagination in boyhood. Professor Fraser's *Essays in Philosophy*, then just published, was the first philosophic book I ever looked into, and I well remember the awestruck feeling I received from the account of Sir William Hamilton's classroom therein contained. Hamilton's own lectures were the first philosophic writings I ever forced myself to study . . . Such juvenile emotions of reverence never get outgrown; and I confess that to find my humble self promoted from my native wilderness to be actually for the time an official here, and transmuted into a colleague of these illustrious names, carries with it a sense of dreamland quite as much as of reality. (James 1902: 1–2)

Just a decade later, however, James Seth, who studied philosophy at Edinburgh under Hamilton's students Calderwood and Fraser, could write that 'it is difficult for us to understand the extraordinary, and we cannot but judge, exaggerated reputation which Hamilton achieved among his contemporaries and immediate successors' (J. Seth 1912: 298). As W. J. Mander says, 'There can be few thinkers who have been the subject of such a massive reversal of fortune as Hamilton, from being heralded in his day as a philosophical genius to being ignored by subsequent generations as a pompous blunderer' (Mander 2020: 9).

Why did this happen? A plausible explanation is that the esteem in which Hamilton was held resulted from the conviction that he had revitalised Scottish philosophy. Alongside recovering the fundamental insights of Reid, he had enlarged them thanks to an unusual familiarity with Kant, and thus restated them more convincingly. That he revitalised philosophical discussion in Scotland can hardly be doubted. His eventual fall into obscurity, the standard view of Hamilton holds, resulted from the assessment, by critics on all sides, that close examination of this 'revitalisation' revealed a valiant but confused and contradictory attempt to combine wholly incompatible ways of thinking. Still, a fresh study by Mander leaves us with a puzzle. 'Taking stock of the whole, we must conclude that Hamilton's philosophy is nothing like as incoherent or contradictory as his current reputation would have us believe. There can be no denying its deficiencies but, virtually all systems of philosophy contain tensions or weaknesses' (Mander 2020: 34). There is reason, consequently, for some further investigation.

III

Apart from his influence in the lecture room, Hamilton's philosophical prestige rested primarily on the three essays that he had published in the *Edinburgh Review*. According to John Veitch, these essays exhibit 'a power of consecutive thinking and trenchant dialectic unequalled in his day', and it is on them that 'his repute as a thinker must, for the most part, ultimately rest' (Veitch 1882: 9). The first of these essays was, ostensibly, a review of Victor Cousin's *Course de Philosophie*, the text of lectures Cousin had given to great acclaim, published in Paris in 1828. It was Cousin who first coined the expression *Philosophie Écossaise* (the title of a work never translated into English), and he represented it as a distinctive answer to the persistent challenge of the philosophical scepticism inaugurated by David Hume. This 'Scottish' answer was to be contrasted with an alternative 'German' one. The first – which appealed to the principle of 'Common Sense' – owed its origins to the empirical moral psychology of Reid's *Inquiry*, while the second – which invoked the concept of 'transcendental apperception' – had developed out of Kant's *Critique of Pure Reason*. Neither answer was deemed wholly satisfactory, and in his *Course de Philosophie*, Cousin aimed to repair their deficiency by an 'eclectic' mix of both, along with other philosophical components.

In 'The Philosophy of the Unconditioned' Hamilton identifies Cousin's eclecticism as one of four logical possibilities, the other three being transcendental Idealism (Kant), mysticism (Schelling), and a 'philosophy of the conditioned' or 'Natural Realism', which was the name he gave to his revitalised version of 'Common Sense Philosophy'. Natural Realism was intended to resolve the problem of scepticism by judiciously combining Kantian insights about the limitations of human thought with the firm foundation which Reid's appeal to the principles of Common Sense was supposed to have supplied. The key to this project lay in seeing that recognising the inescapably 'conditioned' nature of human knowledge did not imply that reality is thereby fashioned by the concepts we employ.

> The conditioned is the mean between two extremes – two inconditionates, exclusive of each other, neither of which can be conceived as possible, but of which, on the principles of contradiction and the excluded middle, one must be admitted as necessary. On this opinion, therefore, reason is shown to be weak, but not deceitful. The mind

is not represented as conceiving two propositions subversive of each other, as equally possible; but only, as unable to understand as possible, either of two extremes; one of which, however, on the ground of their mutual repugnance, it is compelled to recognize as true. We are thus taught the salutary lesson, that the capacity of thought is not to be constituted into the measure of existence; and are warned from recognizing the domain of our knowledge as necessarily co-extensive with the horizon of our faith. And by a wonderful revelation, we are thus, in the very consciousness of our inability to conceive aught above the relative and finite, inspired with a belief in the existence of something unconditioned beyond the sphere of all comprehensible reality. (Hamilton 1853: 15)

The 'inconditionates' to which Hamilton here refers are the Infinite and the Absolute. The Absolute is that which admits of no further division or analysis, and the Infinite is that which admits of unlimited division. This was a novel use of the terms 'absolute' and 'infinite', because for the most part, philosophers had hitherto used them interchangeably. An important, and subsequently highly contended, step in Hamilton's philosophy was to employ them as opposites. His key premise, accordingly, is that the 'Infinite' and the 'Absolute' are mutually exclusive conceptions of 'the Unconditioned'. At the same time, they exhaust the possibilities; either reality is without limit – the Infinite – or it has some limit which human thought cannot penetrate – the Absolute. We know that one must be true, but we cannot know which one. That is what is meant by saying that 'the domain of our knowledge' is not necessarily co-extensive with 'the horizon of our faith'. This necessary combination of affirmation and ignorance means that all human knowledge must fall, and be content to fall, between the two, while at the same time acknowledging 'a belief in the existence of something unconditioned beyond the sphere of all comprehensible reality'.

This argument about the necessary either/or of the Absolute and the Infinite reveals the way in which Hamilton's thought was influenced by Kant. The 'antinomies' to which Kant draws attention uncover the inescapable limits of the human mind's endeavours. The question is whether, and how, Hamilton's assertion differs from the Kantian postulation of a world of unknowable 'things-in-themselves'. And in what relation, if any, does the 'mean' which this 'philosophy of the conditioned' commends stand to Reid's

'Principles of Common Sense'? Hamilton's answer to the first of these questions is as follows: 'Kant has clearly shown, that the Idea of the Unconditioned can have no objective reality – that it conveys no knowledge – and that it involves the most insoluble contradictions' (Hamilton 1853: 17). However, the distinction that Kant draws between Reason (*Vernunft*) and Understanding (*Verstand*) creates a difficulty. *Vernunft*, supposedly, gives us access to the Unconditioned, while *Verstand* give us access to the Conditioned. This lends a spuriously positive character to the Unconditioned, Hamilton contends. It suggests that at some level or other we could have knowledge of things-in-themselves – which is to say, knowledge of the unknowable, a plainly contradictory supposition. It is thus essential, Hamilton thinks, that the 'Unconditioned' should be defined purely negatively – as 'containing nothing even conceivable'. Employing Kant's distinction, Hamilton argues, shows Understanding to be 'weak', but it shows Reason to be 'deceitful'.

> The imperfection and partiality of Kant's analysis are betrayed in its consequences. His doctrine leads to absolute scepticism. Speculative reason, on Kant's own admission, is an organ of mere delusion. The idea of the unconditioned, about which it is conversant, is shown to involve insoluble contradictions, and yet to be the legitimate product of intelligence. Hume has well observed, 'that it matters not whether we possess a false reason, or no reason at all.' If 'the light that leads us astray, be a light from heaven' what are we to believe? If our intellectual nature be perfidious in one revelation, it must be deceitful in all . . . Kant annihilated the older metaphysic, but the germ of a more visionary doctrine of the absolute, than any of those refuted, was contained in the bosom of his own philosophy. He had slain the body, but had not exorcised the spectre of the absolute; and this spectre has continued to haunt the schools of Germany even to the present day. (Hamilton 1853: 18)

It is in the sentence 'If our intellectual nature be perfidious in one revelation, it must be deceitful in all' that we can find the connection with Reid. Reid argues, against Hume, that rational arguments in favour of scepticism about the external world presuppose that reason is reliable, while concluding that our senses are deceptive. But this preference for reason over experience is groundless. If our perceptual faculties truly are 'perfidious', to use Hamilton's term, then we have no grounds for thinking that our rational faculties are not 'perfidious' also.

Kant figures prominently in Hamilton's first *Edinburgh Review* essay. Reid figures even more prominently in the second. 'The Philosophy of Perception' takes as its starting point the recently published French edition of *Reid's Works*, translated by Jouffroy and Royer-Collard, his two leading proponents in France. A few pages in, however, the essay becomes an attack on Thomas Brown, Dugald Stewart's successor in the Chair of Moral Philosophy at Edinburgh. Brown's well-known criticisms of Reid, Hamilton argues, are a result of the fact that 'he has completely misapprehended Reid's philosophy, even in its fundamental position' (Hamilton 1853: 46). In part, however, Reid himself is at fault by failing to articulate his central insight adequately, and Hamilton's essay is a sustained attempt to make good this deficiency. There are, he holds, two major errors in Reid's analysis of the human mind. First, like Kant, he drew a distinction where he ought not to have done – between consciousness and perception. According to Hamilton, consciousness is not a faculty of the mind comparable to perception, imagination, memory and so on, but simply the generic name for all of these. We can certainly draw a logical distinction between seeing on the one hand, and our awareness that we are seeing on the other. But it is a profound mistake to confuse this with a psychological distinction, because it is in fact psychologically impossible to be conscious that we are seeing (a horse, say) without at the same time being conscious of what it is (a horse) that we are seeing.

This first error is not a very grave one. It is of significance chiefly because it misleads people like Brown.

> Reid's erroneous analysis of consciousness is not perhaps of so much importance in itself, as from causing confusion in its consequences. Had he employed this term as tantamount to immediate knowledge in general, whether of self or not, and thus distinctly expressed what he certainly taught, that mind and matter are both equally known to us as existent and in themselves; Dr Brown could hardly have so far misconceived his doctrine, as actually to lend him the very opinion which his whole philosophy was intended to refute, viz. That an immediate and consequently a real, knowledge of external things is impossible. (Hamilton 1853: 52)

The second error (by Hamilton's account) is much more significant. Reid's 'superstitious horror of the ideal theory' led him to deny what seems incontestable – that memory and imagination 'are of necessity, mediate and representative'.

> There exists, therefore, a distinction of knowledge – as immediate, intuitive, or presentative, and as mediate or representative. The former is logically simple, as only contemplative; the latter is logically complex, as both representative and contemplative of the representation . . . Representative knowledge is purely subjective, for its object known is always ideal; presentative may be either subjective or objective, for its one object may be either ideal or material . . . Considered in relation to each other: immediate knowledge is complete, as all-sufficient in itself; mediate incomplete, as realized only through the other. (Hamilton 1853: 53)

Perception tells us about the world around us; imaginary objects are in the mind only, and in this sense these objects of knowledge are purely subjective. Accordingly, and *pace* Reid, knowledge can be of mental 'ideas' as well as external 'objects'. On the basis of this emendation of Reid, Hamilton elaborates the version of Common Sense that he calls 'Natural Realism'. At its heart lies a conviction in the 'veracity of consciousness'. In precisely the same spirit as Reid, Hamilton writes:

> As we did not create ourselves, and are not even in the secret of our creation, we must take our existence, our knowledge *upon trust*: and that philosophy is the only true, because in it alone *can* truth be realized, which does not revolt against the *authority* of our natural *beliefs* (Hamilton 1853: 63, emphasis original)

The watchword of the Natural Realist is 'the facts of consciousness, the whole facts, and nothing but the facts', and an inescapable fact is this: in any act of consciousness we are aware, and cannot but be aware, of a distinction between 'Ego' and 'Non-ego'. We apprehend this distinction immediately as a fact of consciousness. The Absolute Idealist denies this distinction and holds that Ego and Non-ego are ultimately identical. The subjective Idealist believes that Non-ego is simply a manifestation of Ego, while the Materialist believes the opposite – that Ego is a manifestation, or a product, of Non-ego. The 'Hypothetical Realist' – or 'Cosmothetic Idealist' – tries to straddle these divisions by supposing that Ego (the contents of mind) somehow mediately represents Non-ego. Hypothetical

Realism, Hamilton declares, 'although the most inconsequent of all systems, has been embraced, under various forms, by the immense majority of philosophers' (Hamilton 1853: 56).

> The scheme of Natural Realism (which it is Reid's honour to have been the first, among not forgotten philosophers, virtually and intentionally, at least, to embrace) is . . . the only system on which the truth of consciousness and the possibility of knowledge can be vindicated; whilst the Hypothetical Realist, in his effort to be 'wise above knowledge,' like the dog in the fable, loses the substance, in attempting to realize the shadow. (Hamilton 1853: 68)

Is Hamilton's 'Natural Realism' truly the solution to the problems that have haunted Scottish philosophers since Hume? And is it a skilful combination of the metaphysics of Kant with the psychology of Reid that breathes new life into Scottish philosophy? Or is it an unholy concoction of radically disparate elements that sounds Scottish philosophy's death knell?

IV

The first full-length criticism of Hamilton appeared in his lifetime. In 1854, one of his most admiring students, Henry Calderwood, later Professor of Moral Philosophy at Edinburgh, published a highly critical volume entitled *The Philosophy of the Infinite, with special reference to the theories of Sir William Hamilton and M Cousin*. Calderwood was only twenty-four years old, still a divinity student, and expressly acknowledged that Hamilton's essay on Cousin 'has afforded to me matter of greater interest and more searching study than any other philosophical production in our language' (W. L. Calderwood and Woodside 1900: 49). So it was an act of considerable courage on his part to venture into print with a sustained attack on such a luminary.

Calderwood's book has nothing to say about perception or Hamilton's version of Reid. It takes issue with Hamilton's starting point, and examines closely the significance of his unusual use of the terms 'Infinite' and 'Absolute'. Calderwood notes that it is not clear whether Hamilton, in describing them as opposites, is merely deploying these terms in a different way to previous philosophical use, which generally treated them as interchangeable, or whether he is declaring this previous use to be radically mistaken. Either

Hamilton and the Revitalisation of Scottish Philosophy

way, however, Calderwood argues that we can make no sense of Hamilton's account of them as opposites.

> Is there such an Absolute as that which Sir William postulates, and which he asserts to be contradictory of the Infinite? Is that which he postulates really absolute, or has it any existence at all? In endeavouring to answer this question, let us recall Sir William's definition of the Infinite and of the Absolute; it is this – the Infinite is the unconditionally unlimited, the Absolute is the unconditionally limited. Now we cannot understand in what sense the Absolute can be called unconditionally limited, in what sense anything can be called unconditioned which is at the same time limited. Is not limitation a condition of existence; to be limited is to be conditioned? May we not as well speak of the unlimitedly limited, or of the unconditionally conditioned, as of the unconditionally limited? If the Infinite is unconditioned inasmuch as it is unlimited, must not the Absolute be conditioned inasmuch as it is limited? (H. Calderwood 1854: 23)

In short, Hamilton has failed to show the existence of two 'inconditionates', and thus failed to establish any extremes between which 'the conditioned' can be the mean. It is just such a mean, however, that underwrites, and is supposed to commend, his 'philosophy of the conditioned'.

Calderwood next goes on to argue that Hamilton's characterisation of 'the Infinite' as a purely 'negative notion' that is 'incognisable and inconceivable' is also mistaken. For a start, it makes the very existence of the term in our language a mystery. If 'the Infinite' really is inconceivable, how can it serve as well as it does, in mathematics for example? More importantly, the idea that it is in some deep way incoherent relies on a failure to distinguish properly between the 'Infinite' and the 'Indefinite'. The latter can only be a property of subjective human thought, since objective reality cannot be 'indefinite'. The Infinite by contrast must signal something independent of thought, since by definition it cannot be contained within thought. To say that it cannot be contained within thought, however, is not to say that it is completely unknowable. The 'indefinite' ideas that certain experiences generate within us – the blue depths of the sky, the impenetrability of a dark night, and the endlessness of causal chains are among Calderwood's examples – can plausibly be interpreted, he argues, as hints or 'traces' of a reality that is infinite. Experience of the 'indefinite' points thought in a direction – the Infinite – which it cannot fully comprehend. But this does not make the thought nugatory. If this is correct, then *pace* Hamilton, it is possible for us to have knowledge of the Infinite. Calderwood's background, but chief, concern is the possibility of knowledge of God which Hamilton's argument excludes. In denying the possibility of any *knowledge* of 'the Infinite', Hamilton does not mean to undermine religious belief because, he says, 'the domain of our knowledge' does not set 'the horizon of our faith'. This claim implies, however, if it does not expressly state, the post-Kantian thought that though we can hold beliefs about God in faith, we can never convert them into knowledge properly so called. The claim that Calderwood wants to press is that, if the concept of the Infinite on which this contention rests is incoherent, there is no need to differentiate faith and knowledge in this way.

Calderwood's criticism of Hamilton is severe, but it is not unsympathetic. He readily acknowledges his intellectual debt to his teacher, and laments that he had 'found it necessary to differ from Sir William Hamilton to a degree that is painful to one who has been indebted to the instructions of that distinguished philosopher' and for whom he felt 'a degree of esteem and respect which can be appreciated only by those who have listened to his prelections' (H. Calderwood 1854: v–vi). Yet Calderwood's book effectively began Hamilton's philosophical demotion. Surprisingly perhaps, given the youth of its author, *The Philosophy of the Infinite* attracted a lot of sympathetic attention. The *British Quarterly Review* even went so far as to say that 'this work of Mr Calderwood furnishes abundant reasons for the modification, *if not the abandonment*, of some of the positions taken by Sir William Hamilton (quoted in W. L. Calderwood and Woodside 1900: 52, emphasis added).

Two further examinations of Hamilton, written from radically different philosophical perspectives, were published a decade after Calderwood's, but unlike his, they were both deeply unsympathetic. The first of them, *Sir William Hamilton: Being the Philosophy of Perception – An Analysis* was written by James Hutchison Stirling, already well known at the time as the author of *The Secret of Hegel*, the first book to introduce Hegelian philosophy to an English readership. Stirling's book on Hamilton is the first part of a larger study never completed, and as its subtitle suggests, it is confined to his analysis of perception. He claims to find in Hamilton's writing 'a certain vein of disingenuousness that ... has probably caused the retardation of general British philosophy by, perhaps, a generation' (J. H. Stirling 1990: vii). Stirling was a student at Glasgow in the dull days of Jardine and Mylne, so this charge rests upon his profound conviction that the old Scottish philosophy was dead, and the future lay with the philosophy of Germany and Hegel in particular. Consequently, Hamilton's attempt to revitalise Scottish philosophy by taking cues from Kant had the double fault of deflecting philosophy in Scotland from the new Idealist dawn. Still, whether Stirling was right about this or not, his accusation is nonetheless striking testimony to Hamilton's standing and influence. Only someone whose work was highly lauded could plausibly be accused of retarding the whole of British philosophy.

Stirling's tone throughout is one of intellectual outrage. He accuses Hamilton of systematically misrepresenting those he claims to expound in order to vacillate on crucial questions, thereby allowing himself to seem to square some philosophical circles. At the heart of his argument is the contention that Hamilton unites the insights of Kant and Reid in an entirely superficial way. He tries to integrate Kantian 'phenomenalism' with Reid's 'presentationism', but massively fails to do so. Kant holds (on this account) that our immediate awareness is of phenomena and never of the 'things-in-themselves' that cause those phenomena. Reid holds that things in the world directly present themselves to our consciousness so that it is correct to say that we are immediately aware of them. Hamilton, according to Stirling, 'holds all our knowledge to be phenomenal' while at the same time 'unequivocally' asserting 'presentationism' (J. H. Stirling 1990: 12). 'It seems', he says, 'never to have struck Hamilton that presentationism is noumenalism, and therefore the logical contrary of phenomenalism. Nowhere does he seem aware that he may appear to have committed the contradiction of directly identifying these opposites' (J. H. Stirling 1990: 13).

This last sentence is not quite right. In the second edition of the *Dissertations*, in which the essay on the philosophy of perception with which Stirling is principally concerned was reprinted, Hamilton directs the reader to his further thoughts on the subject in the appendix on perception that he included in his edition of Reid's collected works. The purpose of this supplementary 'dissertation' is to elaborate at much greater length a distinction between 'sensation' and 'perception'. The former is 'subjective', the latter 'objective', but both can be said to occur 'within' the mind of the human organism.

He notes, however, that 'it may appear, not a paradox merely, but a contradiction that the organism is, at once, subjective and objective, Ego and Non-Ego'. Nevertheless, he contends, it is a fact, though 'how the material can be united with the immaterial is "the mystery of mysteries to man"' (Hamilton 1872: 880).

The identification of a 'mystery' can scarcely be said to be a solution to a philosophical problem, but this passage is sufficient to show that Stirling was wrong to accuse Hamilton of being blithely unaware of the problem. Indeed, this supplementary dissertation is a very lengthy, and somewhat laboured, attempt to address the relationship of sense experience to the apprehension of objects, by contrasting the bare experience of sights and sounds with their occurrence in perceptual judgements. Hamilton thinks (1) that we *must* draw such a distinction, and (2) that we can do so without running the risk of scepticism about or ignorance of the objects that we see and hear. Sensation invariably accompanies perception, but perception is sensation with an 'assertory judgment', which is to say, 'the recognition by Intelligence of the phaenomena presented in or through its organs' (Hamilton 1872: 878). 'In *or* through' is the key phrase here, since it allows him to assert that we are immediately aware of our immaterial sensations, and no less immediately aware of material objects.

How can this be? Surely if we are aware of material objects *through* sense perceptions, we are thereby *mediately* aware of them. And if this is the case, how does Hamilton's 'Natural Realism' differ from the position of the 'Hypothetical Realist', who thinks that material objects are to be inferred from sensitive experience, thereby, according to Hamilton, losing the substance, in attempting to realise the shadow? The difference lies, or is supposed to, in Hamilton's invocation of Common Sense, interpreted as an intuitive conviction of the identity of the immaterial sensation and the material object.

> When I concentrate my attention in the simplest act of perception, I return from my observation with the most irresistible conviction of two facts, or rather, two branches of the same fact; that I am – and that something different from me exists. In this act I am conscious of myself as a perceiving subject, and of an external reality as the object perceived; and I am conscious of both existences in the same indivisible moment of intuition. The knowledge of the subject does not precede nor follow the knowledge of the object; – neither determines, neither is determined by, the other . . .

> Such is the fact of perception revealed in consciousness, and as it determines mankind in general in their equal assurance of the reality of an external world, and of the existence of their own minds. *Consciousness declares our knowledge of material qualities to be intuitive.* Nor is the fact, *as given*, denied even by those who disallow its truth. So clear is the deliverance, that even the philosophers . . . who reject an intuitive perception, find it impossible not to admit, that their doctrine stands decidedly opposed to the voice of consciousness and the natural conviction of mankind. (Hamilton 1853: 54–5, emphasis original)

Hamilton's crucial claim, then, is that the perception of external objects is no less immediate than sensitive experience because the two are united 'in the same indivisible moment of intuition'. But what exactly is this moment of intuition? Is it a psychological experience? If it is, then there remains the question of its logical force. Let us agree that there is a natural conviction that the objects we seem to see do in fact exist. This much Hume was happy to agree with. The issue is whether that natural conviction is rational or merely psychological. What Hamilton calls Reid's 'superstitious horror of the Ideal theory' was really Reid's determination to resist the supposition that mental images authoritatively warrant a belief in their existence in a way that perceptual judgement cannot. It is the rational authority of perceptual judgement that he focuses upon, not the role of sensation in perception. Reid's 'direct realism' is compatible with our saying, if we wish, that sense impressions are 'immediate' in a way that perceptual judgements are not. The error is to suppose or imply that this 'immediacy' gives them privileged epistemological status.

Unfortunately, in another supplementary dissertation on Common Sense, Hamilton appears to say precisely this.

> [T]o argue from common sense, is simply to show, that the denial of a given proposition would involve the denial of some original datum of consciousness; but as every original datum of consciousness is to be presumed true, that the proposition in question, as dependent on such a principle, must be admitted . . . Here, however, . . . it is proper to take a distinction . . . the neglect of which has been productive of considerable error and confusion. It is the distinction between the data or deliverances of consciousness considered simply, in themselves, as apprehended facts or actual manifestations, and those deliverances considered as testimonies to the truth of facts beyond their own phaenomenal reality. (Hamilton 1872: 743–4)

Hamilton goes on to argue that while scepticism in regard to this 'phaenomenal reality' is impossible, we still have to consider the merits of Common Sense as an argument for the truth of facts 'beyond' that reality. In the end his contention appears to be that Common Sense requires us to presume the truth of such facts, and to hold this presumption as vindicated unless we can be shown that there is something contradictory about doing so.

The problem is that this seems to be a position the 'Hypothetical Realist' can happily accept. If so, this shows it to be at odds with the 'Natural Realism' which it had been Reid's 'honour' to embrace before anyone else. As Baruch Brody has argued, Reid's argument from Common Sense does not rest upon widely held convictions, as Hamilton's does, but on deeply rooted human practices of thinking, arguing and judging.

> Reid claimed that there are three elements in any act of perception.
>
>> First, some conception or notion of the object perceived; Secondly, a strong and irresistible conviction and belief in its present existence; and, Thirdly, that this conviction is immediate, and not the effect of reason (*EIP*, II/5.)
>
> What Reid wanted to claim is that [the second element], which is universally held and whose denial seems absurd and leads to paradoxical consequences if acted upon . . . is a common-sense belief. In other words Reid is not claiming that some general belief about the external world is a common-sense belief. Such a claim would be false since such a belief is usually not even formulated by most people, much less held by them. What is universally believed, and what is a common-sense belief, is that the object I see now exists. (Brody 1971: 429)

Philosophers may set about formulating 'the principles of Common Sense' that underlie the practices of reason, as Reid himself does, but this should not be taken to mean that ordinary people in any sense 'believe in' those principles, or could even articulate them.

Stirling is wrong, then, to contend that Hamilton is oblivious to, and does not address, the difficult issues confronting any attempt to transcend the phenomenal/noumenal distinction. He does do so, and believes that his account of 'sensation' and 'perception' held together by 'intuitive conviction' can provide a resolution to them. On the other hand, Stirling is right in his belief that Hamilton's solution does not work. His use of 'intuitive conviction' to forge an identity between the phenomenal and the noumenal fails. Furthermore, it is not true to the Reidian insights he claims to employ.

John Stuart Mill's *Examination of Sir William Hamilton's Philosophy*, first published in two volumes, is a much more comprehensive treatment than either Calderwood or Stirling. Mill investigates not only the philosophy of the conditioned and Hamilton's treatment of perception, but his account of causation and his logic, as well as the extension of his thought to religion that H. L. Mansel had undertaken in the Bampton Lectures he delivered in Oxford in 1858.

Mill does not contest Hamilton's extraordinary erudition, but he does accuse him of constant vacillation on key points, amounting to flat contradiction, baldly declaring that 'Sir W. Hamilton forgets in one part of his speculations what he has thought in another' (Mill 1979: 408). Though his two volumes range over a large number of topics, it is striking that six out of fourteen chapters are devoted to the role of psychology in Hamilton's philosophy. The reason is that Mill's deepest criticism of Hamilton is methodological. He thinks that Hamilton's 'interpretation of consciousness' is an unscientific mix of psychological introspection and a priori speculation, resulting in questionable generalisations about the human mind, which are then lent a specious authority by being declared the universal deliverances of 'Common Sense'.

> Idealists, and Sceptics, contend that the belief in Matter is not an original fact of consciousness, as our sensations are, and is therefore wanting in the requisite which, in M. Cousin's and Sir W. Hamilton's opinion, gives to our subjective convictions objective authority. Now, be these persons right or wrong, they cannot be refuted in the mode in which M. Cousin and Sir W. Hamilton attempt to do so – by appealing to Consciousness itself. For we have no means of interrogating consciousness in the only circumstances in which it is possible for it to give a trustworthy answer . . . [W]e have no means of now ascertaining, by direct evidence, whether we were conscious of outward and extended objects when we first opened our eyes to the light.
>
> . . .
>
> The proof that any of the alleged Universal Beliefs, or Principles of Common Sense, are affirmations of consciousness, supposes two things; that the beliefs exist, and that they cannot possibly have been acquired. The first is in most cases undisputed, but the second is a subject of inquiry which often taxes the utmost resources of psychology.

> Locke was therefore right in believing that 'the origin of our ideas' is the main stress of the problem of mental science, and the subject which must be first considered in forming the theory of the Mind ... [W]e cannot study the original elements of mind in the facts of our present consciousness. Those original elements can only come to light as residual phenomena, by a previous study of the modes of generation of the mental facts which are confessedly not original ... This mode of ascertaining the original elements of mind I call the psychological, as distinguished from the simply introspective mode. It is the known and approved method of physical science, adapted to the necessities of psychology.
>
> ...
>
> That we cannot imagine a time at which we had no knowledge of Extension, is no evidence that there has not been such a time. (Mill 1979: 140–2)

V

According to a common assessment, Mill's *Examination* constituted the complete destruction of Hamilton's philosophical pretensions. According to W. J. Mander, however,

> if we look closely ... we quickly see that Mill was as careless as an interpreter as he was uncharitable, and on many points Hamilton could easily have set him straight. Any appearance of 'victory' is in no small part due to the fact that Hamilton was by that point long dead, with only his students and admirers left to point out the weaknesses and misunderstandings of Mill's attack. (Mander 2020: 11–12)

One of the most distinguished of these admirers was Henry Mansel, who published a vigorous response to Mill. In *The Philosophy of the Conditioned* (1866) Mansel accused Mill of wholly misunderstanding the position he meant to attack. Mill takes Hamilton's contentions about the *nature* of consciousness to be contentions about the *history* of consciousness. This is an evident misunderstanding. As Mansel correctly points out, Hamilton nowhere makes any claims about 'what Consciousness told us at the time when its revelations were in their pristine purity' (Mill 1979: 139). To suppose that he does is to reject Reid's basic insight on which Hamilton was building, namely, that any serious intellectual investigation must either presuppose the reliability of conscious awareness from the outset, or be self-vitiating. How could 'a study of the modes of generation of the mental facts', such as Mill supposes psychology to be, be undertaken without a prior exercise of consciousness? We can only assemble, arrange and theorise facts that we have first been able to ascertain. And how does Mill imagine we are to ascertain the facts his study requires, unless we hold it to be incontestably true that our acts of consciousness, though no doubt erroneous from time to time, generally give us reliable access to facts that are not of our own manufacture?

From the perspective of Hamilton, then, Mill inevitably slides back into some version of sterile Lockean 'sensationalism'. All we have access to are mental sensations. The Hypothetical Realist declares these to be the product of an objective world we cannot access. Mill, it seems, does not even go this far. By his account the only intelligible conception of 'matter' is 'a Permanent Possibility of Sensation', which, he thinks, 'includes the whole meaning attached to [the concept] by the common world' (Mill 1979: 184). However, possibility, even if it is permanent, is not reality, from which it would appear to follow that mental sensations are the substance of reality. If so, we are back to a version of 'the ideal theory' that wholly vindicates Reid's 'superstitious horror'.

In the course of his attack on Mill, Mansel takes notice of Stirling as well. 'It is curious', he writes in a footnote, 'that the very passage which Mr Mill cites as proving that Hamilton, in spite of his professed phenomenalism, was an unconscious noumenalist, is employed by Mr Stirling to prove that, in spite of his professed presentationism, he was an unconscious representationalist' (Mansel 1991: 85). The passage in question is to be found in the first volume of Hamilton's posthumously published lectures, where he says:

> It is, therefore, of the highest moment that we should be aware that what we know is not a simple relation apprehended between the object known and the subject knowing, – but that every knowledge is a sum made up of several elements . . . In the perception of an external object, the mind does not know it in immediate relation to itself, but mediately in relation to the material organs of sense. If, therefore, we were to throw these organs out of consideration, and did not take into account what they contribute to, and how they modify, our knowledge of that object, it is evident that our conclusion in regard to the nature of external perception would be erroneous. (Hamilton 2001: 146)

No one can deny that we need eyes to be able to see, and that poor eyesight can get in the way of our seeing objects properly. But how are these facts about the 'organs of sense' relevant to the construction or modification of knowledge? It is difficult not to conclude that it is neither Mill nor Stirling but Hamilton, with his abstruse account of the relations between mental image, physical object and sense organ, who is primarily responsible for the 'curiosity' Mansel notes. It does not clearly come down on one side or the other of the presentationist/phenomenalist dichotomy, but neither does it adequately transcend that dichotomy. Stirling's Idealism and Mill's empiricism are at odds, certainly, and both might be expected to attack a position that sought to occupy middle ground. The fact that they could cite the same passage in support of competing positions is evidence, *pace* Mansel, of Hamilton's failure even to articulate clearly a third possibility.

Mansel, however, does identify a deeper and ultimately more important difference between Mill and Hamilton. This is their contrasting conceptions of the inquiry in which they are engaged.

> Psychology, which with Hamilton is especially the philosophy of man as a free and personal agent, is with Mill the science of 'the uniformities of succession; the laws, whether ultimate or derivative, according to which one mental state succeeds another'. (Mansel 1991: 61, quoting Mill's *Logic* VI 4 §3)

The contrast between 'philosophy' and 'science' in this passage is significant. Hamilton, successfully or unsuccessfully, is attempting to do something that lies at the heart of Common Sense philosophy – namely, establish a philosophical conception of mind and matter that avoids the errors of both sensationalism and materialism. Reid's *Inquiry into the Human Mind upon the Principles of Common Sense*, and everything that took a lead from it, aimed to construe the relation between the mental and the material worlds properly, by doing justice to the facts of both. In this sense it seeks a middle ground between the traditional dichotomy of mind and matter, while at the same time connecting the facts of human psychology with the norms of rational thought. For Mill, however, this is a necessarily fruitless endeavour since there is no middle ground. The 'laws of the mind', he tells us, are either 'the laws of association according to one class of thinkers, [or] the Categories of the Understanding according to another' (Mill 1979: 140). If, taking our lead from Hume, we pursue the former, then the future

Hamilton and the Revitalisation of Scottish Philosophy 43

lies with empirical associationist psychology. If, following Kant, we pursue the latter, we will engage in logic. The speciousness of any Reidian 'middle ground' is revealed by the fact that it necessarily trades in simple opinion. This is the charge that Mill ultimately brings against Hamilton.

> In the mode he practises of ascertaining [the primary facts of consciousness], there is nothing for science to do. For, to call them so because in his opinion he himself, and those who agree with him, cannot get rid of the belief in them, does not seem exactly a scientific process. It is, however, characteristic of what I have called the introspective, in contradistinction to the psychological, method of metaphysical inquiry. (Mill 1979: 147)

This accusation – that the 'method' of Common Sense is anti-intellectual – is a recurrent theme among the critics of 'the Scottish School'. It is one to which John Veitch expressly offers a reply in his 1883 exposition of Hamilton.

> In ordinary usage, common-sense of course means a general shrewdness and sobriety of intelligence in the affairs of life, native rather than acquired. Because, apparently, of this one sense of the term . . . it has actually been supposed that the thinkers of the Scottish school meant to leave the problems of philosophy to be dealt with by the shrewd practicality of ordinary intelligence . . . [I]s not this the abandonment of the scientific or speculative intelligence, which is our true help to pure knowledge . . .? Of course, no thinker who can fairly be taken to be representative of the Scottish school ever thought of elevating common-sense in its ordinary usage of native shrewdness to the place of a judge in philosophy . . . The method of common-sense, as interpreted almost uniformly by Reid, and always by Hamilton, is 'not an appeal from philosophy to blind feeling' or to ordinary belief. 'The first problem of philosophy,' says Hamilton, 'is to seek out, purify, and establish by intellectual analysis and criticism, the elementary feelings and beliefs in which are given the elementary truths of which all are in possession. This is dependent upon philosophy as an art.' (Veitch 1883: 37)

The principles of Common Sense, Veitch goes on to argue,

> are found to be embodied in consciousness, in language, in action, in science, in art, in religion. A philosophy which is true, sound, and complete, must recognize those notions, and seek their guarantee, try

> to determine their meaning and applications; or if it says they are illusions, it is bound consistently with its pretensions to show how those illusions have grown up in the common consciousness of mankind. (Veitch 1883: 38)

Philosophy, we might say, is the art of making sense of common sense; it is not the attempt to identify 'uniformities of succession; the laws, whether ultimate or derivative, according to which one mental state succeeds another', which, as Mill and others hoped, would form the demonstrable results of a new science. Hamilton, in fact, expressly rejects the establishment of truths as the proper end of philosophy. In commenting on philosophy in France before the advent of Cousin, he observes that 'discussion had ceased', not because Condillac had demonstrated the truth of his psychological theories beyond reasonable doubt, but because his sensationalism was widely accepted as true. *But*, he then goes on to add,

> Nor would such a result have been desirable, had the one exclusive opinion been true, as it was false, – innocent, as it was corruptive. If the accomplishment of philosophy is simply a cessation of discussion, – if the result of speculation be a paralysis of itself; the consummation of knowledge is the condition of intellectual barbarism. Plato has profoundly defined man, – 'The *hunter* of truth;' for in this chase, as in others, the *pursuit* is all in all, the success comparatively nothing. 'Did the Almighty,' says Lessing, 'holding in his right hand *Truth*, and in his left *Search after Truth*, deign to proffer me the one I might prefer; – in all humility, but without hesitation, I should request – *Search after Truth*.' We *exist* only as we energise; . . . In *action* is . . . perfection of our being; and knowledge is only precious, as it may afford a stimulus to the exercise of our powers, and the condition of their more complete activity. Speculative truth is, therefore, subordinate to speculation itself . . . Every *learner* in science is now familiar with more truths than Aristotle or Plato ever dreamt of knowing; yet, compared with the Stagirite or the Athenian, how few, even of our *masters* of modern science, rank higher than the intellectual barbarians! Ancient Greece and modern Europe prove, indeed, that 'the march of intellect' is no inseparable concomitant of 'the march of science'. (Hamilton 1853: 40–1, emphasis original)

If speculative truth is indeed subordinate to speculation itself, at least as far as philosophy is concerned, then we may say that the esteem in which Hamilton's contemporaries held him was indeed warranted. 'I am and always have been a disciple of Hamilton,' Veitch writes, 'not in the sense of following his opinions, or teaching these; . . . but in the way of the spirit of the man.'

> What I have felt as the greatest thing about Hamilton is, not his philosophy, powerful as this is, but the man himself . . . For there is even a higher standard by which we may test . . . the intellectual power of a man than the real or supposed correctness of the conclusions he has sought to establish . . . The electric force of intellect is not to be measured merely by the degree of illumination which it casts over the field of human knowledge; it is to be gathered as well from the amount of vitality which it imparts to the minds through which it passes, and which it quickens to the life of thought. (Veitch 1883: 27)

There are thus two different standards of success by which Hamilton's status can be assessed. In his chapter on 'The Development and Consequences of the Scottish Philosophy of Common Sense', James Seth makes the point succinctly.

> [Hamilton's] reputation has been finally discredited for us by Mill's relentless *Examination* and Hutchison Stirling's still more caustic *Analysis* . . . Mill indeed finds that 'the enormous amount of time and mental vigour which he expended on mere philosophical erudition [left] only the remains of his mind for the real business of thinking,' part of the explanation of Hamilton's failure to contribute more effectively to the solution of philosophical problems. Yet even his erudition has been to some extent discredited. Apart from errors in points of detail, he often fails entirely to grasp the system or to appreciate the point of view of the several philosophers to whom he refers . . . [Yet] the fact remains that Hamilton gave a new and a strong impulse to the study of philosophy . . . and it is rather as the originator of such an impulse than in virtue of the importance of his own contributions to the solution of its problems that his significance is to be found. (J. Seth 1912: 298–300)

It is worth noting that Seth's book is dedicated to his teacher Alexander Campbell Fraser, 'distinguished alike as a representative and as an expositor of English [language] philosophy', who had expressly said that he owed 'more to Hamilton than to any other intellectual influence'. Seth resigned from the Sage Chair of Moral

Philosophy at Cornell in order to become Professor of Moral Philosophy at Edinburgh as successor to his other principal mentor in philosophy, Henry Calderwood, who had also recorded his debt to Hamilton. From the ranks of Hamilton's students who became distinguished occupants of Scottish philosophical Chairs we can add the names of John Veitch and Thomas Spencer Baynes. In *Memories of Two Cities* David Masson, who in later years became Professor of Rhetoric and English at Edinburgh, and Historiographer Royal for Scotland, recalls the astonishing impression that Hamilton had on his students, and especially 'the ablest young minds native to the University'. At the time of his appointment to the Chair of Logic, Masson says,

> All that Hamilton was to be, and all the honour that was to come to the University of Edinburgh from its having possessed him, were not foreseen. It was not foreseen that to him, more than any contemporary of his in Britain, would be traced a general deepening and strengthening of the speculative mood of the land . . . [but] the little student-world round the University quadrangle had already ascertained its own good fortune in possessing Hamilton among its teachers. When he was named or thought of, it was as the Kant or Aristotle of the place . . . His grasp, his very fingermarks, if I may say so, were visible on the young minds that had passed through his teaching. (Masson 1911: 114–16)

Judged by the degree to which Hamilton quickened the life of thought in his own time, then, he can be heralded as a major figure in 'the march of intellect' in Scotland and abroad. Mill's *Examination*, of course, is based exclusively on the 'supposed correctness of the conclusions [Hamilton] sought to establish', and, even allowing for Mill's prejudices, by this standard it does seem correct to say that Hamilton's contribution to 'the march of science' – the resolution of the intellectual problems with which he was concerned – is at best limited and perhaps nugatory. If, on the other hand, we question Mill's implicit preference for a contribution to the 'results' of 'psychology as a science', and make our criterion the intellectual stimulation of a generation in the practice of 'philosophy as an art', there is reason to conclude that his *Examination* is ill-conceived. It is as a philosopher, not as a scientist, that Hamilton should be judged.

This cannot be the final word, however. Philosophical influence arises, and endures, from books as well as lectures. There is no doubt that several of Hamilton's students went on to publish works of considerable philosophical significance, and in their turn stimulated further generations to do so as well. The century across which Hamilton's Chair was held by Alexander Campbell Fraser, Andrew Seth Pringle-Pattison and Norman Kemp Smith is a striking illustration of this. Nevertheless, it remains the case that Hamilton himself published very little philosophy. Leaving aside his posthumously published lectures, his contribution to the literature of philosophy consists in just three review essays, with copious notes and supplementary 'dissertations' in his edition of Reid. More importantly, this small corpus has not proved to have enduring philosophical interest. This is not because it lacks 'results', or defends positions that have proved erroneous. This is true of almost all philosophy ever written. Plato's dialogues, for instance, are eminently worth reading even though almost everyone acknowledges that there is not much 'correctness' about 'the conclusions he sought to establish'. But the modern reader who is interested in the philosophical problems that exercised Hamilton and his contemporaries will gain relatively little by returning to the philosophical texts he left behind. This marks an important difference between Hamilton and other Scottish philosophers such as Hutcheson, Hume, Reid and Smith. It is in his contribution to the activity of philosophy in his own day, and his influence over subsequent generations, that Hamilton's accomplishment is to be found, not in his repository of texts. A similar assessment might be made of Socrates, of course, and as in that case, it is perhaps in the writings of some of Hamilton's students and successors that we should seek to find a more lasting philosophical legacy.

3

James Frederick Ferrier and the Course of Scottish Philosophy

I

In Part 4 of his highly acclaimed book *The Democratic Intellect*, George Elder Davie tells a dramatic and riveting story about the decline of Scottish Enlightenment philosophy in the course of the nineteenth century. A central role in the story is given to James Frederick Ferrier, Professor of Moral Philosophy at St Andrews from 1845 until his death in 1864. *The Democratic Intellect* was published in 1961, but Davie's fascination with Ferrier, he tells us, had begun nearly thirty years earlier in 1936, when he first read about Ferrier in Torgny Segerstedt's book *The Problem of Knowledge in Scottish Philosophy*.[1] As a result, he found himself

> caught up in the problem as to why this St Andrews Professor of Moral Philosophy . . . should be completely neglected in the philosophy classrooms of twentieth-century Scotland in favour of contemporaries or near contemporaries of his such as J. S. Mill or F. H. Bradley, who, whatever their merits, were in no wise his superiors in the quality of their philosophy . . . [and] . . . greatly inferior to him in the matter of anticipating and offering illumination on the principal innovations of twentieth-century thought. (Davie 1991: 89)

Davie's estimate of Ferrier was not eccentric. Ferrier's contemporary, Principal John Tulloch, a scholar of great distinction and philosophical acumen, concludes a long commemorative essay, 'Professor Ferrier and the Higher Philosophy', with this fine tribute.

---

[1] Davie misremembered the title and called it 'The *Theory* of Knowledge in Scottish Philosophy'. In later publications he corrected this.

> [W]e feel warranted in saying of Professor Ferrier – whatever estimate may be formed of his philosophical system – that he is one of those thinkers who are likely to leave their mark upon the course of metaphysical opinion. There is life in all that came from his pen, – the life which springs out of intense conviction and of a rare, brilliant, and penetrating faculty of thought. (Tulloch 1884: 374)

Fifty years on, the estimate of Ferrier's distinction had not diminished. In 1911, the University of St Andrews marked its 500th anniversary with a special publication – *Votiva Tabella*. The chapter on philosophy was written by G. F. Stout, then Professor of Logic and Metaphysics. He says this of Ferrier.

> Ferrier stands out as *the* representative of St Andrews philosophy ... the fifteen years he spent in St Andrews were the fruitful years of his life. In them all his most valuable and characteristic work was produced; and it was produced in immediate connexion with his activity as a teacher ... Further, his thinking was no mere derivative stream having its primary source in other minds. He was himself a fountain head ... 'Whatever my dominion over truth may be, I have conquered every inch of it myself.' In this somewhat boastful utterance he does not mean to disown indebtedness to his predecessors. What he intends to assert is, that he adopted from them no ready-made doctrines, but that what he derived from them was rather stimulus, suggestion, and material for the development of his own thought. This is true more or less of all whose names deserve to appear in the History of Philosophy. But it held good in a special degree of Ferrier. (Stout 1911: 154–5)

These testaments to Ferrier's brilliance are impressive, and they serve to intensify Davie's puzzle. Why has his work been so neglected?

II

A major part of the purpose of *The Democratic Intellect*, as well as most of Davie's later publications, was to explain and understand this near disappearance from the history of philosophy. It was, Davie contends, a consequence of the intellectual, educational and cultural circumstances that surrounded Ferrier's rejection for two professorial positions at the University of Edinburgh, in 1852 as a candidate for the Chair of Moral Philosophy, and especially in

1856 as a candidate in the Chair of Logic and Metaphysics. What made these rejections so surprising was that on both occasions Ferrier was, by almost any reckoning, the most philosophically distinguished candidate. Already a professor of philosophy in a Scottish university with a very substantial record of publication and a European-wide reputation, he was supported in his candidature for the Chair of Moral Philosophy by Sir William Hamilton, arguably the most reputable philosopher in Britain at that time. It was Hamilton's death in 1856 that then left the Chair of Logic vacant, and to many minds it was obvious that Ferrier was the person best fitted to be Hamilton's successor. Yet again, though, he was rejected.

On both occasions, the decision lay with Electors appointed by Edinburgh's Town Council. Inevitably this introduced a political element, but Davie sees the politics of the appointment as simply one aspect of what he repeatedly refers to as a cultural, educational and philosophical *crisis*. The roots of this crisis stretched back over a century to the union between England and Scotland, but it finally came to a head with the 'Disruption' of 1843, when the national Church of Scotland split over longstanding differences about the proper relationship between Church and State. According to Davie, this division had crucial consequences for philosophy in Scotland, and these consequences showed themselves most dramatically in certain key university appointments. 'The epoch of the Disruption – as the Scottish collapse has been termed – was characterized by a series of bitter and prolonged public disputes about appointments to philosophy chairs, and about the character of the philosophy to be taught from them' (Davie 1961: 287).

Why should this be so? *The Democratic Intellect* elaborates a twofold explanation, part institutional, part intellectual. The institutional aspect arose from the fact that, under the leadership of Thomas Chalmers, Professor of Moral Philosophy at St Andrews from 1823 to 1828 and Professor of Divinity at Edinburgh from 1828 until the schism, the 'Free' church resolved to establish alternative 'Free' universities that would not be subject to political interference. Chalmers died in 1847, and by 1852 only New College in Edinburgh had come anywhere near to establishing a range of subjects other than theology. Consequently, when religious tests in the ancient universities fell into abeyance, Free Church clergy were eligible for appointment, and anxious to return to the larger intellectual context of a well-established and famous university. This is what happened in Edinburgh. In 1852, and again in 1856, Ferrier's successful rivals were both New College professors.

But, according to Davie, the real explanation lay beyond this institutional rivalry, in deep philosophical differences that had been growing over many decades.

> Scottish philosophy owed to Hume above all, on its own confession, the conception of a fundamental role in metaphysical inquiry of a peculiar set of mental facts, intermediary between the all-embracing One of the rationalists and the fragmented and atomized Many of the empiricists – namely the *natural beliefs* or principles of common sense, such as the belief in an independent external world, the belief in causality, the belief in ideal standards, and the belief in the self of *conscience* as separate from the rest of one.
>
> Reid and his followers had very much the same conception of the task of philosophy as had Hume. They all tended to agree with Hume that the traditional problems of philosophy were concerned with a question whether a given natural belief, although unable to be justified by a straightforward appeal to experience, might nevertheless be defended in terms of a reference to experience taken in some wider sense; and it was, in fact, the diverse possible modes of conducting the defence which gave rise to the chief philosophical division among the Scots. On the extreme left we find the characteristic answer of Hume that the common-sense beliefs, for all that they can never be renounced, are sometimes nevertheless ultimately indefensible being in fact contradicted by experience. Then somewhat to the right, the middling answer of Reid, Stewart, Hamilton and the bulk of the school was that while beliefs of common sense are not inconsistent with experience . . . they contain in fact an irreducible element of mystery.
>
> Finally, thinkers such as Brown and Ferrier regarded the mystery-mongering of Reid and Hamilton as a very ineffective reply to Hume's scepticism, and proceeded to exploit the possibilities of a full-scale rational defence of common sense . . .
>
> It is to be expected that the distinctions drawn here between the skeptical, the intuitionist and the rational tendencies profess to be accurate only in a general, approximative way. In particular, while it applies fairly well to the position of the philosophers in question in reference to the School's favourite problem of belief in an external world, it does not hold so rigorously in reference to other problems. (Davie 1961: 274–5, emphasis original)

This threefold division of philosophical opinion sets the stage for 'the greatest of all the academical crises of Victorian Scotland – the crack-up of the Common Sense school' (Davie 1961: 277) and with it the 'battles' that surrounded the competition for philosophical Chairs – not only in Edinburgh, but in St Andrews and Aberdeen as well.

Davie uses this dramatic background to explain both Ferrier's significance within the Scottish philosophical tradition, and his disappearance from its history. Ferrier, he holds, 'thanks to Sir William Hamilton's stimulus', 'was redefining the tasks and problems of philosophy' and 'as a result of their joint efforts, the common sense tradition seemed to be undergoing a renovation destined to adapt its sagacity and moderation to the conditions of the modern world, and it looked for a time as if the burning bush of Scottish philosophy might continue to be a beacon to the nations' (Davie 1961: 276–7). The product of Ferrier's 'renovation' was a long series of articles published in *Blackwood's Magazine* between 1838 and 1843. It was on the strength of these substantial essays that Ferrier had been appointed to the St Andrews Chair. In rejecting Ferrier for a philosophical Chair at Edinburgh, then, the Electors were effectively rejecting a revitalised version of Scottish philosophy. As a consequence of that rejection, the 'old' version of Scottish Common Sense philosophy faded from view as it became ever more passé, to be overshadowed before too long by an imported version of German Idealism.

But if Ferrier was giving new vigour to the philosophical tradition that stemmed from Hume and Reid, why was his application for the Edinburgh Chairs rejected? Davie has an explanation for this also. Ferrier's aim, he says, was to frame a 'new philosophy of common sense' that would be 'anti-intuitive and consistently rational', and thereby 'provide a more effective answer to the irrationalist Evangelical doctrines of unverifiable illuminations and uncommunicable inspirations' (Davie 1961: 288). Among the three versions of Scottish philosophy that Davie earlier identified, the 'middling' version of Reid and Stewart had become a 'tepid, halfhearted rationality of official common sense philosophy' (ibid.), powerless against the religious dogmatism and emotional preaching to which the Evangelicals of the Free Church had given new life. Ferrier's new version could have better served the purpose, but for this very reason invited religious opposition. His double failure at Edinburgh put paid to the prospect of a reinvigorated Common

Sense philosophy, and, importantly for Davie's story, that failure was engineered by the most powerful Evangelical figure of the period – the Revd John Cairns, successor to Chalmers as Principal of the still fledgling university, New College.

III

How persuasive is Davie's account of Ferrier's rise and fall? For present purposes the central question is his relationship to the history and development of Scottish philosophy, but there is also the matter of the political analysis Davie offers us, and it is worth saying something about this first. To begin with, it should be acknowledged that appointments to Chairs in the Scottish universities had often been the subject of political machination. This was especially true of the Chair of Moral Philosophy at Edinburgh. Exactly 100 years before Ferrier, Hume had been rejected for the position. It is quite widely assumed that this was a consequence of his philosophical views and their unacceptability to the religious and philosophical establishment. No doubt this played some part, but detailed research by Roger L. Emerson has shown that Hume's candidature fell foul of the then deep political division between two Scottish factions, the Squadrone and the Argathelians (see Emerson 1994). It was politics more than religion that kept Hume out of the Chair.

Similarly, in 1820, following the death of Thomas Brown, politics determined the appointment of his successor. At this time a no less factional divide persisted, but it was now between Whig and Tory. In 1810 Brown had been appointed to succeed Dugald Stewart, whose protégé he was, and Stewart was well known for his Whig sympathies. In 1820 William Hamilton was without question the academic front-runner for the Chair, but he too was a Whig sympathiser, and by then the political tide had turned. Tories were in the ascendant. Consequently, the appointment went to John Wilson, better known as 'Christopher North', the pen-name under which he authored his highly partisan contributions to *Blackwood's Magazine*. This had been established as the arch-Tory rival to the arch-Whig *Edinburgh Review*, edited by Francis Jeffrey. Wilson, Davie says, with a measure of understatement, 'was for the most part a very unprofessional person so far as philosophy was concerned' (Davie 1961: 282). It would be more accurate to say, in fact, that despite the great popularity of his lectures, Wilson was not a philosopher at all. Yet he occupied the Chair for over thirty years.

These precedents must serve to mitigate the powerful sense that Davie so successfully conjures up of the highly fraught nature of the competitions in which Ferrier took part. Moreover, he adds to this sense by exaggerating the Evangelical fervour, both of those who were appointed and of those who supported them. Patrick Campbell Macdougall, who was appointed to the Chair of Moral Philosophy in preference to Ferrier, had taken 'On Moral Philosophy – its Province, Limits and Leading Divisions' as the subject for his inaugural lecture as Professor of Moral Philosophy at New College a few years before. It does not make for exciting reading, but it sticks very closely to the combination of ethics and moral psychology that had long been the staple of the subject as taught in the Scottish universities. And though he remarks at the outset that 'the subject of Christian ethics . . . constitutes the last and highest division, and completes the whole' subject, he is insistent that this part can be conducted 'without any sacrifice of scientific rigour'. In the lecture itself he barely touches on the topic, saying that he has run out of time (Macdougall 1852: 314–442). In short, there is nothing in his lecture that could be called fervour, still less fanaticism.

Macdougall died in 1868 and the competitors to succeed him included Robert Flint, Ferrier's successor at St Andrews, and Henry Calderwood, a minister of the United Presbyterian Church (not the Free Church) in Glasgow, alongside James Hutchison Stirling, author of *The Secret of Hegel*. Davie is determined to portray the competition in the starkest of terms. He ignores Stirling's candidature, describes Flint as 'the last original thinker of the Scottish School', and casts Calderwood in the deepest dye – 'a man of hard, sectarian stamp . . . whose one-sided loyalty could be depended upon' – and 'thus the narrow-minded extremist was appointed instead of the broadminded man of the centre' (Davie 1961: 319). This could only be written by someone who knew nothing of Calderwood's life and had read nothing of his work. Moreover, opposition to Flint (who was only thirty-four at the time) cannot have been very deep-seated, because eight years later Edinburgh appointed him to the Chair of Divinity. When Flint and Calderwood were colleagues, James McCosh hailed them *both* as admirable advocates of Scottish philosophy against the reductivist materialism of Bain in Aberdeen and the alien Idealism of Edward Caird in Glasgow. Davie, one is inclined to say, has not allowed historical detail to get in the way of the cultural 'crisis' by which he is enthralled.

He is undoubtedly right about this, however. The opposition to Ferrier was indeed orchestrated by the leading intellectual light on the Evangelical side, John Cairns, who combined a considerable intellect with intense pietistic feeling. But importantly, Cairns's charge against Ferrier was not his religious moderation, but his abandonment, betrayal even, of the Scottish philosophical tradition. This brings us back to the aspect of *The Democratic Intellect* that is of greatest interest. What was Ferrier's relationship to Scottish philosophy?

IV

Did the neglect of Ferrier's philosophy in the half-century after his death result, as Davie contends, from a blind (and religiously convenient) adherence to the 'old' Scottish philosophy and a refusal to acknowledge that Scottish philosophy needed a 'new' direction? In the aftermath of the second competition, Ferrier himself addressed this issue in the pamphlet *Scottish Philosophy: The Old and the New*, billed as 'a statement' but running to fifty-nine pages. Written with considerable passion, the statement is a polemic rather than an academic essay, and its somewhat purple prose is probably the reason that Blackwood's, Ferrier's regular publisher, declined to undertake its publication, leaving Ferrier to have it privately printed. In it, Ferrier excoriates the Town Council Electors and their advisers, while at the same time strenuously defending his philosophical position as a metaphysical transformation of Scottish philosophy and not, as he thought his critics alleged, a Germanic-inspired rejection of the 'old' psychological approach pioneered by Hume and Reid.

After Ferrier's death, a shortened version of this pamphlet, purged of rhetorical excess, was included in the first edition of his collected *Philosophical Remains*. This was omitted from the new edition that appeared in 1883, presumably because the pamphlet, having been occasioned by a highly context-specific issue, was regarded as of little continuing philosophical interest. Who, thirty years after the event, would be concerned with the debates and rivalries surrounding a university appointment? Whether Edinburgh Town Council made the right choice, and whether the grounds upon which it was made were legitimate, were central issues for the participants, but questions that inevitably lost their interest as the years passed.

Curiously, though, interest in *Scottish Philosophy: The Old and the New* persisted, and indeed the pamphlet has been quoted by almost everyone who has written about Ferrier. This reveals that while the immediate issue was specific to one time and place, a more wide-ranging philosophical question underlay it. Between the two professorial competitions, Ferrier published the work he regarded as his magnum opus – the *Institutes of Metaphysic*. In *The Democratic Intellect*, Davie asserts that 'To the last Ferrier remained a common-sense philosopher', and he goes on to quote a passage from the *Institutes* in support of this claim (Davie 1961: 284). Cairns and others, including James McCosh some twenty years later, took quite the opposite view. They held that in the *Institutes*, Ferrier had departed so radically from the fundamental ideas at work in Reid and Hamilton that he had in effect abandoned Scottish philosophy. It was in response to such an allegation that Ferrier published his pamphlet, arguing strenuously that though his philosophy was indeed 'new', it was nonetheless 'Scottish to the very core . . . national in every fibre and articulation of its frame' (Ferrier 1856: 12). Who was in the right on this matter?

The wrath of those who opposed Ferrier's appointment to the Chair of Logic was roused not simply because Ferrier disagreed with Thomas Reid, but by the fact that he expressed this disagreement in terms so extreme that they transgressed the norms of philosophical debate. In an essay published in the year of the competition for the Logic Chair, Alexander Campbell Fraser, the successful candidate, expressed a wide consensus when he wrote, 'Dr Reid's philosophical works have long been recognized in this country as the type and standard of the Philosophy of Scotland, and they are now regarded by the most thoughtful men of Europe and America as constituting a conspicuous land mark on the wide sea of modern speculation' (Fraser 1856: 35). In sharp contrast, Ferrier in the *Institutes* wrote, 'At home in the submarine abysses of popular opinion, Dr Reid, in the higher regions of philosophy, was as helpless as a whale in a field of clover' (Ferrier 2001a: 495). It is not hard to see why his readers should regard this as the abandonment of criticism in favour of contemptuous abuse. Reid may not have accomplished as much as those who admired him believed, but the comparison of his precise and careful thinking with 'a whale in a field of clover' is absurdly wide of the mark. Many years later Fraser, writing about this matter, remarked that Reid himself 'could hardly recognize the stuffed figure put up by

Ferrier to be knocked down' (Fraser 1898: 153). Even Davie, who is broadly sympathetic, thought that Ferrier wrote with 'a vibrant fury of quite appalling vehemence' (Davie 1961: 297).

Despite his contempt for Reid, Ferrier never ceased to regard Sir William Hamilton, Reid's most ardent defender, as 'among the greatest of the great'. But his denigration of Reid could not fail to imply criticism of Hamilton as well, with the result that opposition was also roused among the people who had held Hamilton in high esteem. These included Cairns, who had been one of Hamilton's most brilliant students. In advance of the second election, Cairns published a pamphlet entitled *An Examination of Professor Ferrier's Theory of Knowing and Being*. In turn this pamphlet prompted another clergyman – John Smith – to produce a reply defending Ferrier. Cairns then issued a second pamphlet, significantly entitled *The Scottish Philosophy; A Vindication and Reply*. It was against the background of these publications that Ferrier composed his self-vindication.

It is likely that this exchange of pamphlets was the first time the expression 'Scottish philosophy' appeared as the focus for academic debate. The derogatory term 'Scotch metaphysics' had been coined by Joseph Priestley in the eighteenth century, and in 1829 Victor Cousin had published a more enthusiastic set of lectures entitled *La Philosophie Écossaise*. But the title of Cairns's pamphlet, and the response it elicited, brought the idea of a distinctively Scottish philosophical tradition to self-consciousness for the first time. By taking up the expression, Ferrier's reply to Cairns, consequently, came to have intellectual significance well beyond the events of 1856, as repeated references to 'Scottish philosophy' over the next half-century showed.

In considering this question, the case that Ferrier makes in the first third of his pamphlet is the obvious focus, since the remainder is devoted to rebutting, point by point, the specific criticisms that Cairns brings in his two pamphlets, as well as those that appear in reviews of the *Institutes* by Alexander Campbell Fraser and Henry Mansel. Essentially, Ferrier's claim is threefold. First, having recently abandoned religious tests for professorial appointments, the Electors have now imposed a philosophical test.

> Chiefly through their liberalism the religious test was abolished, and entirely through their illiberalism, a philosophical test of the most exclusive character has been substituted . . . [A] candidate for a philosophical

chair in the University of Edinburgh need not be a believer in Christ or a member of the Established Church; but he must be a believer in Dr Reid, and pledged disciple of the Hamiltonian system of philosophy. (Ferrier 1856: 7)

Secondly, this kind of restriction is based on 'a mistake about the true nature and spirit of philosophy. Philosophy is not traditional. As a mere inheritance it carries no benefit to either man or boy. The more it is a received dogmatic, the less is it a quickening process' (Ferrier 1856: 9). Thirdly, if the Electors' decision was based on the opinion 'that the old Scottish philosophy is truer than the new', then they failed to understand the kind of truth that philosophy properly so called seeks. It is on this third point that Ferrier ultimately rests his case.

Truth, under the relation in which we have at present to consider it, is not truth *simply*, but truth *in philosophy* . . . Suppose that we are discussing the subject of salt, and that we say 'salt is white and gritty, it is in some degree moist, it is sometimes put into a salt cellar and placed on the dinner table . . .' These statements about salt are all truths; they are truths, as we may say, *simply*, but they are not truths *in chemistry*. No man would be considered much of a chemist, who was merely acquainted with these and other such circumstances, concerning salt. So in philosophy no man can be called a philosopher who merely knows and says, that he and other people exist, that there is an external world, that a man is the same person today that he was yesterday, and so forth. These are undoubtedly truths, but I maintain that they are not truths in philosophy, any more than those others just mentioned, are truths in chemistry. Our old Scottish school, however, is of a different way of thinking. It represents these and similar facts as the first truths of philosophy, and to these it has recourse in handling the deeper questions of metaphysics. [My] system . . . denies that the first truths of the old Scottish school are truths in philosophy at all. This is one very fundamental point of difference between the old and the new Scottish system of metaphysics. (Ferrier 1856: 10)

[O]ne thing is certain, that the first principles of philosophy are not the elementary truths which have been enunciated as such by our old Scottish philosophy. These, I conceive, must be set aside, as good for nothing in science, however indispensable they may be in life . . . [T]he fundamental difference between the two Scottish philosophies, the Old and the New, is this, that while I hold that philosophy exists for the sole purpose of correcting the natural inadvertencies of loose, ordinary thinking – that this is her true and proper vocation; the old school, on the contrary, are of the opinion that philosophy exists for the very purpose of ratifying, and, if possible, systematising these inadvertencies. This is held by Reid and his followers to be the proper business of metaphysical science. (Ferrier 1856: 11–12)

It is essential here to distinguish between several different questions. Is Ferrier's conception of philosophy one we should endorse? Does he correctly characterise the 'old' Scottish philosophy as falling short of philosophy properly so called? Is there sufficient continuity between 'new' and 'old' to warrant identifying them both as 'Scottish'? And, by extension, does it matter whether we do so or not?

V

On the first of these questions there seems little difficulty in agreeing with Ferrier. Who could or would deny that dogmas are antithetical to philosophy? Philosophical inquiry is an activity and its practitioners must always be free to follow an argument wherever it leads. Ferrier infers from the decision of the Electors that they failed to appreciate this. Perhaps they did, though he does not adduce any specific evidence for this inference, but this would not make their mistaken attitude an intrinsic aspect of 'old' Scottish philosophy. It is also easy to agree with Ferrier that people engaged in philosophy are seeking an understanding that goes beyond everyday thought and opinion. Why else would anyone take up the study of philosophy? Ferrier implies that Reid and the 'old' school thought otherwise, but this is simply not the case. It had long been observed that 'Common Sense' is easily mistaken for 'native wit' (to use Dugald Stewart's expression) and that Reid might have done better to choose some other term. But it is impossible to read the *Inquiry* and the *Essays* with any degree of objectivity without seeing that Reid's purpose is not ratifying 'loose, ordinary thinking'. Rather, his purpose is to arrive at a better understanding of the human mind.

Cairns, in *The Scottish Philosophy*, his second pamphlet, does not undertake the defence of dogmas or 'truths'. Nor does he claim that Ferrier denies what Reid asserts. His focus is on method rather than doctrine. Ferrier's principal departure from the Scottish philosophy, Cairns claims, is his reliance on pure deduction. In arguing the point, he too draws an analogy with chemistry.

> Mr Smith [Ferrier's defender] seems to think that the Scottish Philosophy has some mortal antipathy to deduction even from established principles. All that it condemns is the attempt to deduce, prematurely and dogmatically, all truths of philosophy from one. It will employ the synthetic method as freely as chemistry; but if any man in the present state of that science proposed to deduce all the chemical elements from one, and stuck to his demonstration in the face of incorrigible fact, instead of attempting by analysis to overcome the difficulties, this would be parallel to that deductive procedure against which the Scottish Philosophy cannot cease to protest. (Cairns 1856: 18)

Thirty years later, in an article published in the *Princeton Review*, James McCosh also makes methodology, not doctrine, the defining characteristic of Scottish philosophy. First, he claims, it proceeds by observation. Second, it observes the operation of the mind chiefly through consciousness, but welcomes any assistance that may come from the study of the brain. Third, it uncovers through observation 'universal and eternal' principles that are 'above' observation. Contra Ferrier, McCosh argues that metaphysical principles have to be discovered by observation through consciousness because 'pure' reason without experience is empty. Now it is of special interest to note here that in one of his *Blackwood's Magazine* essays – 'The Crisis of Modern Speculation' – Ferrier does appeal to the idea of metaphysical discovery by observation. He heralds a 'new' philosophy that gives 'the finishing stroke' to the 'old' antithesis between Realism and Idealism (Ferrier 2001c: 286) precisely because it is based on a 'more rigorous observation of facts' about 'man's intercourse with the external world' (269). But as Davie eventually concluded, this is at odds with the method of the *Institutes*, which Cairns reasonably describes as 'an attempt to deduce . . . all truths of philosophy from one'. Douglas McDermid, a much more recent commentator on the *Institutes*, comes to the same conclusion. Ferrier is a 'committed rationalist' who 'maintains that philosophy is a purely a priori discipline, that its premises and conclusions must be necessary truths, that the only form of reasoning it can employ is deduction, and that its arguments must be proofs or demonstrations in the strict and proper sense of the term' (McDermid 2018: 168). This is unquestionably a radical methodological departure from Hutcheson, Hume, Smith, Ferguson, Stewart, Hamilton and all the other figures associated with 'the Scottish philosophy'. On what basis, then, could Ferrier's 'new' philosophy, as exemplified in the *Institutes*, still count as Scottish?

Ferrier's own answer makes no appeal to conceptual or methodological continuity, but to autobiography. He learned how to think philosophically in the shadow of Reid and with the guidance of Hamilton. He then forged his own philosophical position, not by recourse to some other group of thinkers, but by means of a sustained and critical investigation of the problems and issues with which they were concerned. Thus, context and history generate a very straightforward sense in which he can claim to be a Scottish philosopher. As a result of his own philosophical labours he eventually arrived at conclusions that diverged very significantly from theirs. But why should such an outcome be disguised or resisted? Philosophy tackles problems of exceptional difficulty in a critical rational spirit. Divergence of opinion is exactly what it must expect and allow, and what, as a matter of fact, his teacher Hamilton encouraged.

This is all plausible, and at one level incontestable. Still, the same claims could be made, for instance, by James Hutchison Stirling, who excelled in the Moral Philosophy class at Glasgow, where Professor Fleming was still basing his lectures on the texts of Reid, Stewart, Brown and, especially, Hume. Some years later, when he returned to philosophy, Stirling judged that 'Europe has continued to nourish itself from the vessel of Hume, notwithstanding that the *Historic Pabulum* has long since abandoned it for another' (A. M. Stirling 1912: 127). Accordingly, he expressly moved on, to Kant and, especially, Hegel. Ferrier made no such explicit admission. Indeed, he explicitly disavowed any debt to German philosophy. In the *Institutes*, while he allows that 'Kant had glimpses of the truth', he is no less dismissive of Hegel than of Reid.

> Hegel, – but who has ever yet uttered one intelligible word about Hegel? Not any of his countrymen, – not any foreigner, – seldom even himself ... unnavigable by the aid of any compass, and an atmosphere, or rather a vacuum, in which no human intellect can breathe ... A much less intellectual effort would be required to find out the truth for oneself than to understand his exposition of it. (Ferrier 2001a: 94–6)

Against this, Henry Laurie remarks in *Scottish Philosophy in its National Development* that Ferrier 'does not appear to have been fully aware of his indebtedness to German philosophy'.

> Yet, when we compare his philosophy to that of Kant, we find the same prominence given to a theory of knowledge, the same separation of philosophy from psychology, the same refusal to follow the guidance of popular thought, and even the same Copernican illustration of the distinction between the ordinary thoughts of men and the results to be obtained by the *savant* or the philosopher. (Laurie 1902: 310–11)

Given the 'Germanic' character of his thinking, why should Ferrier be so insistent that his 'new' way of thinking had a claim to the label 'Scottish'? Here, I am inclined to speculate, he was driven by the personal hurt he felt at being rejected for the Chair of Logic that Hamilton occupied. He had no doubt, and rightly or wrongly nor had many others, that his intellectual qualifications for this Chair greatly exceeded those of his rival, and he more than hints at that belief in his protesting pamphlet. Still, rather than baldly asserting such a claim, it was easier to contend that those members of the Town Council who voted against him (a relatively small majority in fact) were misled by Cairns. To reveal and counter the misguided nature of their judgement, therefore, it proved necessary to assert that Cairns's understanding of what could count as 'Scottish philosophy' was narrowly parochial and closed to innovation.

But even if it was, that possibility is quite compatible with Ferrier having rejected everything that could plausibly be called 'Scottish philosophy'. The question at issue, and the one that continues to lend Ferrier's pamphlet philosophical interest, is a conceptual one: does Ferrier's 'new' philosophy have sufficient continuity with the 'old' to warrant retention of the label 'Scottish'? On this score, the most plausible answer is 'no'. This was the conclusion that McCosh reached in *The Scottish Philosophy*.

> Mr Ferrier, who was supported by Hamilton in the competition for the moral philosophy chair in Edinburgh when Professor Wilson retired, and with whom Hamilton (as he assured the writer of this article) was in the habit of consulting, published the 'Institutes of Metaphysic,' which is a complete revolt against the whole of Scottish philosophy. (McCosh 1875: 422)

Ferrier and the Course of Scottish Philosophy

The key issue is the proper place of psychology. Ferrier, like Kant, insists upon a radical division between psychology and metaphysics. Psychology is based on observation, and tells us how human beings form beliefs about reality, and how those beliefs enable them, through the medium of desires and feelings, to accommodate and manipulate their environment. Metaphysics, by contrast, is founded on reason rather than observation or experience, and thus aims to tell us what we *ought* to think about reality. Its peculiar task, accordingly, is that of establishing what is truly real. Clearly human beings can hold false beliefs, may hold fast to them despite their falsehood, and may nevertheless make their way through life satisfactorily. Much that passes for 'common sense' is belief of this kind, and Reid's great failing, in Ferrier's eyes, was to think that strong convictions widely held are a proper basis for the apprehension of reality. Reid's 'philosophy', by Ferrier's account, is nothing more than low-level psychological observation masquerading as metaphysics.

It is difficult not to regard this as a gross misrepresentation of Reid, with whom Ferrier seems to have been strikingly out of sympathy, but the main point to be made here is that the invocation of a radical division between metaphysics and psychology is in effect a rejection of the philosophical method propagated by Hume and Reid and pursued by their successors. It is precisely on this ground that Victor Cousin opposed Ferrier as the successor to Hamilton and supported Fraser instead. 'When the psychological approach is given up at Aberdeen, at Glasgow and at Edinburgh, on that day, we do not hesitate to predict, it is all up with Scottish philosophy' (quoted in Davie 1961: 313).

Rejecting this method was not unique to Ferrier. His younger contemporary Alexander Bain, whose application for the Logic Chair in St Andrews in 1858 Ferrier strongly supported, employs the very same distinction some twenty years later in an article in *Mind*, the journal Bain had founded.

> We are, at this moment, in the midst of a conflict of views as to the priority of Metaphysics and Psychology. If indeed the two are so closely identified as some suppose, there is no conflict; there is in fact one study ... It is said [as it would have been said by Ferrier] that if we embark on the promiscuous field of mental facts, with a bad Metaphysics, that is, with wrong notions as to External Reality, Cause, Substance, and so on, all our results will be vitiated and

> worthless; nevertheless, I do not see any mode of attaining a correct Metaphysics until Psychology has at least made some way upon a provisional Metaphysics which it returns to after a time to rectify and improve. (Bain 1903: 37–8)

Ferrier thinks that it is the role of metaphysics to correct psychology. Bain thinks that, for a time at any rate, psychology is needed to correct metaphysics. Now if we take Hume, Reid and Hamilton to be among 'those who suppose' that metaphysics and psychology are 'closely identified', then Bain can be seen to be departing from the Scottish philosophy no less than Ferrier, but in the opposite direction. If this is correct then Bain (though he made no such claim) has as much reason as Ferrier to declare his approach to be a 'new' Scottish philosophy. Both claims, of course, could not be correct. The more obvious inference to draw is that Ferrier and Bain, for quite different reasons, came to the conclusion that 'the Scottish philosophy' of Reid and Hamilton had run into the sand.

Davie, after almost half a century studying Ferrier, had come to a rather different conclusion from the one advanced in *The Democratic Intellect*. In *Ferrier and the Blackout of the Scottish Enlightenment* (2003) he retracted his earlier assertion that Ferrier had remained a Common Sense philosopher to the last.

> The difficulty that occupied me was how to make sense of the apparent contradictions between Ferrier's early philosophy in his *Blackwood's* articles and his later philosophy as contained in the *Institutes of Metaphysic* some fourteen years afterwards. For many years I tried to find a way of reconciling the later philosophy with the earlier philosophy, a way of squaring what Ferrier calls the 'New' Scottish philosophy with the 'Old' Scottish philosophy. Ultimately, I came to the conclusion that what Ferrier calls the 'New' Scottish philosophy – that is, the *Institutes* – is not merely irreconcilable with his version of the 'Old' Scottish philosophy, but is a contradictory and indefensible position. (Davie 2003: 1)

The book ends with this sentence: 'A career which begins in philosophical genius concludes in contradiction, and we witness in Ferrier not the renewal of the Scottish Enlightenment, but its intellectual blackout' (Davie 2003: 73).

VI

In Davie's final estimation, then, Ferrier sank into philosophical oblivion because he failed to complete the renewal of Scottish philosophy of which his earlier writings showed such promise. But if a 'blackout' of some sort did descend, this evidently did not mean the end of philosophy in Scotland. On the contrary, attention simply turned in a new direction. From the 1860s onwards, the attractions of Hegelian Idealism had greatly diminished the status of Reid and Common Sense in the Scottish universities, so much so that by 1885 Andrew Seth could write, 'It will hardly be denied that the philosophical productions of the younger generation of our University men are more strongly impressed with a German than with a native stamp' (Seth Pringle-Pattison 1885: 2). This turn to Idealism, interestingly, has prompted a quite different assessment of Ferrier's influence on the course of Scottish philosophy, and a correspondingly different explanation of his neglect.

In *The Rise and Fall of Scottish Common Sense Realism*, Douglas McDermid makes no reference to Davie, but he give expression to exactly the same sort of puzzlement about Ferrier's neglect in the history of the subject.

> An acute reasoner and a forceful stylist, Ferrier was the author of several works remarkable for their ambition and élan . . . For the most part, these works – witty, argument-rich, and written with panache and pugnacity – still make for very good reading. But who today has heard of their author, let alone glanced at his works? (McDermid 2018: 137)

For McDermid, like Davie, at least part of the explanation lies in the affair of the Edinburgh professorial competitions.

> Ferrier's reputation in Scotland suffered as a result of the events of 1856. When he died less than a decade later (in 1864) at St Andrews, he had founded no school, inspired no movement, attracted no followers . . . Had Ferrier been appointed to the Chair of Logic and Metaphysics at Edinburgh, however, he would have almost certainly exerted significantly greater influence upon the intellectual life of his country, and his magnum opus would very likely have attracted considerable interest abroad . . . And if that had happened, more universities outside Scotland would have made the *Institutes* required

reading ... and more historians of philosophy would have felt obliged to relate his mature system to the production of greater and lesser minds. In short Ferrier could have been a contender and not a footnote, had he only received a few more votes in the summer of 1856. (McDermid 2018: 207)

This, of course, is speculation – the 'history' of the 'might have been' – but McDermid goes on to find what might be called Ferrier's *hidden* intellectual influence.

One way of summing up Ferrier's achievement would be to say that the *Institutes of Metaphysic* finishes what Hamilton started, and that its author did unto Hamilton what Hamilton did unto Reid ... [W]hat Ferrier has done is to refine Hamilton's qualified realism until the realist elements have been eliminated from it like so much dross, and all that remains is an unalloyed idealism which is simultaneously post-Kantian and neo-Berkeleyan. Locke's material substances, Reid's mind-independent objects, Kant's things-in-themselves, Hamilton's unconditioned: these dreadful spectres and frightful phantoms have been exorcized by Ferrier, and philosophy need no longer be haunted by them ... Realism is now an exotic relic, a faded dust-covered curio; idealism is the new Scottish philosophy, born from the womb of the old, and the future belongs to her children. (McDermid 2018: 198)

[B]y the end of the nineteenth century, several of the once-unpopular causes championed by Ferrier in the 1840s and 1850s had triumphed: Thomas Reid was no longer the *beau ideal* of most Scottish philosophers, the old meta-philosophy of common sense was decidedly out of favour, and idealism had supplanted realism as the metaphysic of choice in many Scottish universities. (McDermid 2018: 207)

In short, thanks to Ferrier's *Institutes of Metaphysic*, 'Idealism had established itself as the new Scottish philosophy' (McDermid 2018: 208).

Jennifer Keefe is of the same opinion. 'Ferrier's work marks a turning point in the history of Scottish philosophy: the end of the Enlightenment. Thereafter there was indeed a new Scottish philosophy, albeit one that Ferrier anticipated rather than took part in' (Keefe 2015: 92). In a similar vein, without special reference to *Scottish* philosophy, W. J. Mander accords Ferrier a key, if hitherto generally unacknowledged, role in the change that came over British philosophy more broadly in the latter part of the nineteenth century.

> There are reasons to regard at least part of the impetus for the Idealist movement as both earlier and more home-grown than the traditional starting gun that is James Hutchison Stirling's *The Secret of Hegel* (1865)...
>
> The British Idealist movement was such a rapid and dramatic shift in the national style of philosophy that it is natural to wonder how it came about, and it has been common to locate its origin in a Kant-and-Hegel-inspired counter-reaction to the native empirical tradition of Hume and Mill. This is not necessarily wrong. But it is interesting to note that many of the Idealists themselves saw the roots of their movement in an earlier and rather different reaction, namely that of James Frederick Ferrier to the Scottish 'common-sense' philosophy of William Hamilton... Ferrier certainly knew and was inspired by German Idealism (his attempts to downplay this influence have more to do with politics than philosophy) but the case he sets out in the *Institutes* owes no significant debt to that tradition. In the light of this, the very fact that the British Idealists saw their own later efforts as continuous with his must begin to modify our perception of *their* relation to German Idealism. (Mander 2020: 207–9)

This relocation of Ferrier within the history of philosophy in Scotland from the fag-end of Common Sense to the vanguard of Idealism can also be found in much earlier commentators. In *Scottish Philosophy in its National Development*, for instance, Laurie writes:

> [T]hough the immediate influence of Ferrier on his contemporaries may not have been great, he anticipated the wave of continental speculation which was destined to change the character of Scottish philosophy in the latter half of the century. And the neo-Kantian speculation of recent years reproduces much that had been more simply said in the *Institutes* of Ferrier. (Laurie 1902: 311)

This view is repeated in *Veterum Laudes*, a volume published in 1950 to mark 500 years of St Andrews' oldest surviving college. Thomas Malcolm Knox, who was at the time Professor of Moral Philosophy and later Principal of the University, declares Ferrier to be 'the most distinguished philosopher in all our history'. He finds the chief significance of Ferrier's work, however, not so much in its intrinsic merits as in its consequences, especially in preparing the ground for Stirling's influential volume.

> It was Ferrier's writings above all others which helped to produce that climate of opinion which made it possible for Scotland to become receptive to the Hegelian influence transmitted through Hutchison Stirling and the Cairds. That is the great contribution which Ferrier made to the intellectual life of his country and for which St Salvator's must venerate him as one of its greatest names. (Knox 1950: 74)

Keefe and Laurie refer to Ferrier's 'anticipation' of Idealism. This is something that chronology is sufficient to confirm. Knox, McDermid and Mander make a stronger claim about historical causation. To validate this, we have to establish a connection of the right kind. When this is attempted, however, the evidence does not offer very much support. As Mander observes, the appearance of James Hutchison Stirling's *The Secret of Hegel*, a year after Ferrier's death, is usually taken to be the first explicit introduction of Hegelianism to Scottish philosophical life. Stirling's book struck its readers and reviewers as a wholly new turn in philosophy, and Stirling was very clear that German philosophers 'required to be understood *before an advance was possible for us*' (A. M. Stirling 1912: 168, emphasis original). This implies, though it does not expressly say, that Ferrier could not have made a significant advance in ignorance of German philosophy, and in a letter Stirling does include Ferrier in the list of philosophers who had *not* successfully mastered, still less transmitted, Hegel (ibid.).

Nor is there much evidence to support Knox's claim about Ferrier and the Cairds. Though a revered and influential figure, Principal John Caird published relatively little. His longest work was an introduction to the philosophy of religion, first delivered as the Croall Lectures in Edinburgh in 1878–9. The Prefatory Note to the published version records his debt to Wallace and Bradley, among others, and 'above all Hegel's *Philosophie der Religion*' but it does not mention Ferrier. The text takes issue with several of the figures identified by Mander as major contributors to nineteenth-century British metaphysics – Spencer and Huxley for instance – but it does not allude to Ferrier. Edward Caird, who was fifteen years younger than his brother, studied for one session at St Andrews University when Ferrier was professor there, but the biography published after his death by Henry Jones and J. H. Muirhead, while endorsing the description of Ferrier as 'one of the most brilliant of Scottish metaphysicians', says that 'it is not known whether Caird attended his class, nor whether Ferrier had any part in . . . introducing him to the great German Idealists' (Jones and Muirhead 1921: 19). It is notable, in this regard, that there is no entry for Ferrier in the indices of Edward Caird's collected *Essays on Literature and Philosophy*, not even in relation to the essay on 'Metaphysic' that runs to almost 200 pages.

A Glasgow student does recall Caird quoting Ferrier in lectures, but Caird's interest in Idealism, it seems certain, was awakened in Oxford by T. H. Green.[2] Moreover, it completely expunged any interest he might have had in the authors who occupied Ferrier so much. Caird's great reputation as a teacher, together with his personal knowledge of and sympathy for the Scottish system of university education, played a significant part in his appointment to the Chair in Glasgow and his remarkable occupancy of it for twenty-seven years. But there was never any doubt that his philosophical enthusiasm and inspiration did not come from Scotland but were a result of his study of Kantian Idealism. His biographers, also his former students, tell us that 'he most rarely referred to philosophical views which were current in Scotland in his time', and that 'session after session passed and no allusion, near or remote, was made to the "Scottish School" of Common Sense, whose psychological doctrines were confused with Metaphysics . . . No Scottish name later than that of David Hume passed his lips' (Jones and Muirhead 1921: 67).

Thomas Carlyle is also a witness to the novelty of Stirling's book. After his move to London in 1834, over several decades Carlyle maintained a connection of sorts with Scottish philosophy, and he agreed to provide Stirling with a testimonial in the 1867 competition for the Edinburgh Chair of Moral Philosophy. The testimonial describes Stirling as 'the one man in Britain capable of bringing Metaphysical Philosophy in the ultimate, German or European, and highest actual form of it, distinctly home to the understanding of British men' (A. M. Stirling 1912: 209). Ferrier was dead by this time, but if he had played a role in preparing

---

[2] Green, interestingly, had been rejected in his application to succeed Ferrier at St Andrews.

the ground for Stirling's book, it seems that Carlyle was entirely ignorant of it.

In short, Knox's claim that Ferrier generated a climate of opinion more favourable to Scottish interest in Hegel is hard to sustain. There is no doubt that Ferrier embraced and articulated a version of Idealism, just as there is no doubt that a few years later prominent Scottish philosophers were enthusiastic Hegelians. The incontestability of these facts, however, is not evidence that the former was the major, or even a contributory, cause of the latter.

McDermid does not enter the question of Ferrier's relationship to Hegel and German Idealism, declaring that 'this particular patch of scholarly territory is not our turf and we prudently refuse to trespass on it' (McDermid 2018: 178). The reverse is true of Mander, a key part of whose narrative is that Ferrier's influence on British Idealism pre-dated the arrival of Hegelianism. Yet his evidential basis, too, is slim. He says that 'many of the Idealists themselves saw the roots of their movement' in Ferrier, but does not cite the names of any leading figures in the movement. He does refer to histories of philosophy by James Seth and W. R. Sorley, the latter of whom there is reason to call 'Idealist'. Both of them do discuss Ferrier, and both remark on the originality of his thought. Naturally, they acknowledge chronological order and so place him before Grote, the Cairds and Bradley. Still, both histories concur with the view, as Seth expresses it, that Stirling's book on Hegel 'marked the inauguration of a new era in English Idealism' (J. Seth 1912: 341). It seems, then, that making Ferrier's claim to distinction his hidden role as the 'root' of British Idealism rests on very slender evidence.

VII

There remains, of course, a separate, strictly philosophical question about Ferrier's neglect among twentieth- and twenty-first-century philosophers. Is ignorance the explanation? Would his writings serve to cast fresh light on the philosophical questions that absorbed philosophers over this period, and thus show themselves to have enduring interest?

It has been a recurring theme of those who have written about Ferrier that, aside from his place in the history of philosophy, his work warrants far greater attention than it has received for the purposes of continuing philosophical discussion. Over the years there have been several attempts to renew interest. Thus, Bernard Mayo, a twentieth-century successor in the Chair of Moral Philosophy at St Andrews, made 'a reappraisal of James Frederick Ferrier' the topic of his inaugural lecture in 1969, and declared his intention to be that of 'trying to rescue him from undeserved obscurity' (Mayo 2007: 159). Perhaps this is what prompted Davie to say in 1985: 'However it may have been formerly, there is something in the air of the age which keeps pushing Ferrier into prominence' (Davie 1991: 96). In 1989, however, John Haldane, another St Andrews philosopher, thought the position largely unchanged. 'Ferrier's life and work have yet to receive the scholarly and philosophical examination they deserve,' he wrote in his introduction to the reprint of Ferrier's *Collected Works* (Ferrier 2001a: xvi).

More recently McDermid and Mander have given Ferrier much more sustained critical attention. McDermid in particular offers a careful, and highly sympathetic, reconstruction of what he calls 'Ferrier's Master Argument for Idealism'. From this argument, he thinks, we can derive not only the necessary 'mindedness' of reality (and thus the falsity of materialism), but the ultimate necessity of theism. These are, obviously, conclusions of considerable interest and importance, and strongly reminiscent of Berkeley, whose ideas Ferrier worked to restore. Mander focuses more directly on his epistemology. The invention of this term is undoubtedly Ferrier's most enduring contribution to philosophy, though he himself thought his most original contribution to metaphysics was to be found in his theory of ignorance (for which he also invented a term – 'agnoiology' – which has not survived) and its relation to ontology. But both McDermid's and Mander's interest is primarily in rescuing Ferrier from neglect within the history of philosophy – *The Rise and Fall of Scottish Common Sense Realism* in McDermid's case, and the nineteenth century's interest in the metaphysics of *The Unknowable* in Mander's case.

Should these attempts at rescue prove ineffective, Ferrier's continued absence from histories of philosophy cannot be taken to show that his writings ultimately fail the test of time. On the other hand, only time will tell whether future metaphysicians and epistemologists do come to find valuable insights and arguments in his work. One preliminary issue, however, relates to which body of writing might be most promising in this respect. Ferrier's *Collected Works* run to three volumes. The first volume is the *Institutes of Metaphysic*, originally published two years before the 1856 Edinburgh competition.

The second volume comprises the *Lectures on Greek Philosophy* that he composed during his final years in St Andrews and after his 'retreat' from philosophical skirmishing. The third volume is entitled *Philosophical Remains*. This volume includes 'Introduction to the Philosophy of Consciousness' (1838–9), the series of papers on the philosophy of consciousness that appeared in *Blackwood's Magazine*, as well as 'The Crisis of Modern Speculation' (1841), 'Berkeley and Idealism' (1842) and 'A Speculation on the Senses' (1843). It is this third, very substantial body of work, in fact, that generated Ferrier's European reputation. In which of these three volumes, then, should we look for his enduring contribution to the subject?

Ferrier regarded the *Institutes* as his culminating philosophical achievement, and it is perhaps for this reason that the editor (his son-in-law, Sir Alexander Grant) ignored chronological order and made it the first volume. G. F. Stout's assessment in *Votiva Tabella* initially seems to confirm this: 'the fifteen years he spent in St Andrews were the fruitful years of his life. In them all his most valuable and characteristic work was produced' (Stout 1911: 154). Yet as Stout's contribution to *Votiva Tabella* unfolds, he gradually undermines his initial high praise. Contrary to Ferrier's own opinion, he describes Ferrier's *Lectures* as 'perhaps his best book', but then tells us that when it came to the history of philosophy, Ferrier's 'dominating interest lay in discovering not so much what his author actually said, as what from his own point of view his author ought to have said', and this characteristic was 'most conspicuous' in the *Lectures* (Stout 1911: 157). His estimate of the *Institutes* is no less importantly qualified.

> What Ferrier regarded as the leading merit of this work was its rigidly deductive method. He intended it to contain and believed it to contain only propositions either self-evident or strictly inferred from other propositions which are self-evident. A careful examination of the book shows that this claim is illusory . . . Thus the deductive form of the work is in the main a mere formality, and contributes little or nothing to its value. Wherein then does its value consist?
>
> . . .
>
> The leading merit and the chief defect of Ferrier's work is bound up with his practice of continually saying virtually the same thing over again in new forms and in varying contexts. There were certain fundamental postulates which formed the light of all his seeing . . . the attentive reader is thus compelled to examine and re-examine them . . . so that he

becomes gradually penetrated with a full and vivid realization of their meaning and importance. Whether he ends by accepting or rejecting, he will at least know clearly and distinctly what it is that he accepts or rejects. (Stout 1911: 158–9)

This is certainly more than damning with faint praise, but it hardly amounts to a resounding endorsement of the *Institutes* as an enduring philosophical classic that will, in Tulloch's words, leave a 'mark upon the course of metaphysical opinion'. Stout's ambivalence, in fact, mirrors a more widespread division of opinion about the *Institutes*. In her 'Famous Scots' biography of Ferrier, Elizabeth Haldane, in the same spirit as Tulloch, describes it as 'the work by which Ferrier's name will descend to posterity'. On the other hand, John Blackwood, its publisher, reluctantly came to the conclusion that it was 'a bottle of smoke', which is to say, all form and no substance. The expression is one that others picked up and endorsed.[3] Indeed, no less a figure than John Stuart Mill took a similar view, declaring Ferrier's 'fabric of speculation' to be a 'romance of logic'. 'It is depressing to me', Mill writes, 'to see a man of so much capacity under what appears to me so deep a delusion . . . The whole system is one great specimen of reasoning in a circle' (Mill 1972: 246–7). Looking back over sixty years at the contest between Fraser and Ferrier for the Edinburgh Chair of Logic, Andrew Seth Pringle-Pattison judged that 'if Fraser did not possess his rival's literary brilliance and incisive statement, there was . . . more staying power in his thinking than in the somewhat meagre results of Ferrier's demonstrative method' (Seth Pringle-Pattison 1915: 8).

Davie, on the other hand, reached the opposite conclusion to Ferrier's own. His final verdict was that Ferrier's career began in 'philosophical genius' but ended in 'contradiction'. If this is so, then it is to the essays in *Philosophical Remains* that attention should be directed. It is to this 'far livelier work of his youth' that Bernard Mayo turns, and he finds the hope of 'rescue' more promising in these because he finds a far greater and more important emphasis on moral philosophy than on epistemology and metaphysics. Ferrier's essays on the philosophy of consciousness, he thinks, pick up on Kantian themes about agency and personhood that, it can

---

[3] Ferrier, in a similar expression, declared Reid's philosophical works to be 'bottled air' (Ferrier 1856: 11).

be argued, the onward march to Hegelian Idealism crowded out in its pursuit of metaphysical and epistemological themes. The Kant that we find in Ferrier, by Mayo's account, is the Kant that stimulated the interest of P. F. Strawson and R. M. Hare in the dry atmosphere of mid-twentieth-century 'Oxford philosophy'. Given the prominence of consciousness and self-consciousness among the topics currently possessing intense philosophical interest, perhaps it is indeed in the 'Introduction to the Philosophy of Consciousness' that Ferrier's originality is most likely to be recovered.

4

Psychology and Moral Philosophy: Alexander Bain

I

The question of Hume's relationship to Scottish philosophy is somewhat problematic. The term 'Scottish philosophy', of course, did not gain much currency until 1875, almost a century after Hume's death, when James McCosh published *The Scottish Philosophy*. McCosh included Hume in his list of forty-nine Scottish philosophers, giving him the longest chapter in fact, because, interestingly, he thought the content of Hume's *Treatise* was not widely enough known. Yet he makes it clear that Hume, to whom he refers as 'the Scotch sceptic', is not to be regarded as belonging to 'the Scottish philosophy'. Rather, 'it has been the aim of the Scottish school, as modified and developed by Reid, to throw back the scepticism of Hume' (McCosh 1875: 158). Hume's role, in other words, is as a stimulus, not a contributor, to 'the Scottish School'. Ten years later Andrew Seth gave expression to the same idea when he subtitled his Balfour Lectures on *Scottish Philosophy* 'A Comparison of the Scottish and German Answers to Hume'. This formulation clearly excludes Hume from the Scottish School, whose principal architect Seth took to be Reid.

Hume's *Treatise* preceded Reid's *Inquiry* by about twenty-five years, but it is plain that McCosh and Seth did not think of Scottish philosophy as a development that *built upon* Hume's *Treatise*. It was, rather, a *reaction* to it. This is indeed how, since the late eighteenth century, many people have seen Hume's relationship to Scottish philosophy, and there is evidently considerable plausibility to the view. Yet there are also important considerations to be brought against it. To begin with, while a key feature characterising Scottish philosophy is the assertion of a radical division between Reid and Hume, that is not how Reid himself regarded matters. Certainly, he and his circle in Aberdeen found Hume's *Treatise* a stimulus to their thinking, as Reid expressly acknowledges in a letter to Hume dated 18 March 1763:

> Your Friendly Adversaries Drs Campbel & Gerard as well as Dr Gregory return their compliments to you respectfully. A little Philosophical Society here of which all three are members, is much indebted to you for its Entertainment ... [Y]ou are brought oftner than any other man, to the bar, accused and defended with great Zeal but without bitterness. If you write no more in morals and politicks or metaphysicks, I am afraid we shall be at a loss for Subjects. (Reid 2002a: 31)

The reference to Hume's being defended as well as accused is worth emphasising, but in any case, the same letter shows that Reid's relation to Hume's philosophy amounted to more than 'stimulus and response'.

> I shall always avow my self your Disciple in Metaphysicks. I have learned more from your writings in this kind than from all others put together. Your System appears to me not only coherent in all its parts, but likeways justly deduced from principles commonly received among Philosophers: Principles which I never thought of calling in Question until the conclusions you draw from them in the treatise of humane Nature made me suspect them. (Reid 2002a: 31)

This letter was sent in reply to a letter from Hume commenting on a draft of Reid's *Inquiry*. In it, Hume acknowledges his role as stimulus, but with some measure of pride and no hint of implacable division.

> If you have been able to clear up these abstruse and important subjects, instead of being mortified, I shall be so vain as to pretend to a share of the praise; and shall think that my errors, by having at least some coherence, had led you to make a more strict review of my principles, which were the common ones, and to perceive their futility. (Hume 1932: I, 376)

Since disagreement and debate are essential to philosophy, remarks like these could easily be made by philosophers regarded as proponents of the very same 'school'. And indeed, there is good reason to think of Hume and Reid as being of one mind in several important respects. First, they shared the same conception of moral philosophy as a 'science of human nature'. Second, they both thought that this 'science' should be pursued in no less an investigative and critical spirit than physics and astronomy. Third, as Reid's reference in his letter to 'morals and politicks or metaphysicks' shows, he and his Aberdonian colleagues were happy to endorse the broad philosophical agenda set out by Hume in the *Treatise*. Fourth, they were of one mind about method, namely a reliance on experience through introspection and observation, rather than the system building by means of axioms and deduction characteristic of Rationalists such as Spinoza and Descartes.

Given this very considerable common ground, why should Hume and Reid have come to be regarded, well before the books by McCosh and Seth appeared, as on opposing sides of some deep division? One familiar answer is this. The way in which Hume pursued the science of human nature resulted in scepticism. It was this that occasioned Reid to his 'more strict review of [Hume's] principles'. This led him to make 'judgement' a more fundamental operation of the mind than Hume's 'impressions', and to identify 'first principles' that underlie the activity of judgement. These have to be endorsed if the science of mind is to proceed at all. He argues at length that such principles (every effect has a cause, for instance) are neither mere opinion nor inductions from experience.

> The power of reasoning ... resembles the power of walking ... Nature prompts to it, and has given the power of acquiring it. After repeated efforts, much stumbling, and many falls, we learn to walk; it is in a similar manner that we learn to reason. But the power of judging in self-evident propositions, which are clearly understood, may be compared to the power of swallowing our food. It is purely natural, and therefore common to the learned and the unlearned; to the trained and the untrained: It requires ripeness of understanding, and freedom from prejudice, but nothing else. (Reid 2002b: 453)

> To judge of first principles, requires no more than a sound mind free from prejudice, and a distinct conception of the question. The learned and the unlearned, the Philosopher and the day-labourer, are upon a level and will pass the same judgement, when they are not misled by some bias or taught to renounce their understanding from some mistaken religious principle. In matters beyond the reach of common understanding, the many are led by the few ... but in matters of common sense, the few must yield to the many. (Reid 2002b: 461)

It is remarks like these that led James Seth (brother of Andrew), a student of Alexander Campbell Fraser and successor to Henry Calderwood in the Chair of Moral Philosophy at Edinburgh, to describe Reid's response to Hume as a 'revival of Rationalism'. It was not, by James Seth's account, a very satisfactory version of Rationalism, however, and quickly 'led to the criticism of the Philosophy of Common Sense as an appeal from the reasoned conclusions of philosophy to the vulgar prejudices of the ordinary man' (J. Seth 1912: 233). Thanks in part to Kant, Reid was lumped together with other, more strident, proponents of 'Common Sense' as a defence against Hume, such as James Beattie and James Oswald, despite being a much better philosopher and superior thinker. Yet, for all Reid's intellectual superiority, Seth thinks,

> It must be admitted that there is another Reid who is fitly coupled with Beattie and Oswald ... There is the Reid who does not hesitate to make play for the uninitiated with the results of the 'theory of ideas'; who asserts against Hume the necessity of that practical belief of which Hume himself had proclaimed the inevitableness; who betrays fatal inability to understand the significance of Berkeleyan idealism, or to distinguish the speculative from the practical aspect of philosophical questions. Even at his best, he is apt to attribute a doctrine of Representationism to philosophers in whose theories there is no such tendency whatever, to confuse the psychological with the philosophical question, and to relapse into the very doctrine of Representationism against which he so earnestly contends. (J. Seth 1912: 236)

In this paragraph, Seth is endorsing several of the criticisms that Ferrier brought against Reid some fifty years earlier. But he then adds an interesting further contention.

> It is, therefore, greatly to the credit of the French philosophers of the earlier half of the nineteenth century that they discovered the deeper elements in the Scottish philosophy, as formulated by its founder – true feeling for the ethical and practical interests, its enthusiastic acceptance of the experimental method, its preference of factual observation to abstract speculation and systematic completeness. (J. Seth 1912: 236)

It is true that these French philosophers looked principally to Reid, but Seth's characterisation of Scottish philosophy's 'deeper' elements could just as easily cite Hume as 'its founder'. In that case an interesting question arises. If Reid is right that Hume's development of the 'science of human nature' led to scepticism, and if the critics of Reid are right that his appeal to 'Common Sense' is ultimately anti-philosophical, might Scottish philosophy be better revitalised by the renovation rather than the rejection of Hume?

II

While Scottish philosophy has undoubtedly been identified most often with Reid's appeal to 'Common Sense', it is not hard to identify an alternative line of thought amongst Scottish philosophers more sympathetic to Hume that aims to develop and build on some central elements in his thought. Thomas Brown held the Chair of Moral Philosophy at Edinburgh in succession to Dugald Stewart. In *The English Utilitarians*, Leslie Stephen describes Brown as being the last in the genuine line of Scottish Common Sense philosophers. At the same time, on many points Brown sided with Hume rather than Reid, and was indeed highly critical, not only of Reid, but of his standing among Scottish philosophers. In his posthumously published *Lectures on the Philosophy of the Human Mind*, Brown distances himself from the Scottish adulation of Reid.

> While by philosophers in one part of the island, [Reid's] merits seem to have been unjustly undervalued, I cannot but think also, that, in his own country, there has been an equal or rather a far greater tendency to over rate them . . . The genius of Dr Reid does not appear to me to have been very inventive, nor to have possessed much of that refined and subtle acuteness which, – capable as it is of becoming abused, – is yet absolutely necessary to the perfection of metaphysical analysis. (Brown 1836: I, 267–8)

Conversely, Brown's treatment of Hume, though critical, strikes a rather different tone. Having quoted from Hume's first *Inquiry*, Brown writes:

> On these paragraphs of Mr Hume, a few obvious criticisms present themselves. In the first place, however, I must observe, – to qualify in some degree the severity of the remarks that may be made . . . that it is evident from the very language now quoted to you, that he is far from

bringing forward his classification as complete. He states, indeed, that though the reality of [the three principles of association – resemblance, contiguity and causation] will not, he believes, be much doubted, it may still be difficult to prove, to the satisfaction of his reader, or even of himself, that the enumeration is complete. (Brown 1836: I, 347)

This more sympathetic treatment of Hume arises from the fact that Brown is a thoroughgoing empiricist. Moreover, in the end he does not see any very deep difference between Hume and Reid, as he comments in a letter to William Erskine.

I confess I do feel much astonishment, that no one should before have discovered, that [Hume] is not that strange sceptic as to the idea of power, which he is uniformly represented to be, and that the theory of Reid is in truth the very same theory as that of Mr Hume which, with so much zealous blundering, he professes to confute. (Welsh 1825: 160)

Even on a sympathetic interpretation, Brown is overstating the case when he says Hume and Reid subscribed to 'the very same theory'. But his broader point is that they both identify what we might call 'bedrock' propositions that are neither observable nor deduced from observation, and are yet inescapable convictions. Reid takes these bedrock convictions to be necessary first principles that the human mind is naturally disposed to believe. They may therefore be called self-evident. Hume takes the same convictions to be factual statements about the habits of the human mind. Reid's first principles are grasped by intuition. Consequently, if there is any dispute about them, the only recourse is to seek a consensus between people who have the requisite open-mindedness and intellectual humility. If anyone professes to doubt them, the only recourse is assertion and ridicule. Hume's statements about psychological habit are discovered by observation, which is to say, empirical investigation into the way human beings characteristically think. This explains why Hume is willing to allow that his conclusions are inevitably provisional and might well be amended by advances in empirical psychology. Viewed in this light, there is indeed a deep and significant difference in how the science of mind is to be pursued. For Reid, while the science of mind is observational, it is bounded by intuitive principles that cannot themselves be validated empirically, but must be grasped intuitively. For Hume, the science of mind is experiential through and through, an investigation that simply goes wherever the evidence leads. Faced with these alternatives, Brown concurs with Hume. Accordingly, he incurs the wrath of Sir William Hamilton, who sides with Reid.

Later in the century, Hamilton in his turn came under attack from John Stuart Mill from the Humean side. He cites this same division between intuition and experience when explaining the underlying thought that motivated his *Examination of Sir William Hamilton's Philosophy* (1865).

> I knew that [Hamilton's] general mode of treating the facts of mental philosophy differed from that of which I most approved . . . yet his strenuous assertion of some important principles . . . made me think that genuine psychology had considerably more to gain than lose by his authority and reputation. His *Lectures* and *Dissertations on Reid* dispelled this illusion . . . My estimation of him was so far altered, that instead of regarding him as occupying a mind of intermediate position between the two rival philosophies ['that of Intuition, and that of Experience and Association'], I now looked upon him as the chief pillar, of that one of the two which seemed to me to be erroneous. (Mill 1971: 161–2)

The School of Experience and Association, Mill goes on to tell us, is a 'better mode of philosophizing'. This 'better mode', he says, had been reintroduced by '[m]y father's *Analysis of the Mind*, my own *Logic*, and Professor Bain's great treatise' (Mill 1971: 163), but credentials stretch much further back. '[A]lmost everything which has been contributed from these islands towards the advancement of psychology since Locke and Berkeley, has, until very lately, and much of it in the present generation, proceeded from Scottish authors and Scottish professors' (Rectorial Address to St Andrews University, 1866, quoted in W. L. Calderwood and Woodside 1900: 166). Mill thereby endorses a body of opinion within Scottish philosophy which, having rejected Reid and Common Sense, looked to a more strictly empirical psychology that took its lead from Hume.

By 'the present generation' Mill meant Alexander Bain and the 'great treatise' he refers to is a two-volume study on *The Senses and the Intellect* and *The Emotions and the Will*. Bain published both these volumes a few years before being appointed to the newly created Regius Chair of Logic at the University of Aberdeen. In a letter to Bain, John Grote, who had succeeded William Whewell as Professor of Moral Philosophy at Cambridge, acknowledges receipt of *The Emotions and the Will* and makes this comment.

> Our worthy Scotch predecessors in the last century talked a great deal about introducing induction and really scientific methods into the science of mind, but I must say it appears to me that you have done it more than most of them did. (Bain 1904: 254)

James Seth makes a similar assessment of the significance of Bain's work.

> When we compare these treatises with the earlier works of the Scottish philosophers, and even with that of James Mill, we cannot help remarking that they are scientific in a sense in which those were not. It is not merely that Bain is the first to use effectively the physiological method, referring psychological phenomena to their correlates in nerve and brain, but that he adopts throughout the genetic, if not the evolutionary method, tracing the complex to the simple and the later to the earlier, and thus explaining, where his predecessors had been content to do little more than describe, the phenomena of the mental life. (J. Seth 1912: 278–9)

Much more recently, Cairns Craig has advanced and defended a similar view. 'What Bain described as 'A Natural History of the Feelings' was, in significant ways, the culmination of that 'science of Man' on which David Hume had embarked in the 1730s' (Craig 2015: 116). Craig is more explicit than Grote or Seth: out of all Bain's 'worthy Scotch predecessors', the one deserving of special mention is Hume.

III

These assessments raise four questions. First, was Bain pursuing the same questions as his Scottish predecessors? Second, was he pursuing them more scientifically? Third, is there reason to think that his 'improved' approach was notably continuous with Hume's? And finally, did his more sophisticated psychology result in significant advances in moral philosophy and the philosophy of mind?

The first of these questions is easy to answer positively. Though his major works were published in London, where he lived for over a decade, Bain was as deeply rooted in the Scottish philosophical tradition as any other holder of a philosophy Chair in nineteenth-century Scotland. Born in Aberdeen into circumstances of considerable poverty, Bain was obliged to leave formal education at the age of eleven and was apprenticed to his father as a weaver. However, his intellectual inclination, ability and application made him a natural autodidact. Thus in 1836, seven years after his schooling ended, he gained bursaries enabling him to attend either of Aberdeen's two universities, King's College or Marischal College. He chose Marischal, where he pursued the usual wide range of subjects – Latin and Greek, Algebra, Geometry, Logic, Natural Philosophy (physics) and Natural History, as well as a class in Anatomy which he says 'made a most valuable groundwork for future studies in Physiology' (Bain 1904: 101). Like every student, he was required to take Moral Philosophy, and having read Hume's *Treatise* in the years between school and university, he was now introduced to Reid by Dr Glennie, James Beattie's successor in the Chair of Moral Philosophy and Logic at Marischal. Glennie's curriculum drew very heavily on Reid, with chapters of the *Essays on the Active Powers* being read verbatim as Glennie's lectures. But Bain, partly through his own efforts, also gained a very wide knowledge of other philosophical writers, and won first prize in the Moral Philosophy class.

After completing his degree, for a time he served officially as Glennie's assistant (effectively his substitute), and taught from the same Reid-centred curriculum. Accordingly, his years at Marischal ensured that the problems in the philosophy of mind which came to interest him were those that lay at the heart of debates between Hume, Reid, Brown and Hamilton. This grounding is confirmed by his 'compendium' on *Mental and Moral Science*. Published a few years after his appointment to the Regius Chair of Logic in Aberdeen, this book is primarily a text aimed at students. It contains condensed versions of Bain's major works – *The Senses and the Intellect* and *The Emotions and the Will*, as well as general surveys of philosophy and ethics. In the introduction he outlines his approach to the study of mind, and explicitly contrasts it with that of Reid, Brown, Hamilton and Stewart. Throughout the book, regular summaries reveal a copious knowledge of the history of philosophy. These include references to all the well-known Scottish philosophers – Hume, Smith, Reid, Ferguson, Stewart, Brown, Hamilton and Ferrier. So we may safely conclude that Bain thought of himself as writing in succession to his Scottish philosophical forebears, and was fully equipped to do so.

Unlike Glennie, however, Bain was not a passive conduit for received philosophical opinion. He was astonishingly prolific from his first year as an undergraduate, with his scientific interests and orientation prompting a steady stream of innovative talks and papers so copious that it is hard to credit the intensity with which he must have been able to read and write. Since many of his essays were published as a means of generating an income, their subjects range very widely – on literature, physics, ethics, travel, meteorology, health, education, grammar and psychology. Of special importance was his connection with John Stuart Mill, which began in 1839, when Bain assisted Mill in the final revision of Mill's *System of Logic*. Getting to know Mill was a major influence on the development of Bain's thinking, and he thereafter became identified as an empiricist, materialist and utilitarian in philosophy. Yet Bain was no mere acolyte of Mill's. He had arrived at most of his major philosophical positions already, and Mill himself remarked (in the *Examination of Hamilton*) that 'Mr Bain did not stand in need of any predecessor except our common precursors, and has taught more to me, on these subjects, than there is any reasonable probability that I can have taught to him' (Mill 1979: 216 n.).

Are there grounds for thinking that Bain's study of the mind took it in a more scientific direction? Again, it is easy to answer in the affirmative. While Bain did expressly endorse and employ the method of introspection, his approach was much more systematic in two respects. First, he regarded the definition of terms as foundational to all good science, and so gave a great deal of attention to formulating definitions clearly and precisely. 'It is a part of the scientific method', he says, 'to take strict account of leading terms, by a thorough and exhaustive inquiry into the meanings of all such' (Bain 1879: 8–9). Second, not content with broad descriptions of his own mental experience, he gave concentrated attention to patterns of association and succession, carefully recording the details in notebooks with a view to framing the laws of the mind's operation more rigorously. Most importantly, he added something his precursors necessarily lacked – a detailed knowledge of current research in physiology, especially the physiology of the brain.

All this labour came together in *The Senses and the Intellect* (1855) and *The Emotions and the Will* (1859), his two major works in psychology. Both volumes went into several editions, each one of which Bain revised thoroughly. The preface to *Senses* makes plain the innovative intention of Bain's endeavour in comparison to previous writers.

> Conceiving the time has now come when many of the striking discoveries of Physiologists relative to the nervous system should find a recognized place in the Science of Mind, I have devoted a separate chapter to the Physiology of the Brain and Nerves. (Bain 1855: iii)

The 'recognized place' for physiology turns out to be foundational. 'No fact in our constitution can be considered more certain than this, that the brain is the chief organ of the mind, and has mind as its principal function' (Bain 1855: 12). A little later in the book he amplifies this in a way that reveals his revision of the Lockean picture.

> The organ of the mind is not the brain by itself: it is the brain, nerves, muscles, organs of sense and viscera . . . The notion that the brain is a *sensorium*, or inner chamber, where impressions are accumulated, like pictures put away in a store, requires to be modified and corrected. (Bain 1855: 52)

Though a materialist, Bain was not an eliminative materialist. In *The Emotions and the Will* he expressly rejects any form of reduction.

> Consciousness is a fact different from the properties of material bodies, but it is nevertheless constantly associated in nature with certain combinations of those physical properties. Consequently, while making no attempt to resolve Mind into Matter, any more than we should endeavour to resolve gravity into extension, or electricity and magnetism into gravity, it is an object of inquiry to ascertain what are the laws and particulars of this alliance, or association. (Bain 1859: 4)

He then applies this associationist conception to emotion broadly understood.

> Everyone knows that emotions manifest themselves in outward acts, gestures, and appearances, called the *expression of feeling*, of which a great part is instinctive, and grows out of the primitive organization of the frame. It is further known that the secretions and other processes of organic life are exceedingly subject to the influence of states of feeling. What is proposed in the ensuing discussion is to represent

this action and reaction of feeling upon the physical framework under general laws and in precise language. (Bain 1859: 5)

This passage reveals that while resisting any reduction of mind to matter, Bain nevertheless seeks, as Seth says, to explain by tracing the complex to the simple and the later to the earlier. When it comes to psychological phenomena, mature expression is not identical with, but nevertheless the outcome of, primitive instinct and organic processes.

IV

The previous quotations from *The Emotions and the Will* also show clearly Bain's strong inclination towards the natural sciences, an inclination that his *Autobiography* records from a very early stage. But is this more 'scientific' approach clearly continuous with Hume's *Treatise*? There is no doubt that Bain was fully versed in the differences between Hume and Reid, and aware of the philosophical division to which they had given rise. Evidence for this is to be found in the 'compendium' of *Mental and Moral Science*, where discussions of both Hume and Reid are scattered throughout. Unmistakably, Hume is expounded more sympathetically than Reid. In, for instance, the section on 'The Perception of the Material World', Bain tells us that the 'celebrated scepticism of Hume' is partly the outcome of his being 'a man fond of literary effects as well as speculation'. As a consequence, '[i]t is no wonder that others have supposed him to deny both the existence of matter and the existence of mind, although, in point of fact, he denies neither, but only a certain theoretic mode of looking at and expressing the phenomena admitted by all'. Reid's appeal to Common Sense, on the other hand, gets short shrift. 'In general it may be said that Reid declaims rather than reasons on the question' and even in the eyes of his disciple Hamilton 'is often at fault, often confused, and sometimes even contradictory' (Bain 1872: 207).

In itself, this greater sympathy for Hume would not be enough to show the sort of continuity that Grote, Seth and Craig identify. However, it is not hard to augment it at a more substantial level. It is striking that there is no reference at all to Hume in either *The Senses and the Intellect* or *The Emotions and the Will*. This is a little strange, since a great deal of the material to be found in these books is effectively a reworking of Hume, even to the point of employing the terminology of 'impressions' and 'ideas'. Here, for example, is Bain on the subject of 'The persistence or continuance of mental impressions of the external agent'.

> When the ear is struck by a sonorous wave, we have a sensation of sound, but the mental excitement does not die away because the sound ceases. There is a certain continuing effect, generally much feebler . . . In consequence of this property, our mental excitement, due to external causes, may greatly outlast the causes themselves; we are enabled to go on living a life in ideas, in addition to the life in actualities . . . After the *impression* of a sound has ceased entirely, and the mind has been occupied with other things, there is the possibility of recovering from oblivion the *idea*, or mental effect, without reproducing the actual sound. This implies . . . that something has been engrained in the mental structure. (Bain 1855: 323–4, emphasis added)

This brief extract is characteristic. There are of course differences, but for the most part they are refinements of the same conception. Thus, the opening sentence of Hume's *Treatise* says: 'All the perceptions of the human mind resolve themselves into two distinct kinds, which I shall call IMPRESSIONS and IDEAS' (Hume 2007: 7). At the start of *The Senses and the Intellect*, Bain says in a very similar fashion, 'The phenomena of the Subject Mind are usually comprehended under three heads, Feeling, Volition, [and] Thought.'

As this suggests, in key respects, Bain's whole endeavour is conducted in what we could call 'the spirit of Hume'. It is empirical, analytical and associationist. That is to say, everything is said to rest on empirically observed facts about human psychology sometimes arrived at by introspection, and sometimes the result of experiment, especially when brain physiology is added to the mix. Once the terms have been defined, these observable facts are analysed, just as Hume analyses them, into 'simple' and 'complex'. Then, the observed regularities between the more fundamental elements are formulated into laws of association, and these are then invoked to explain the generation of more complex phenomena. Both of Bain's major works proceed along these lines, with a certain relentlessness. The result is more detailed, and in some ways more sophisticated, than Hume's, but it is not much different in essentials.

Returning to the four questions outlined at the start of section III, then, we can now confidently answer the first three in the affirmative. Bain was continuing the study of the human mind that

Scottish philosophers had engaged in for over a century, but pursuing it in the light of more recent advances in anatomy and physiology. At the same time, he was employing more or less Hume's empirical, analytical and associationist philosophical framework. It remains then to address the fourth question. Did Bain do this more successfully than Hume had done?

V

To answer this question something needs to be said about criteria of success, and this immediately complicates matters. The eighteenth century's conception of a 'science of mind' did not distinguish, as later periods came to do, between psychology and the philosophy of mind. But as empirical psychology developed over the course of the nineteenth century, this distinction became more important. So the question is whether, and to what extent, empirical psychology could advance a more satisfactory resolution of the problems about the mind and its relation to reality that had exercised philosophers. For anti-materialists, such as Ferrier, the answer was 'not at all'. In Ferrier's eyes, every attempt to psychologise metaphysics (especially Reid's) is misconceived. Bain sometimes writes as though he took the opposite view, and supposed that with the advent of physiologically based psychology, the older philosophical approach to the study of mind could be abandoned. In one place, indeed, when advising on courses of study, he appears to use the terms 'moral philosophy' and 'psychology' interchangeably. But in a relatively late paper on 'Associationist Controversies', he endorses a more modified view.

> [A]s to the priority of Metaphysics and Psychology ... I believe that ... a disinterested Psychology should come first, ... revise its fundamental assumptions ... [and] when so revised, should resume consideration of the wide field of mental facts ... that deal with practical applications rather than with the metaphysical groundwork. After a few further strides we might come back again to the foundations. (Bain 1903: 38)

Bain's own work exhibits the trajectory that he here describes. His earlier interest in the metaphysics of mind was gradually displaced by a more markedly psychological orientation. This is why he has often been credited with serving as a bridge between the old and the new, enabling modern psychology to emerge from under the shadow of philosophy of mind, while not himself making a permanent contribution to either. It is also true, as this passage suggests, that he became more interested in 'practical applications' than in metaphysical 'foundations'. With respect to the enduring metaphysical debate about freewill and determinism, for instance, Bain thinks that there are no moral implications, whichever side we take.

> It seems to me ... that the meaning and scope of Moral Consciousness and Responsibility should be argued apart from the Freedom of the Will ... [A]s to the nature of Conscience: I do not see what either Freedom or Necessitation has to do with it. In responsibility to God or to Man, I for one see everything that is distinctively meant by 'moral'; those that hold otherwise need not introduce Free-will in order to say what moral is or includes ... If a man's conduct is ruled by motives, the way to control him is to supply such motives. (Bain 1903: 13)

It is for this reason that Bain sees psychology as a richer resource. 'As a problem of the psychology of the Active Powers of the mind, all that I have ever contended for is that our actions are governed by our feelings, as motives, according to the law of uniformity of sequence; so that the same situation as regards the feelings is always followed by the same voluntary action' (Bain 1903: 11).

This appeal to psychology as a resource for shaping human conduct finds its most extended treatment in Bain's guide for teachers, *Education as a Science* (1879). The book runs to over 450 pages, and aims to draw implications from psychology for school education. It begins with a list of definitions, followed by a short chapter entitled 'Bearings of Physiology' and a very much longer one on the 'Bearings of Psychology', thus laying the foundation for detailed chapters on teaching science, mathematics, natural history, logic and language, as well as moral and aesthetic education. There is virtually no mention of philosophy, and the section entitled 'The Science of Mind' refers exclusively to psychology.

Viewed in this way, here too Bain is following Hume's agenda in the *Treatise*. Book 1, 'Of the Understanding', concerns metaphysics, Book 2, 'Of the Passions', begins with restatement of the division between impressions and ideas, but is chiefly a psychological investigation that does not much rely on metaphysics, and leads to Book 3, 'Of Morals', which for the most part is even further removed from the debates of Book 1. Given the similarity between Bain's direction of thought and Hume's, we are now in a position to refocus the question of success. Is Bain's moral philosophy an improvement on Hume's in virtue of being better informed about advances in psychology?

The treatment of moral and aesthetic education in *Education as a Science* is instructive on this question. In accordance with his dictum 'If a man's conduct is ruled by motives, the way to control him is to supply such motives', Bain effectively construes education as training. That is to say, good teaching is a matter of motivating someone to behave in accordance with certain precepts. With regard to motivation, Bain is a Benthamite. People are moved to action by the promise of pleasure and the threat of pain. His list of pleasures and pains is more extensive, and more sophisticated, than Bentham's, but the psychology is the same. And he is more sanguine about the hedonic calculus than Mill.

Education as training is an instrumental conception. Consequently, the adoption of means, however well grounded in a properly scientific human psychology, requires a set of ends to which those means can be directed. What are those ends, and how do we determine them? With respect to what he calls 'the theoretical or knowledge-giving sciences', Bain's answer is fairly straightforward.

> These subjects present the scientific method and spirit in the greatest perfection, and impart the greatest amount of accurate information. Whatever scientific culture can do, is done by the curriculum thus laid down. Of this culture, perhaps the greatest result is embraced under the devotion to TRUTH, which, allowing for human infirmities, must emerge as a consequence of being initiated in all the devices of modern research. (Bain 1879: 161–2)

There are important philosophical questions to raise about whether 'truth' and 'knowledge' will do the work that Bain requires here, but he does not consider them. Indeed, despite his belief that a key aim of education is to give pupils and students the ability to assess critically the things they are asked to believe, Bain mostly takes conventional values for granted.

With respect to moral education, the chief end to be pursued is sociability. The teacher's task is to bring it about that the individual becomes a valued and valuable member of 'the Family, . . . the State and the World'. This involves inculcating virtues that can all be grouped under three traditional heads – Prudence, Justice and Benevolence. How are these to be taught? Bain is, especially by the standards of his time, highly enlightened about method. He is sceptical of the value of fear and punishment, and no less sceptical about moral 'lectures'. Far better to appeal to the incipient 'motives of Sociability'. These include a mix of the self-regarding and the other-regarding. 'To get the most we can out of life, we must behave well to everyone that has the power to help or to thwart us' (Bain 1879: 405). The 'cravings for Love, Affection, Pity', he declares, 'are perhaps the most powerful instrument of moral suasion' (408). If this sounds a little too manipulative, Bain is quick to add that the 'briefest glance at moral teaching must not omit the topic of Moral Ideals'. 'It is in Morality, more especially, that the teacher works by putting forward grand, lofty, and even unapproachable Ideals; the supposition being that the charm and attractiveness of these will make a far more powerful impression than any unvarnished statement of consequences'. Nevertheless:

> While in the Ideal, self-devotion or self-sacrifice is depicted so as to kindle a momentary glow, the hard reality warns us that only a very small portion of this can be engrained in the average individual. Rivalry, competition, over-grasping and supplanting – are what we have to deal with on the one side; and on the other, we have to set the tendencies to the social, the sympathetic and the amiable; and close is the game we have to play in the encounter. (Bain 1879: 410)

This passage is revealing in two important respects. First, it is profoundly inegalitarian (which Bain would not have denied) and divides humanity into two groups – those who inculcate social virtues (by whatever means), and those in whom these virtues need to be inculcated. It is the former group, presumably, who have to determine the ends to which moral education should be directed. This raises a related question. What is the role of psychology here? It is reasonably easy to see how a more detailed knowledge of human psychology could throw light on more and less promising *means*, and validate Bain's objection to punishment and moral lecturing. But how do we know to what *ends* these improved means should be directed? The answer cannot be the maximisation of pleasure and the minimisation of pain. Bain does subscribe to Bentham's 'two great masters' psychology. But elsewhere (and against F. H. Bradley) he claims that there is such a thing as pure malevolence, and he defines it in terms of pleasure taken in cruelty, mockery and so on. Not all pleasures, then, are to be endorsed, still less promoted. 'If a man's conduct is ruled by motives, the way to control him is to supply such motives,' Bain has told us, but when psychological investigation has revealed all that can be known about motivation, we still have to decide which motivational buttons to press.

In short, Bain's division between the theoretical and the practical sciences, the first focused on truth and knowledge, the second on motivation and conduct, leaves him in exactly the same position as Hume at the end of the section in the *Treatise* entitled 'Of the influencing motives of the will'. Having declared that 'Reason is, and only ought to be the slave of the passions and can never pretend to any other office than to serve and obey them' (Hume 2007: 266), Hume can only conclude that there is 'great difficulty of deciding concerning the actions and resolutions of men, where there is any contrariety of motives and passions' (267). The additional problem for Bain is that this is just what his conception of moral education as a science requires him to do.

VI

A similar sort of weakness becomes apparent in his account of aesthetic education.

> It needs little examination to discover that the strongest stimulation of Art productions is in the direction of illimitable appetite and desire – the passions of love, malevolence, ambition, sensibility . . . The highest Art and the highest Art education check and control the outgoings of the fiery passions . . . The proper aim of Art education and Culture is to enable us to feel these higher artistic effects at the least possible expenditure of gross and grovelling passion. (Bain 1879: 431)

Leaving aside the implicit invocation of an emotivist conception of art, which there is good reason to question, how are we to tell the difference between 'higher' and 'gross and grovelling' feeling? Since by his account, the purpose of art, and by extension art education, is the stimulation of aesthetic emotion, why might this not be accomplished as much (or more) by exposure to kitsch as by exploring the art of the great masters? If the criterion of success is 'feeling emotion', it is hard to see how one would differentiate between inspiration and titillation. Only *qualitative* judgement can do this – not what we *do* feel, but what we *ought to* feel. Here the same problem confronts Bain as confronts Mill in his vain effort to distinguish between 'higher' and 'lower' pleasures in chapter 2 of *Utilitarianism*.

The sections on poetry, music and art are amongst the weakest in *Education as a Science*. Probably this is because Bain did not have much feel for such things. Admiring students, who appreciated his lectures greatly, nevertheless recorded a certain blindness when it came to the arts. G. Watt Smith writes:

> Poetry – to Bain it was a mystery. 'There was the door to which he found no key.' What to many rendered his English class repellent was his possession by one idea: 'Grammar is a science or it is nothing'. Bain did but reflect the characteristics of a country which was 'a layer of peat-moss spread on a bannock of granite'. (*Aberdeen University Review* 1960: 176)

Bain also reflected the characteristics of his country in another respect – his attitude to religion. The grim austerity of the Calvinism his father embraced affected him greatly. His *Autobiography* records an avid interest in religious questions that faded as his education progressed. In the end, though never an outspoken atheist, and a friend of many former students who had become ministers, he effectively lost interest in the subject, and perhaps never had any feel for the things that drew people to religion. By his request, his burial was without a religious ceremony of any kind.

This explains, no doubt, why religious education gets the most cursory treatment in *Education as a Science*. 'The essence of Religion', he says, 'must always be something Emotional; and the culture of Emotion is not carried on advantageously in ordinary school teaching.' In particular, he was anxious to separate moral education from religious instruction.

> Religion, working in its own sphere, does not make full provision for all the moral exigencies of human life. The precepts of morality must be chiefly grounded on our human relations in this world, as known by practical experience. Religion has precepts of its own, and motives of its own; and these are all the more effectively worked, when worked in separation. (Bain 1879: 421)

Given this commitment to separation, Bain, even if he had seen them, would not have turned to religion to make good the deficiencies in his moral philosophy. It is notable that, for all his admiration of Mill, Bain was highly critical of his posthumously published essay on 'Theism' which in his estimation was 'not only short, but extremely unsatisfactory' (Bain 1882: 135–6).

To the question did Bain's more robustly empirical 'science of mind' psychologise philosophical questions more successfully than Hume had done, the proper conclusion seems to be 'no'. *The Senses and the Intellect* and *Emotions and the Will* can without too much distortion be regarded as his reworking of Books 1 and 2 of Hume's *Treatise*. They remain firmly within the conceptual framework of 'impressions', 'ideas' and the principle of 'association'. Bain's knowledge of the physiology of the brain and nervous system is vastly superior to anything Hume could have acquired. Yet it does not add much more to the Humean enterprise than fresh, more 'scientific' examples. *Education as a Science*, which takes up some of the topics of Book 3 of the *Treatise*, as well as topics in aesthetics and religion that Hume dealt with elsewhere, perpetuates, without noticeably making more sophisticated, utilitarian instrumentalism of a largely Humean kind.

Bain's sidelining of religion carries a slightly different implication. It marks him out from almost all his contemporaries in Chairs of Philosophy at Scottish universities between, say, 1850 and 1920, and even from his successors in the Chair at Aberdeen. In their efforts to address the fundamental debates that continued to dominate philosophy in Scotland and further afield, most of them saw reason to return to theism, or at least to reopen the metaphysical questions surrounding it. This is true of Hegelian Idealists such as Edward Caird and Henry Jones, as well as those such as Alexander Campbell Fraser and John Veitch who persisted with the inheritance from Reid and Hamilton. In one way, this further serves to identify Bain as a successor to Hume, whose views, as Reid's letter shows, were respected by, but at odds with, prevailing opinion amongst Scottish philosophers. However, it also marks a difference, because Bain seems to have shared none of Hume's life-long fascination with religion. Perhaps this reflects a difference between eighteenth- and nineteenth-century Scotland. The cultural world of which Bain was a part remained religious, but it had lost the passionate interest in theological issues that so exercised the inhabitants of Hume's world.

5

Thomas Carlyle and the Philosophy of Rhetoric

I

It would be difficult to exaggerate the degree to which Thomas Carlyle was lionised in the last years of his life. No fewer than 119 eminent people signed the list assembled by David Masson in celebration of his eightieth birthday. It included prestigious scientists (Charles Darwin and Thomas Huxley), poets (Alfred Tennyson and Robert Browning) and novelists (George Eliot and Anthony Trollope), as well as almost all the professors of philosophy in Scotland. This was in 1875, despite the fact that after the death of his wife Jane Welsh Carlyle in 1866, Carlyle published very little. The little he did publish, however, was avidly seized upon by the reading public. What might be considered his 'last word', the anti-reform pamphlet *Shooting Niagara*, published in 1867, sold 4,000 copies in just three weeks. The London house he had occupied for forty years became a place of pilgrimage for a constant stream of people from the highest social, political, literary and even royal circles. They all wanted to see 'the Sage of Chelsea' and hear the long monologues on cultural and political themes that had become his trademark.[1]

---

[1] The long monologues were nothing new. On a trip to London in 1850, Alexander Campbell Fraser recalls his first meeting with Carlyle, when he spent an evening at the house in Chelsea in the company of David Masson. 'I seem to see, in the lurid firelit chamber, the weird-like figure of the sage, now and again replenishing the fire, while discharging merciless denunciations of the political and religious vices of his generation . . . the turgid monologue now and then relieved by occasional coruscations of Mrs Carlyle's ready wit' (Fraser 1904: 141).

II

Carlyle spent the first thirty-eight years of his life in Scotland. Self-employed for more than a decade, he had been trying to gain recognition and acceptance as a writer and thinker. In 1834, when the struggle was beginning to succeed, he and his wife left the isolation of Craigenputtock, a small farm in Dumfriesshire, and moved to Chelsea, then a suburb on the edge of London. Their new location did not change things immediately, but the tide finally turned in Carlyle's favour when he published his history of *The French Revolution* in 1837.[2] Thereafter he steadily came to be accorded immense intellectual stature, and towards the end of his life was held worthy of receiving the highest academic awards and political honours (most of which he declined).

The Cambridge edition of his *Collected Works* runs to thirty volumes, and the peak of this literary achievement was a six-volume biography of Frederick the Great. Carlyle devoted thirteen years to its composition, an enormous endeavour undertaken at considerable personal cost, especially to his wife. When it was finally published, it proved a huge success and made him rich. The first two volumes appeared in 1858 to critical acclaim. *The Spectator* declared that their appearance was not only the event of the year but one of lasting literary significance. 'All that Mr Carlyle writes at once takes its place among our standard English literature, without waiting for the suffrages of criticism, and is as sure to be read thoroughly and calmly studied generations hence as now' (quoted in Heffer 1995: 317).

As a prediction, the last part of this sentence could hardly have been more erroneous. Although translations and further editions of *Frederick* did appear, it is safe to say that 'generations hence' no one reads it thoroughly, still less studies it. Indeed, aside from a small group of Carlyle specialists, almost no one reads it at all. This is not the fate of *Frederick* alone. Out of all the books Carlyle published, just two are available in Oxford's *World's Classics* series. Nor is this simply a reflection of the distance in time between his world and ours. Carlyle's fall from grace

---

[2] The publication was set back considerably when the manuscript of the first volume, temporarily in the custody of John Stuart Mill, was accidentally used by a maid to light the fire.

was not long in coming. As Simon Heffer memorably expresses it, Carlyle's death was quickly followed by his assassination. 'Society was polite enough to this elderly sage to wait until he was dead – though only just – before taking apart his reputation and achievements' (Heffer 1995: 361).[3]

But what exactly were those achievements? In 1856, before the publication of *Frederick*, George Eliot had written:

> It is an idle question to ask whether [Carlyle's] books will be read a century hence; if they were all burnt as the grandest of the Suttees on his funeral pile, it would only be like cutting down an oak after its acorns have sown a forest. For there is hardly a superior or active mind of this generation that has not been modified by Carlyle's writings; there has hardly been an English book written for the last ten or twelve years that would not have been different if Carlyle had not lived. (Quoted in Clubbe 1976: 182)

With hindsight, this assessment also seriously overstates the case, but it does neatly circumvent the fact that his books are no longer read. It is entirely plausible to hold that an author's influence may ultimately be found in works that he did not himself write, and perhaps this was indeed the case with Carlyle. But even if it was, we are still left with this question. What was the nature of the influence, and how did it show itself? Was it his style of writing, or the content of his thought?

A significant obstacle in the way of answering this question is the further matter of Carlyle's intellectual classification. There is a notable ambivalence about this amongst commentators. Though his most extensive works by far were histories – of the French Revolution, Oliver Cromwell and Frederick the Great – when *The Spectator* review places 'all that he writes' in the category of English Literature, it anticipates a widespread inclination to identify him as a 'literary' figure. On the other hand, as his moniker 'the Sage of Chelsea' suggests, Carlyle was also expressly referred to as a 'philosopher', an early work having been an account of the life and thought of the philosopher/poet Friedrich Schiller.

---

[3] In 'Carlyle Personally', the first of two lectures given to the Philosophical Institution of Edinburgh, David Masson, who knew him well, recounts and seeks to reverse this speedy and dramatic change.

Carlyle's immediate intellectual circle cannot settle the question, because it included notable figures from both sides of the divide – Browning, Dickens and Tennyson in literature, and John Stuart Mill and Ralph Waldo Emerson in philosophy.[4]

From an early stage, some commentators responded to this issue by refusing to classify him in either way. In *Carlyle and Scottish Thought*, Ralph Jessop devotes a whole chapter to the late-nineteenth-century debate about 'Categorizing Carlyle – Literature or Philosophy?', and in the end inclines to the view that 'his diversity may elude our attempts to categorize him finally within one discipline or genre' (Jessop 1997: 25). More recently, Lowell T. Frye, in his 2012 T. H. Green Lecture on Carlyle, reaffirmed this resistance to classification.

> Carlyle himself never could – or would – define exactly what it was he did or wrote – and nor can we, the readers and scholars who have responded to Carlyle's work and have tried to *fix* it and him during the past 180 years. We are unsuccessful in pigeonholing Carlyle no matter how hard we try ... During his lifetime Carlyle refused all labels, whether political or literary/stylistic, thriving in the interstices between parties and genres. (Frye 2012: 22, emphasis original)

Yet, while Jessop's and Frye's response to the question of classification might appear to be the most plausible, it runs counter to an important consideration. To ask how Carlyle relates to the distinction between 'literature' and 'philosophy' is not an aprioristic 'pigeonholing' for the purposes of tidiness, but an inquiry about how his work is to be understood in relation to a significant historical development. The distinction between 'philosophy' and 'science', for example, is one for which Hume and Reid would have had no use, but the intellectual developments of the following century came to lend it a significance that they might have been expected to appreciate.[5] Similarly, differentiating between literature and philosophy is more than the arbitrary imposition of labels. It reflects a process of intellectual clarification that makes

---

[4] Wikipedia is even more uncertain about his proper classification – 'historian, satirical writer, essayist, translator, philosopher' (<https://en.wikipedia.org/wiki/Thomas_Carlyle>).

[5] See Chapter 6.

the distinction important and valuable. The issue, then, is not whether Carlyle is being 'pigeon-holed', but whether he was ahead of his time in transcending such a distinction, or whether, rather, his works were shaped by a conceptual landscape that was undergoing significant change.[6] Did his taste for the 'interstices', if that is what it was, lead him to thrive, but only for a time? And does it do something to explain his subsequent neglect?

There is light to be shed on this issue by considering Carlyle's relationship to Scottish philosophy. Ralph Jessop has made a detailed study of the works that Carlyle wrote before he left Scotland in order to uncover 'one strand of discourse important to Carlyle's art, namely a Scottish philosophical discourse informed by the works of Hume and Reid' (Jessop 1997: 122). The result of this study, in the end, is somewhat tentative and speculative because, as Jessop admits, 'Carlyle's explicit remarks on the Scottish school are few and characteristically brief and vague or cryptic' (Jessop 1997: 23). Nor were they altogether well informed; he seems not to have understood that Hume and Reid were on different sides with respect to the 'theory of ideas', for instance. My purpose in this chapter is to identify an alternative way in which Carlyle may be said to be related to Scottish philosophy, not by spotting 'Scottish' elements in his thought or writings, but by following the changing relationship between logic and rhetoric in the development of Scottish philosophy after the period of the Scottish Enlightenment. This provides, I shall argue, an interesting intellectual context within which Carlyle's endeavours can be located and assessed.

III

Hume's *Treatise of Human Nature* is subtitled 'Being an attempt to Introduce the experimental method of reasoning into moral subjects'. In the introduction he identifies four 'sciences' as most likely to benefit from this approach because their 'connexion with human nature is more close and intimate', namely 'Logic, Morals, Criticism, and Politics'. In these four sciences, he says 'is

---

[6] This changing conceptual landscape is the subject of *The Scottish Invention of English Literature*, ed. Robert Crawford, Cambridge University Press, 1998.

comprehended almost everything, which it can in any way import us to be acquainted with, or which can tend either to the improvement or ornament of the human mind' (Hume 2007: 4). In the *Treatise* itself, there is not much about 'Criticism', but it would still be accurate to say that in this passage Hume sets a philosophical agenda that the occupants of Chairs of Philosophy in the Scottish universities generally followed. With some modification in the case of Aberdeen's two universities, King's and Marischal, 'Morals' and 'Politics' fell to the Professor of Moral Philosophy, while 'Logic' and 'Criticism' (under the label 'Rhetoric') fell to the Professors of Logic and Metaphysics.

We are now inclined to think of 'criticism' as a rather high-level activity, largely confined to art exhibitions, book reviews and concert programmes. But for the Scottish philosophers of the eighteenth century the primary purpose behind formulating 'principles of criticism' was not to assess literary or artistic merit, but to serve the practical needs of politics, law and religion. Good 'taste' was crucial to the formation of citizens for participation in those worlds, and the education of the rising generation of citizens was the social function, and hence the professional duty, of university professors.

This central concern with 'educated taste' is most evident in the special attention that was given to rhetoric – traditionally understood as the art of using language well. Almost all the philosophers who held university posts in eighteenth-century Scotland taught rhetoric to their students, or assisted in its teaching. Though rhetoric was an ancient subject with classic texts, and had long been the responsibility of the teachers of logic, the project of a science of human nature led to a change, and an interest in what subsequently became known amongst intellectual historians as a 'new' rhetoric. It is a point of some scholarly debate as to just how 'new' this rhetoric was. Its most famous teachers had all had a traditional education in the classics, and their writings make frequent reference to the orators of the ancient world. It is also true that some of the interest in a 'new' rhetoric was not primarily philosophical or theoretical. It arose as a consequence of the 1707 Act of Union between Scotland and England. For legal and political purposes Scottish representatives now had to make themselves heard in Parliament, where the distinctive vocabulary and accent of broad Scots would not serve the purpose. Consequently, teaching and mastering an altered, more anglicised, manner of speech had a strictly practical dimension.[7] Still, this dimension can be exaggerated because there was undoubtedly renewed interest in the theory or philosophy of rhetoric (or 'eloquence'). This is evidenced in the fact that over the years 1748–50, Lord Kames organised popular public lectures on rhetoric by Adam Smith. These were delivered in Edinburgh before Smith became Professor at Glasgow. They constitute his first major contribution to Scottish intellectual life and were influenced in part by his interest in French 'belles lettres'.

Further evidence of the close connection between philosophy and rhetoric is to be found in lecture notes for an advanced class on eloquence by Smith's successor at Glasgow, Thomas Reid.

> Of all the fine Arts Eloquence is undoubtedly the Noblest. The force and Energy of all the others, are in this concentred, and brought, as it were, into one Focus. The harmony of sound, the power of Description, the force of Action, & the charms of good breeding, operate in this Art with united force. Eloquence paints to the imagination in more lively colours than the pencil does to the Eye. It exhibits the noblest passions and Movements of the Soul in a visible form, while at the same time it enlightens the Understanding, fills the Imagination with beautiful elegant and noble forms, awakens every affection by its proper object and calls forth our moral Powers to their natural Exercise . . . Eloquence, when possessed in the highest degree seems to be of all kinds of human power the Noblest and the greatest. (Reid 2005: 197)

This great panegyric to eloquence, it is worth noting, goes along with a style of philosophical thought marked by its care, precision and clarity. Eloquence, by Reid's account, is set within a larger context which he entitled 'the culture of the mind'. The expression has classical origins, and was also used by Reid's teacher in Aberdeen, George Turnbull. The constituents of rhetoric that he highlights – the sound of the voice, power of description, cogency of thought, use of gesture – were thus to be combined in the art of public speaking for a dual purpose: to bring about *both* intellectual

---

[7] Carlyle's acquaintance Francis Jeffrey, jurist and founding editor of the *Edinburgh Review*, went to Oxford for just this purpose: 'The only part of a Scotchman I mean to abandon is the language; and language is all I expect to learn in England' (quoted in Greig 1948: 57).

understanding *and* practical resolution on the part of the audience that the speaker was addressing. In short, rhetoric was not simply pandering to the emotions of an assembly of people, or even rousing passions within them. It was an important contributor to the cultivation of their minds.

This 'new' conception of rhetoric as intellectual cultivation and not merely persuasion aimed to rescue it from both philosophical contempt and empty sophistry. Its intention was to bridge any gap that might be thought to open up between speaking effectively and thinking cogently. The 'old' conception of rhetoric took its cue from debates between Plato and the Sophists. These debates, embodied in such dialogues as *Gorgias* and the *Republic*, were structured around a division between proving (or demonstrating) the truth of a proposition and persuading (or convincing) the audience to believe it. Persuasion was the aim of rhetoric, and thus relied on an appeal to interest and the emotions. Demonstration was the aim of philosophy, and thus relied on rational argument. Behind this division lay a deeper one – the distinction between *physis* and *nomos*, or in modern terms, fact and value. For the Sophists (at least as Plato represents them) no appeal to 'the truth' could move an audience to action, since facts in themselves could not motivate. Accordingly, orators must speak to the 'values' to which their audience subscribed, which was to say, appeal to their interests and play on their emotions. This conception of the rhetorician's ambition had invited philosophical scorn, from Plato to Locke, whose *Essay* describes rhetoric as 'that powerful instrument of error and deceit' (Locke 1975: 508). The 'new' rhetoric of the eighteenth century was new principally because it rejected the dichotomy on which this old debate rested.

Part of the challenge that Hume's *Treatise* presented to his contemporaries lay in its restatement of a characteristically sophistic position.[8] This is most explicit in Book 2 of the *Treatise* where he asserts that 'reason alone can never be a motive to any action of the will . . . [and] . . . can never oppose passion in the direction of the will' (Hume 2007: 265). This assertion plainly runs counter to Reid's contention that the power of rhetoric lies in enlightening the understanding, filling the Imagination and wakening affection, all 'at the same time', and on this point the two most influential

---

[8] The Sophists were philosophically diverse and in some places Plato himself seems to agree with them.

Scottish philosophers of rhetoric – George Campbell and Hugh Blair – agreed with Reid.

George Campbell was Principal of Marischal College from 1759 to 1795 and a founder of the Aberdeen Philosophical Society of which Reid, Alexander Gerard and John Gregory were also members. This was the group that Reid in a letter to Hume referred to as 'Your friendly adversaries'. Campbell's first major publication as Principal was a sophisticated philosophical work on miracles in which he took issue with Hume's famous essay. Over the same period he was working on the philosophy of rhetoric, and delivered a series of papers on the subject to the Society. These papers eventually became a book, *The Philosophy of Rhetoric*, published in 1776. In the opening chapter, Campbell expressly endorses the aim of the 'new' rhetoric.

> Would we not only touch the heart, but win it entirely to cooperate with our views, those affecting lineaments must be so interwoven with our argument, as that, from the passion excited our reasoning may derive importance, and so be fitted for commanding attention; and by the justice of the reasoning the passion may be more deeply rooted and enforced; and that thus may both be made to conspire in effectuating the persuasion which is the end proposed. (Campbell 1963: 6)

The Philosophy of Rhetoric was a considerable publishing success and widely used as a text, especially in American colleges. After a time, it came to be overshadowed by Hugh Blair's *Lectures on Rhetoric and Belles Lettres*. Blair, a friend of Hume's, was Minister of St Giles, the High Kirk of Edinburgh, and himself a highly regarded preacher. He became even more famous, however, for the lectures he gave at the University of Edinburgh as Regius Professor of Rhetoric and Belles Lettres.

Blair's lectures appeared in published form in 1783 (with a second, corrected version in 1785). Their popularity and influence proved enormous – with more than seventy complete editions, plus innumerable extractions and abridgements, published in Europe and America. They had no serious rival until the publication of Richard Whateley's *Elements of Rhetoric* in 1828. Blair emphatically embraces the 'new' rhetoric and declares that

> to be an Eloquent Speaker is [not] to compose a florid harangue on some popular topic, and deliver it to amuse an Audience . . . [but something] . . . much higher. It is a great exertion of the human powers . . .

the Art of being persuasive and commanding; the Art not of pleasing the fancy merely, but of *speaking both to the understanding and to the heart*. (Blair 2005: 380, emphasis added)

The creation of Blair's professorial Chair in 1762 marked a notable departure. Hitherto at Edinburgh, as at the other Scottish universities, rhetoric had been taught by the Professor of Logic, and Blair himself had attended classes on rhetoric by John Stevenson, who held that position. Now, somewhat contrary to the spirit of the 'new' rhetoric, the subjects became separated. A second important aspect of this departure was linking rhetoric to belles lettres, or the study of literature with an emphasis on eloquence in writing. It is for this reason that the Chair of Rhetoric and Belles Lettres at Edinburgh is generally taken to mark the birth of English Literature as a university subject. While the other Scottish universities did not follow Edinburgh's example by the creation of separate Chairs, English Literature did become the more explicit responsibility of the Professors of Logic, late into the nineteenth century. As Professor of Logic at St Andrews, for instance, Andrew Seth gave lectures on poetry, as did John Veitch in Glasgow and Alexander Bain and William Minto at Aberdeen. A similar development is discernible in America where, once more, many of the older colleges continued to model themselves on the Scottish universities. Over the course of the nineteenth century, classes and professorships in 'rhetoric' came more and more to mean the use and study of English language and literature. Eventually, relatively late in the day, Aberdeen, Glasgow and St Andrews followed Edinburgh's early example and separated the professorial provision for the study of philosophy and the study of language and literature. Philosophy returned to its traditional concerns, and literature replaced rhetoric.

IV

Some light is cast on why the thought and writings of Carlyle lost their interest for 'generations hence' if we view them against the history of philosophy and rhetoric. Carlyle himself makes the connection. He writes: 'we have lived to see all manner of Poetics and Rhetorics and Sermonics . . . as good as broken and abolished . . . [I]f you have any earnest meaning, which demands to be not only listened to, but believed and done . . . one leaves . . . Blair's

Lectures quite behind' (Carlyle 1970b: 264). This passage reveals both Carlyle's familiarity with and his rejection of the eighteenth-century philosophy of rhetoric of which Blair was the iconic representative. But by what did he mean to replace it? If the mutually reinforcing combination of logic (good reasoning) and rhetoric (effective expression) does not serve an author or thinker with 'earnest meaning, which demands to be . . . believed', what does?

Carlyle's resolve to leave Blair's *Lectures* 'quite behind' occurs in a letter to Ralph Waldo Emerson, written in 1834 in response to one he had received from Emerson. Emerson, who encountered Carlyle before he became famous, was so impressed by the text he had seen of Carlyle's serialised novel, *Sartor Resartus* ('The Tailor Re-tailored'), that he wanted to arrange for its publication in America. At the same time, he wondered whether the important philosophical ideas embodied in it might have been more effectively communicated in a less obscure form. It is this suggestion that Carlyle rejects.

Sartor Resartus is Carlyle's most philosophical work and arguably the work of most enduring interest. It is highly unusual in content, style and structure, and unsurprisingly, given this degree of novelty, it had difficulty in finding a publisher. In a letter to its (eventual) publisher, Carlyle describes *Sartor Resartus* as 'a kind of Didactic Novel; but indeed properly like nothing yet extant' (Carlyle 1970a: 396). The expression 'didactic novel' might be taken to suggest that the book straddles the philosophical/literary divide, but if so, it is in a wholly new way. For Carlyle, the 'earnest meaning' of the work was radically new, so that a radically different style of presentation was required.

The book's structure is exceptionally strange and complex. It purports to be the edited version of a philosophical treatise by a German professor. The unnamed editor has interspersed explanatory and critical remarks, and in doing so claims to have been greatly aided by biographical material with which he was fortunately supplied. This twofold source – academic treatise and biographical information – explains the subtitle: 'The Life and Opinions of Herr Teufelsdröckh'. From the start, Professor Teufelsdröckh's treatise is set in a recognisably philosophical context. The opening 'Preliminary' cites names specially identified with early-nineteenth-century exponents of the Scottish philosophical tradition – Stewart, Cousin, Royer-Collard – and as the work proceeds there are many explicitly philosophical references – to the Cartesian cogito, the metaphysics of space and time, personal identity, the debate about miracles, Utilitarianism, Rousseau's state of nature, and several other longstanding philosophical topics. At the same time, the deliberately created gap between author and editor allows scope for a degree of humour and satire somewhat at odds with philosophical writing. This extends to the governing conceit – that Teufelsdröckh's book is a treatise on 'The Philosophy of Clothes', which, it is said, is its principal claim to novelty in the history of philosophy. Clothing becomes an extended metaphor for the historical accumulation of ideas and institutions in which human nature is 'dressed'. Rousseau's ideal of the noble savage invites us to return to the state of nature, but this is declared to be both impossible and undesirable. If clothing is dated or worn out, it is with re-tailoring, not a return to nakedness, that the solution lies, hence the title of the book. In the second to last chapter, Teufelsdröckh gives voice to his 'conviction'.

> [L]ooking away from individual cases, and how a Man is by the Tailor new created into a Nobleman, and clothed not only with Wool but with Dignity and a Mystic Dominion, – is not the fair fabric of Society itself, with all its royal mantles and pontifical stoles, whereby, from nakedness and dismemberment, we are organized into Polities, into nations, and a whole co-operating Mankind, as has here been often irrefragably evinced of the Tailor alone? – What too are all Poets, and Moral Teachers, but a species of Metaphorical Tailors? (Carlyle 1894: 187)

It is here that we can find a connection between Carlyle's *Sartor* and the Scottish philosophical tradition, a connection signalled by the fact that a few lines later on, Teufelsdröckh recounts his experience when, 'turning the corner of a lane, in the Scottish Town of Edinburgh, I came upon a signpost', which may be an oblique reference to Carlyle's own moment of 'revelation' on Leith Walk. Philosophy since Hume, grounded as it is in a science of human nature, has hitherto, and mistakenly, sought the truth about humanity beneath or behind its cultural clothing. The resulting naturalism is 'mechanical', in Carlyle's eyes, because it removes human action from its historical context, and conceives of it simply as an aspect of the machine that is the universe. Such naturalism thus strips humanity of its spirituality, and accordingly Carlyle identifies the contrasting vision presented in *Sartor* as 'natural supernaturalism'. This somewhat oxymoronic expression provides a title for the chapter that forms the heart of the book.

Though *Sartor Resartus* is perplexing in many ways, it is evident that the book's 'earnest meaning' was conceived and intended as a powerful counter to what Carlyle regarded as the deeply erroneous mechanistic conception of reality that had prevailed in the eighteenth century. This conception was reflected in the Lockean sensationalism of which Hume was a leading exponent. If this is indeed his target, a question naturally arises as to just how Carlyle's 'didactic novel' might be expected to correct or challenge the errors of a 'mechanical' philosophy. The issue is one that he addresses in the work itself when the 'editor' asks about the 'author': 'Still the question returns to us: How could a man occasionally of keen insight, not without keen sense of propriety, who had real Thoughts to communicate, resolve to emit them in a shape bordering on the absurd? . . . One conjecture is that perhaps Necessity as well as Choice was concerned in it' (Carlyle 1894: 190).

Let us suppose that the point in history at which Carlyle was writing in some sense necessitated a 'shape bordering on the absurd'. How was this necessary absurdity supposed to induce belief in its earnest meaning on the part of the reader? How was conviction in 'natural supernaturalism' to be secured if the established methods of philosophy and rhetoric were abandoned? This question invites us to look a little more closely at Carlyle's relationship to philosophy.

V

Carlyle was a student at the University of Edinburgh from 1810 to 1814. He went there with the purpose of studying theology and entering the ministry of the Church of Scotland. This was an ambition frequently entertained by academically able boys from poor backgrounds, but Carlyle soon abandoned it. Like the majority of students at that time, he did not graduate with a degree. He was nonetheless a very serious student, and a voracious reader. While his preferred classes were in mathematics and the sciences, he followed the usual course of study and took classes in philosophy. The celebrated Thomas Brown was among his professors, though Carlyle did not share in the general admiration that Brown attracted. Twenty years later he fleetingly made the acquaintance of Sir William Hamilton, not long before Hamilton's appointment to the Chair of Logic and Metaphysics at Edinburgh. Carlyle recalls that,

> though he stood so high in my esteem as a man of intellect and knowledge, I had read nothing by Sir William nor indeed did I ever read anything considerable of what has sent his name over the world; – having years before, for good reasons of my own, renounced all metaphysical study or inquiry, and ceased altogether (as a master phrases it) to 'think about thinking.' (Carlyle 1997: 432)

It was a claim he had made some years earlier in a letter to James Hutchison Stirling, declaring himself to be 'quite an alien from all Metaphysic for the last forty years' (A. H. Stirling 1912: 201).

If Carlyle is recalling correctly, this explicit 'renunciation' turned out to be less final than might have been expected. In the late 1820s he still referred to himself as a 'philosopher' and expressed interest in a position teaching philosophy at the newly founded University College London. A year later he applied (unsuccessfully) for the Chair of Moral Philosophy at St Andrews University. Even as late as 1868, and despite his disavowal, he felt sufficient resonance between his intellectual endeavour and philosophy in Scotland to provide James Hutchison Stirling with a testimonial in the competition for the Chair of Moral Philosophy at Edinburgh. In the same year he accepted the (honorary) position of President of the Edinburgh Philosophical Institution.

None of this was merely whimsical. From an early stage, the 'earnest meaning' he meant his works to have was located within a philosophical background with which he expected his readers to be familiar, and the German sources in which he found the antidote to the 'Scotch metaphysics' he had renounced included philosophical and quasi-philosophical writers. In fact, Carlyle was among the first people in Scotland to look beyond the philosophy of Hume and Reid and seek fresh intellectual stimulus from a German alternative. For Carlyle, it was Goethe who provided the main source of inspiration, and he was gratified to win Goethe's approval for his work as a translator and exponent.[9] But it was

---

[9] Goethe agreed to provide a testimonial for Carlyle as a candidate for the Chair of Moral Philosophy at St Andrews, but it arrived too late to be of service.

Thomas Carlyle and the Philosophy of Rhetoric 109

Goethe as thinker, not simply writer or story-teller, in which he found the resources for a post-Christian re-spiritualisation of the world. His version of this is what he elaborates as 'natural supernaturalism' in *Sartor*.

The more widespread importance of Carlyle's translations and essays on Goethe, and other German literary figures, is remarked upon by Edward Caird.

> Carlyle was the first in this country [i.e. Scotland] who discovered the full significance of the great revival of German literature, and the enormous reinforcement which its poetic and philosophic idealism had brought to the failing spirit of man ... in addition to his own great genius, he had the advantage of being thus the first from whom we heard the great words of Goethe and Fichte, of Schiller and Richter and Novalis. Nor was he content to speak of the significance of German thought from an abstract point of view; he was continually trying to show what it meant *for us*. (Caird 1892: 232–3, emphasis original)

Caird made this assessment in a talk on 'The Genius of Carlyle' that he gave to the Dialectical Society of Glasgow University a decade or so after Carlyle's death. Caird, who held the Chair of Moral Philosophy at Glasgow from 1866 to 1893, was himself a leading figure in the rising generation of Scottish philosophers inspired by German Idealism. Yet it was not Carlyle but T. H. Green who brought Caird to a much deeper and more philosophical appreciation of German philosophy, especially the works of Kant and Hegel. Carlyle had whetted Caird's appetite, we might say, but his works provided nothing in the way of a sustained and critical understanding. From the point of view of Caird's own philosophical development, they could be ignored. Why was this?

Caird identifies *Sartor Resartus* as 'the most authentic exposition of [Carlyle's] view of life in its most general principles' (Caird 1892: 243). Yet if anyone asks how *Sartor*'s thesis about the nature of human existence is supported and developed, the answer, if obvious, is disappointing.

> It is almost needless to say that you will not find in [the book] an attempt to demonstrate anything logically, either by old or new logical methods. As to the former, Carlyle never loses an opportunity of, so to speak, insulting the syllogism and all the weapons in the old armoury of Logic. And though he owes much to the later German

philosophy, especially to Fichte's popular works, he seems to have cared only about the results, and nothing at all about the process. Metaphysical theories in general . . . he regards as absurd attempts to measure the immeasurable, or weigh with earthly scales that infinite reality, which we can, he thinks, imaginatively symbolize, but which we cannot scientifically define or determine. (Caird 1892: 248)

Caird summarises Carlyle's purpose as a writer as that of making us 'see through the external puppet-show of human life, to the internecine struggle of good and evil which it half reveals and half conceals' (Caird 1892: 259). The central conceit of *Sartor Resartus*, however – that it is a 'philosophy of clothes' – makes it plain that this is to be done by replacing abstract philosophical inquiry with 'imaginative symbol'. Now as Caird points out, Carlyle's central metaphor in *Sartor* did not originate with him. It has a precursor in Swift's fierce satire 'A Tale of a Tub' published in 1704. The parodies in the Tale include a sect that 'held the universe to be a huge suit of clothes, which invests everything' (Swift, quoted in Caird 1892: 244). To note this earlier source is not to diminish the originality of Carlyle's use of the image, but it does suggest that its philosophical matter, stripped of philosophical reasoning, places it firmly in the category of literature.

Here too, however, Caird identifies an obstacle in another of 'Carlyle's paradoxes, the doctrine, namely, that poets, at least in the present age, should cease to "invent anything but reality." By this he means that they should henceforth cease to produce what is called fiction, and should confine themselves to the task of throwing the light of their imagination upon history and biography' (Caird 1892: 259). This was the course that Carlyle himself pursued. He wrote no more 'novels' after *Sartor Resartus*, and turned to histories and biographies. Importantly, none of the major literary figures whom he knew and admired – Browning, Dickens and Tennyson, for instance[10] – followed him in this, or showed any inclination to do so. In effect, Carlyle discounted imaginative literature no less than metaphysical philosophy, and to make the point more forcefully, was willing even to question the value of Shakespeare's literary legacy.

---

[10] He also knew Wordsworth, but is very dismissive of his accomplishments in *Reminiscences*.

> Of Shakespeare too, it is not the fiction I admire, but the fact. To say the truth, what I most of all admire are the traces he shows of a talent that could have turned the history of England into a kind of *Iliad*, almost perhaps, into a kind of Bible. (Quoted by Caird 1892: 260, no reference to source)

In Scotland over the course of the nineteenth century, philosophy extended its horizons not merely by becoming familiar with but by properly appreciating the revolution in thought initiated by Kant and extended by Hegel. In a related movement, the study of rhetoric was replaced by the study of poetry, drama and the novel. Both these developments can be intelligibly situated within an intellectual trajectory that began with the Scottish Enlightenment philosophers, following, for the most part, the agenda set by Hume's *Treatise*. By contrast, while Carlyle's intellectual labours were immense, and lauded by his contemporaries, they were conducted in indifference to this trajectory. Ironically, since Carlyle was so insistent upon speaking to 'the Present', in retrospect his works can be seen to have been out of keeping with their time. It was Carlyle the living 'Sage' rather than considered thinker by whom his contemporaries were attracted and enthralled.

Caird admired Carlyle, and speaks repeatedly of his 'genius'. Yet in the end his concluding assessment serves to explain why Carlyle neither integrated nor transcended the philosophy/literature divide.

> Carlyle's great faculty of penetrative insight, his power of seeing the poetry of life through the most ordinary details, and, we must add, his want of the highest power, either of abstract thinking on the one side or of creative imagination on the other, produced in him a kind of intolerance of every form of literary utterance except that in which he himself was strongest. (Caird 1892: 260)

Yet there is something more to be said about the disappearance of Carlyle's vast output into near obscurity. This resulted not only from his insistence on a peculiar form of literary utterance, but from the nature of oratory. David Masson classes Carlyle with the great Scottish churchman Thomas Chalmers (1780–1847), as the two greatest men he had ever been privileged to know. The combination is memorable because there is this striking difference between them. Whereas Carlyle sought to move on from the 'new' rhetoric promoted by Campbell, Blair and other Enlightenment philosophers, Chalmers may be said to have exemplified it. As the most powerful orator of his time, possibly in the whole of the nineteenth century, he attracted vast audiences to his sermons, speeches and lectures. Yet this was never the result of crowd pleasing, Masson tells us. Rather, 'there was always substance in what Chalmers spoke or wrote; nothing that he spoke or wrote but was the result of real cogitation; no mind was more incapable of commonplace even for an instant' (Masson 1911: 82). This explains how he could move so easily from the pulpit to the classroom. When he took up the Chair of Moral Philosophy at St Andrews in 1823, Masson says, 'for him, as for every one else over Europe undertaking a course of speculative thought, Hume furnished a necessary point of departure', followed by 'readings or re-readings in Reid, Campbell, Adam Smith and Dugald Stewart' (Masson 1911: 82). 'As an effective expositor of his ideas in discourse from the pulpit or the chair I have never known any one comparable to Chalmers' (Masson 1911: 83).

Chalmers, then, is in a sense almost the polar opposite of Carlyle and, like Carlyle, wrote and published copiously. Yet in his case, no less than Carlyle's, very little of it proved of enduring interest for the generations that came after. Masson thinks he can 'explain why it should be that the interest in Chalmers's writings and the attention now given to them should be far less than might seem due to the worth of the living man'. Part of the answer lies in the simple fact that he was an orator. Writings 'of that oratorical order to which Chalmers's mainly belonged . . . are addressed to moods and emergencies, and moods and emergencies pass away' (Masson 1911: 81). So too with Carlyle, it might be said. Not only his pamphlets, but his massive histories and biographies were 'addressed to moods and emergencies'. That is what gave him the status of 'Sage', but the moods and emergencies to which Carlyle's writings spoke so powerfully also passed away.

6

Hegelianism and its Critics

I[1]

'Hegelianism and its Critics' was the title of an article by Andrew Seth, published in the journal *Mind* in 1894. Seth was writing in response to a two-part article in *Mind* by Henry Jones, published the previous year, which was itself a response to previous articles by Seth in the *Philosophical Review*. Seth's article was preceded by a short piece by R. B. Haldane, and followed by a comment from David G. Ritchie, both of which also appeared in *Mind* under similar titles. These vigorous and extended exchanges can be regarded as the focal point for an argument about the place and role of Hegelianism, and Idealism more broadly, in the trajectory of nineteenth-century Scottish philosophy. This chapter will trace the genesis of the argument, identify its key points, and seek to assess its wider philosophical significance.

Kant knew about philosophy in Scotland well in advance of Scottish philosophers knowing much about him. Yet even before Kant's death, selections from his works had been translated into English by a Scot, John Richardson. Since Richardson was very familiar with Hume, he may have been a Scottish graduate, but his continuing Scottish connections were tenuous. He spent most of his life in Germany, his translations and 'recensions' of Kant were published in London, and his efforts seem to have had little or no impact in Scotland (or anywhere, for that matter). It was not

---

[1] The first few paragraphs of this section owe much to J. H. Burns, 'Scottish Kantians: An Exploration', *Journal of Scottish Philosophy*, 7.2 (Autumn 2009): 115–131, and Paul Guyer, 'The Scottish Reception of Kant', in Gordon Graham (ed.), *Scottish Philosophy in the Nineteenth and Twentieth Centuries*, Oxford: Oxford University Press, 2015.

until the mid-nineteenth century that accurate English translations of some of Kant's works were widely available, two of the most enduring being by Scottish graduates. J. W. Semple's translation of Kant's *Metaphysic of Ethics*, with commentary, first appeared in the 1830s, but attracted a much larger readership when it was reprinted in 1867. This was on the initiative of Henry Calderwood, recently appointed to the Chair of Moral Philosophy at Edinburgh, who wanted his students to learn about Kant's moral philosophy. J. M. D. Meiklejohn's translation of Kant's *Critique of Pure Reason* was published in 1856. For a long time, it served as the standard text and was the version included in the *Everyman's Library*. Eventually Meiklejohn was displaced by the work of another Scottish philosopher, Norman Kemp Smith, whose translation is still regarded as authoritative.

Though German was not widely read in Scotland in the first half of the nineteenth century, and adequate translations were slow in appearing, some knowledge of Kant's philosophy had filtered through to the Scottish universities via France. In 1803, the first volume of the *Edinburgh Review* included a lengthy article on a newly published French book about Kant. The reviewer was Thomas Brown, who was to succeed Dugald Stewart as Professor of Moral Philosophy at Edinburgh in 1810. Based on this second-hand acquaintance, Brown found Kant's philosophy to be an unsatisfactory mix of Reid's Common Sense, Leibniz's innate sensibilities, and Hume's denial of causal necessity and external reality. Ten years later, in another *Edinburgh Review* essay, James Macintosh reverted to the subject and argued that Kant and Reid were concerned with the same ultimate laws of thought as the boundaries of reasoning, and that the differences between them were of style more than substance. At this time (despite Brown's well-known strictures) Reid was still a dominant presence in Scottish philosophy, and so it was natural that the question of Kant's relation to Reid in the task of responding to Hume should arise. But even when Reid's star was no longer in the ascendant, the topic continued to occupy philosophers in Scotland, finding its most extended treatment in 1885 with the publication of Andrew Seth's first set of Balfour Lectures on *Scottish Philosophy: A Comparison of the Scottish and German Answers to Hume*. In the interval, Kant's influence on Scottish philosophical debate in Scotland had increased greatly, thanks in the first instance to Sir William Hamilton. Hamilton studied in Germany for a time and acquired an unusually good knowledge of German philosophy.

He combined this with an adherence to Reid, and drew on his knowledge and understanding of Kant only insofar as this would serve to remedy the deficiencies he detected in Reid. The 'Natural Realism' that Hamilton articulated and defended was in effect an attempt at amalgamating the two.[2] During his twenty-year tenure of the Chair of Logic and Metaphysics in Edinburgh, Hamilton attracted and inspired a large number of students, some of whom later came to occupy professorial positions. But in Hamilton's hands, while the introduction of Kant broadened the philosophical curriculum, it resulted in no major radical changes or innovations in philosophical thinking.

One of the thinkers inspired by Hamilton, though never strictly a student of his, was James Frederick Ferrier. Whereas Brown had inclined to Hume over Reid, Ferrier was the first significant figure in Scottish philosophy to abandon Reid in order to embrace a version of Idealism. It is unclear, however, what part Kant's philosophy played in this. In his essay 'The Crisis of Modern Speculation' (1841) Ferrier hailed, and sought to articulate, the advent of a 'new philosophy'. Hitherto, he held, 'the great endeavour of philosophy, in all ages', namely explaining 'the nature of the connection which subsists between the mind of man and the external universe', had led to a stalemate between Hypothetical Realism, Idealism and Scepticism, the three philosophical positions outlined by Hamilton. None of them had been able to solve the central problem, so 'it is to speculation of a very late date that we owe the only approach that has been made to a satisfactory solution' (Ferrier 2001c: 262). An important result of this 'new philosophy', he says, 'is the finishing stroke which it gives to the old system of dogmatic Realism and dogmatic Idealism' since 'this new doctrine shows that these systems are investigating a problem which cannot possibly be answered in the affirmative or the negative'. That is because the question they ask 'is an irrational and unintelligible one' (Ferrier 2001c: 286). To understand the immense significance of this new philosophy is 'to catch the dawning rays which are now heralding the sunrise of a new era of science, the era of genuine speculation' (Ferrier 2001c: 288).

In this essay, Ferrier does not identify the source of this revolutionary speculation, and he may in fact have been referring to his own endeavours. While it is plausible to hold that it owed something,

---

[2] See Chapter 2.

perhaps a great deal, to Kant, there is no explicit reference to Kant in the essay. Kant is indeed discussed at some length in Ferrier's *Institutes of Metaphysic: The Theory of Knowing and Being*, the major work he published about a decade later. There, however, while Kant is declared to be 'sometimes very nearly right', he ultimately fails, in Ferrier's estimation, to escape the thraldom of the 'old' philosophy.

> [O]ur conclusion is, that instead of [Kant's] system having destroyed sensualism, the sensualism latent in his system has rather destroyed it . . . [T]he misinterpretation of the Platonic analysis . . . which, as we have seen, has played such havoc in philosophy in general, has carried its direful influence even into the psychological museum of Kant, and exhibits its fatal presence in all his elaborate preparations. (Ferrier 2001a: 286)

On a plain reading, this passage suggests that wherever Ferrier thought the 'genius of modern thought' originated, it was not in Kant. If so, however, his opinion was somewhat eccentric. Greater familiarity with Kant brought many English language philosophers to the view, soon widely held, that 'the Critical Philosophy' inaugurated by Kant was the dawning of a new era, something genuinely revolutionary in the history of philosophy. It was comparable, as Kant himself claimed, to the Copernican Revolution that had transformed physics and astronomy. At the same time, growing familiarity with Kant's writings brought an awareness of their deficiencies, as well as increasing knowledge of subsequent German attempts to address these deficiencies by Fichte, Schelling and Hegel. It was Hegel, ultimately, in whom sufficiently many Scottish philosophers found the completion of the revolution begun by Kant to form a group identified as 'Scottish Hegelians'.

II

The Secret of Hegel by James Hutchison Stirling was the first book on Hegel to be published by a Scottish philosopher. It appeared in 1865, and according to Alexander Campbell Fraser, who held the Edinburgh Chair of Logic and Metaphysics at the time, its publication marked 'an epoch in our insular philosophy, with corresponding enlargement in subsequent religious thought' (Fraser 1899: 226). In the same year Stirling published his critical attack on Hamilton's philosophy, thus bringing the rejection of Hamilton's

Reid and the endorsement of Hegel's Kant into sharp focus. Stirling had been a student at Glasgow in the 1830s when philosophy was in its post-Reidian doldrums. His intellectual interest was awakened, but he quickly became convinced that there was no life left in the philosophy of Common Sense and its cognates. Accordingly, he took up medicine, and practised as a doctor for a number of years until an inheritance allowed him to become an independent scholar. He devoted eight years to the study of Kant and Hegel, and *The Secret of Hegel* was the outcome. It was well received and sold a good number of copies for a book of its kind. Nevertheless, despite Fraser's encomium, it is hard to assess its real influence on the course of philosophy in Scotland, and significant perhaps that, though Stirling was able to secure a testimonial from no less a figure than Thomas Carlyle, he was unsuccessful in his application for a Chair of Moral Philosophy both in Glasgow and in Edinburgh.

In the competition at Glasgow, the successful applicant was Edward Caird. He held the position from 1866 to 1893, and his influence during this long tenure in the Chair is much easier to trace. Caird's *Philosophy of Kant* appeared in 1877, and was then developed into *The Critical Philosophy of Kant*, a two-volume study published in 1889, a few years before he left Glasgow to become Master of Balliol. Though this magnum opus retained Kant in the title, the book interpreted the project of Kantian Idealism as completed in Hegel. Caird had himself been a student at Glasgow, but was so enamoured of German philosophy that he ignored Reid and Hamilton entirely. His effectiveness as a lecturer to the large Moral Philosophy class was remarkable, and together his teaching and publications generated a new generation of 'Hegelian' philosophers. This group included some of his most brilliant students, notably his successor in the Chair, Henry Jones. But he also inspired graduates from other Scottish universities who went on to hold Chairs of Philosophy – Andrew Seth at Edinburgh, David Ritchie at St Andrews and W. R. Sorley at Aberdeen, for instance. Another of the new Hegelians was the philosopher-politician R. B. Haldane. Though a prizewinning philosophy graduate from Edinburgh, Haldane never held an academic post. Nevertheless, over the course of thirty years he sustained his philosophical proficiency sufficiently to publish several papers, and even to be appointed Gifford Lecturer at St Andrews at the height of his political career.

The first contribution of these Scottish 'young Hegelians' to philosophical literature was a volume published in 1883 entitled

Essays in Philosophical Criticism. Its publication resulted from a dissatisfaction with the journal *Mind*, established by Alexander Bain, but edited from the outset by his student George Croom Robertson. The authors of the *Essays* believed (probably wrongly) that *Mind*, under Robertson's editorship, was too narrowly focused on philosophy's relationship to empirical psychology, and not sufficiently open to new trends in philosophical thought. Initially their idea was to establish an alternative philosophy journal, but this was abandoned in favour of a single volume, and in fact it was principally in the 'New Series' of *Mind* that the subsequent debate about Hegelianism was conducted.

The *Essays* declared their allegiance to Idealism at the outset by being dedicated to the memory of T. H. Green, and by opening with a preface by Edward Caird (most of which was itself devoted to remembering and extolling Green). Alongside essays by the editors Seth (Pringle-Pattison) and Haldane, there were papers by Ritchie, Sorley and Jones, as well as W. P. Ker and James Bonar, who had also been students of Caird's and were now at Oxford.

In his preface, Caird expressly indicates the writers' orientation.

> [T]he Essays have been written quite independently by their several authors, and . . . any agreement which exists among them is due, not to an intention to advocate any special philosophical theory, but rather a certain community of opinion in relation to the general principle and method of philosophy . . . The writers of this volume agree in believing that the line of investigation which philosophy must follow, or in which it may be expected to make its most important contributions to the intellectual life of man, is that which was opened up by Kant, and for the successful prosecution of which no one has done so much as Hegel. (Seth Pringle-Pattison and Haldane 1883: 1–2)

The essays were neither historical nor simply expository. On the contrary, though taking their cue from Kant and Hegel, they aimed to address philosophical questions of contemporary interest in a fresh and insightful way. As Caird remarks,

> the literal importation of Kant and Hegel into another country and time would not be possible if it were desirable, or desirable if it were possible. The mere change of time and place, if there were nothing more, implies new questions and a new attitude of mind in those whom the writer addresses, which would make a bare reproduction

unmeaning. Moreover, this change of the mental atmosphere and environment is itself part of a development which must affect the doctrine also, if it is no mere dead tradition, but a seed of intellectual life. Anyone who writes about philosophy must have his work judged, not by its relation to the intellectual wants of a past generation, but by its power to meet the wants of the present time . . . A volume of *Essays* such as the present . . . can only be a small contribution to that critical reconstruction of knowledge which every time has to accomplish for itself. But it will, I believe, serve the purpose of its writers, if it shows in some degree how the principles of an idealistic philosophy may be brought to bear on the various problems of science, of ethics, and of religion, which are now pressing upon us. (Seth Pringle-Pattison and Haldane 1883: 2–3)

As this last sentence indicates, one notable feature of the volume was that, in the spirit of Hegel, it expressly widened the scope of philosophy beyond topics in metaphysics, logic and epistemology to critical philosophical explorations of the presuppositions of history, art and politics, as well as those that Caird identifies. This flowed directly from the underlying conception of 'Philosophy as the Criticism of Categories', the subject of Seth's opening essay, and in this way, interestingly, it returned philosophical debate in Scotland to the wide-ranging agenda of Hume, Kames, Reid and Smith, an agenda that had progressively narrowed in the hands of Brown, Hamilton and Ferrier.

Caird allows that, though united by 'a certain community of opinion' about the most promising direction for philosophical inquiry, '[s]uch an agreement is consistent with great and even vital differences' (Seth Pringle-Pattison and Haldane 1883: 1). It was not long before these differences emerged. The 'renegade', from some points of view, was Andrew Seth. In his first set of Balfour Lectures on *Scottish Philosophy*, delivered just as the volume of essays appeared, Seth not only registered his reservations with respect to Kant, but also went some way towards rehabilitating Reid. In his second set of Balfour Lectures, on *Hegelianism and Personality*, he went further and elaborated what he took to be a crucial flaw in the Hegelian alternative to Realism – the inability of the Absolute to accommodate the individuality of persons. This uncovered a major difference with several of his fellow contributors to the *Essays*, most notably Ritchie, Haldane and Jones. Reviewing *Hegelianism and Personality* in *Mind*, Ritchie wrote '*Et tu, Brute!* The kindly rehabilitation of Reid in Prof. Seth's first series of Balfour Lectures and their suggestions in their concluding paragraph of problems unsatisfactorily treated by Hegelianism had hardly prepared us for the fierce blows here bestowed upon the "Neo-Kantians"' (Ritchie 1888b: 256). A few months later and in the same journal, Seth's co-editor Haldane published a second response to the book entitled 'Hegel and his Recent Critics'. Haldane makes express mention of Seth's contribution to the *Essays*.

> One would have expected the author of the essay on 'Philosophy as Criticism of the Categories' to have been most careful while condemning what was bad to separate out and defend what was good in the source of his own inspirations. And yet it is only at the end of the book, in the concluding words of a chapter which contains a lecture to the gallery, that Prof. Seth has anything approaching a good word to say for the Hegelian method. (Haldane 1888: 589)

It was, however, Seth's third set of Balfour Lectures, on Realism, that called forth the most strenuous criticism from a former *Essays* ally, this time Henry Jones. Unlike the first two sets, Seth's *Lectures on Realism* did not appear as a book (except posthumously). Seth expected to revise them (though he never did) and so published them provisionally as a series of articles in the *Philosophical Review*. It was these articles which Jones attacked in his two-part contribution to *Mind*, to which Seth then replied.

III

Jones directed his main criticism at 'epistemologists' who think that a theory of knowledge is and must be prior to any philosophical account of reality. Seth is taken to be a leading representative of these epistemologists, and Jones brings more directly to the fore than either Ritchie or Haldane the contention that Seth's retreat from Hegelianism is a reversion to Reid and Common Sense, albeit with some attempt to incorporate elements of Kantianism.

> The difficulties urged against a philosophy should have some higher source than the commonplace empiricism of ordinary consciousness . . . [The epistemologists, however,] occupy the attitude of ordinary consciousness, except that critically they are better equipped . . . They have certainly gone 'back to Kant', and I believe, much further, even to

> Dr Thomas Reid ... Philosophy seeks a principle of unity in differences; and that principle is scarcely brought to the surface by a theory that combines the dogmatism of Reid with the ontology of Hegel ... Those who advance [such a theory] ... are really objecting to the theory of Hegel from the point of view of Reid. (Jones 1893a: 290–3)

In his response to Jones and what he calls 'the vials of his wrath', Seth also takes the opportunity to reply to Ritchie and Haldane. He rejects the label 'epistemologist' but in the end, while distinguishing epistemology from psychology, reaffirms its independence from metaphysics.

What, ultimately, does this protracted, and heated, disagreement amount to? It is striking that the parties to it emphasise how much they have in common. Both distinguished themselves sharply from the Associationism that can be traced from Hume through Brown and Mill to Bain.[3] In Hume, psychology is mingled with metaphysics to the confusion of both and, as Jones says, the resulting mix 'regards ideas as capable of hanging on to one another like a swarm of bees' (Jones 1893a: 296). Or it separates the two, as Bain does quite explicitly, opening the way for a strictly empirical investigation into the mind, but effectively leaving all the metaphysical questions behind, even if Bain did not quite see it this way. The common ground between Seth and the Hegelians, however, extends beyond a shared opposition to empirical psychology mistakenly employed as a philosophical method. It rests upon a shared supposition that 'the genuine impulse of philosophy' lies in a desire 'to comprehend the Universe as a revelation of a single principle' (Jones 1893a: 289). It is for this reason, according to Seth in his first set of Balfour Lectures, that Kant is to be regarded as a greater philosopher than Reid, and this further supports Ritchie's observation in his review of the second set of lectures that, whatever changes of mind Seth may have undergone, he continued to accept Kant's analysis of the problem as the starting point of philosophy. Haldane in his short article identifies this shared starting point, amplified by Hegel, as an agreement about method, one that

> accepts Kant's criticism of Hume [but] goes further than Kant in asserting that not only can we not go outside the closed circle of consciousness, but that there is no outside which has really any meaning. All that

---

[3] See Chapter 4.

> is, is for – not the self which is a particular object in space and time, not yet any transcendent self, but – knowledge. (Haldane 1888: 589)

It seems a little odd to describe this as articulating a 'method', but at any rate the proposition 'there is no outside which has really any meaning' is one that, on a certain interpretation, Seth does endorse. Conversely, Ritchie is no slower than Seth to identify the unwarranted ontological excesses into which Hegel is tempted, and which some of his followers especially savoured.

Given that all the participants in this debate were signatories, as it were, to the Idealist agenda advanced by the *Essays*, it is not surprising that they should concur in many matters, but so close do the agreements come, in fact, that it becomes hard, even for the authors themselves, to discern where the key difference lies. In his response to Jones, for example, Seth remarks that there is 'a certain satisfaction in seeing one's own views expressed almost in one's own language, but there is also a feeling of topsy-turvydom in seeing them elaborately proved as a refutation of one's own contentions' (Seth Pringle-Pattison 1894: 5). Part of the reason for this is the difficulty of distinguishing clearly between legitimate and illegitimate versions of dualism. All agree that philosophical adequacy rests upon being able to articulate 'a single principle' that somehow underlies both truth and reality. They also agree that there is an obvious distinction to be drawn between knowledge and belief, which is to say, between 'reality' and 'thought about reality'. Seth holds that in its singularity, the Hegelian endeavour to unify thought and reality in the Absolute nullifies the distinction. Jones thinks this amounts to attributing to Hegel 'the preposterous mistake of taking knowledge of reality for reality itself' (Jones 1893a: 305), and he on the other hand claims that Seth's epistemological efforts to avoid this mistake result in necessarily elevating the distinction into a metaphysical duality, thereby failing in the search for a single principle. Given the possibility of error, our thoughts about reality can evidently deviate from reality itself. Given the ultimate unity of experience, however, reality must be comprehended within thought. Kant's unknowable things-in-themselves are the ghostly traces of an 'outside which has really no meaning' but which he was unable to escape. The question remains, though. How are we to make the distinction between thought and reality fundamental without making it metaphysical?

Hegelianism and its Critics

For the purposes of following the trajectory of philosophical debate in Scotland, fortunately, it is not essential to resolve this perplexing issue. The key point of difference between the Hegelians and their critics[4] lies in the contrasting conceptions of philosophical inquiry and the role of a philosophical system. Jones follows the sentence previously quoted – 'The difficulties urged against a philosophy should have some higher source than the commonplace empiricism of ordinary consciousness' – with this noteworthy claim. 'The duty to criticise must be based upon a right to criticise, and that right can only be derived from some consecutive and ultimately constructive theory of existence' (Jones 1893a: 290). In response, Seth says he must 'protest most strongly against this convenient and wholly unwarrantable assumption', and counters it by quoting 'the fine words of Mill': 'If I am asked what system of philosophy I substituted for that which, as a philosophy, I had abandoned, I answer, No system; only a conviction that the true system was something much more complex and many-sided than I had previously had any idea' (Seth Pringle-Pattison 1894: 3, quoting Mill's *Autobiography*). Seth amplifies the grounds of his protest by repeating a widely held criticism of Hegelianism – that it is aprioristic and inclined to manipulate or massage any matters of fact that its theoretical presuppositions cannot easily accommodate.

> Many critics hold that, as a theory, Hegelianism runs far in advance of insight, and that there are awkward facts in the universe to which it cannot be said to do justice. It is surely open to critics in these circumstances to call for reconsideration, for a wider and more elastic theory. Some of them are content to believe where they cannot prove; but if pressed by Hegelian dogmatism, they are equally entitled to take up the purely critical attitude of a suspension of judgment. As Kant says: 'When delusive proofs are presented to us, it is our duty to meet them with the *non liquet* [not proven] of a matured judgment'. (Seth Pringle-Pattison 1894: 3)

---

[4] The most vociferous critic of Hegel from the perspective of adherence to Reid and Hamilton was John Veitch, who held the Chair of Logic at Glasgow for much the same period as Caird held the Chair of Moral Philosophy. His volume of essays on *Knowing and Being* (1889) was also reviewed by Ritchie in *Mind*, but dismissively, and Veitch's criticisms were never lent anything like the same significance as Seth's.

In endorsing this reservation Seth is, probably consciously, echoing something of Reid's suspicion of system building in philosophy. But the disagreement comes to more than this. The implications of Haldane's summary of the Hegelian advance on Kant's fundamental insight – that 'not only can we not go outside the closed circle of consciousness, but that there is no outside which has really any meaning' – admit of variation. On one interpretation, if the circle of consciousness is closed, it is indefinitely malleable. That is to say, reflective consciousness may arrange the encircled contents to secure the greatest degree of coherence, thereby interpreting the deliverances of experience in whatever way seems most satisfactory. This is what Jones has in mind when he insists that criticism must emanate from a constructive theory. Against this Seth holds that, though the circle of consciousness is indeed 'closed' – because there is no sense to the idea of stepping 'beyond' consciousness – this is consistent with asserting that, at certain points, the content of consciousness carries the authority of 'the immediately given'.

> We cannot overstep our knowledge to compare it with any reality beyond; the only possible test of the truth of our knowledge is its internal coherence, the fact that it works out, and that there are no refractory facts or aspects of experience which refuse to be worked into a system. But on the other hand, the truth is true of reality; and that there should be any reality at all, of which it could be true, depends on the immediate assurance ... which accompanies our experience ... A philosophy which tries to escape from the acknowledgement of existence as somehow immediately given seems to me to be constantly in danger of putting a system of predicates (which as predicates are necessarily abstract) in place of the subject to which they refer. Unless we are immediately rooted in fact somewhere, our whole system is in the air. (Seth Pringle-Pattison 1894: 22–3)

In addition to the fact of existence, other 'immediately givens' that can never be explained away in the interests of theoretical coherence include the distinction between self and other, and the conscious exercise of deliberative agency. This appeal to the authority of what is 'given' in experience has evident resonance with Reid's invocation of Common Sense. In the first set of Balfour Lectures, Seth acknowledges that in Reid this basic insight is mixed up with a great deal of what he calls 'extraneous psychological matter', but Reid's confusion on this score too easily leads Neo-Kantian and

Hegelian critics to dismiss the insight as no more than an appeal to elementary psychological observation or, worse, common opinion.

> Prof. Jones . . . has fallen victim to 'the psychologist's fallacy' . . . He confuses, that is to say, the attitude of the reflective critic of knowledge with the unreflective attitude of the plain man in knowing anything. Both these attitudes, taken apart, are intelligible and consistent, but the result of confusing the two is the hybrid and impossible position assigned by Prof. Jones to 'the Epistemologist' of his fancy. (Seth Pringle-Pattison 1894: 16)

Perhaps Reid, from the other side of the debate, was no less a victim of 'the psychologist's fallacy' than Jones. Thanks to Kant, the new Hegelians and their critics agree, philosophy has been rescued from this error. However, this does not license the epistemological omnipotence of theorising that Hegelians embrace. While it is true that philosophy is not answerable to the opinions of 'the vulgar' in the way that some exponents of the philosophy of Common Sense seemed to suppose, this does not mean that the facts of experience set no limits to philosophical construction. On the contrary, there are some 'givens' that have to be acknowledged if our philosophical theories are not to be 'all in the air'. Seth's appeal to these 'givens', however, introduces another aspect to the Scottish debate between Hegelianism and its critics – the nature and role of theism.

IV

'The myth of the given' is an idea made familiar by the twentieth-century American philosopher Wilfred Sellers. In declaring 'the given' to be a myth, Sellers meant to undermine any version of the supposition that there are epistemologically privileged 'facts' or sense experiences that can form an incontrovertible foundation for knowledge. There are, he claims, no such things. But why, we might ask, refer to such supposed facts as 'the given' rather than, say, 'elementary propositions', the language that Wittgenstein uses? One answer is this. The language of the 'given' is the unrecognised residue of a metaphysic now largely abandoned, one in which all things derive from a divine 'giver', and human beings have been created (or have evolved) in such a way that their ability to know anything at all rests upon elements they have, quite literally, been 'given'. Within this theistic framework the 'given' provides a secure metaphysical foundation for human knowledge, but it does so in virtue of its source, not in virtue of its intrinsic character. To invoke a concept of 'the given' in the context of an entirely secularised metaphysic is indeed to trade on a 'myth', as Sellers alleges.

In more recent times the idea of a theologically grounded theory of knowledge has been revived by the proponents of 'Reformed Epistemology', notably Alvin Plantinga and Nicholas Wolterstorff. Interestingly, some Reformed Epistemologists have drawn inspiration from Reid and their aim, in part, is to uncover the theoretical advantages of a theistic metaphysic over a thoroughly secularised one. However, this development does not bear directly on the debate between Seth and Jones. Both of them subscribed to a broadly theistic metaphysic, as the Gifford Lectures that they subsequently gave reveal, so that this is not where the most fundamental difference between them could lie. The issue, rather, is about the scope of philosophical understanding within a theistic framework. Can philosophy, in its pursuit of a unitary explanation of experience, ultimately arrive, as Hegel supposes, at 'the perfect rational articulation of the Universe in the Universal Reason called God? . . . Or must we all still bear . . . a burden of mystery, which neither [Hegelian thought] nor any other interpretation of the universe that is comprehensible by man is able to eliminate?' (Fraser 1899: 228–9).

This quotation is not from Seth, who does not address the issue directly in his debate with Jones, but from his teacher, mentor and predecessor in the Edinburgh Chair, Alexander Campbell Fraser. Fraser devotes two of his Gifford Lectures on the *Philosophy of Theism* to investigating 'the power of man as a thinker to think all mystery out of his universe as from the Divine Centre'. Hegel and the Hegelians suppose that we have this power, but Fraser is conscious of Locke's warning in the *Essay Concerning Human Understanding* against letting 'loose all our thought in the vast ocean of Being; – as if all that boundless extent were the natural and undisputed possession of human understanding, wherein there was nothing exempt from its decisions, or that escaped its comprehension' (Locke 1975: I, I, §7, quoted in Fraser 1899: 235). Fraser is inclined to heed Locke's warning.[5]

---

[5] Fraser was the author of the volume on Locke in the *Blackwood's Philosophical Classics* series (as well as the volume on Berkeley) and editor of a new Clarendon Press edition of Locke's *Essay*.

> The inquirer who recognises that he already knows something, may perhaps find points at which reason itself forbids further approach to completeness, under the inevitable human conditions of thought and experience ... by the discovery that there are indispensable constituents and convictions of human nature which are spoiled when they are taken as rendered in the professedly all-comprehensive philosophy. (Fraser 1899: 235)

By making this appeal to the 'indispensable constituents and convictions of human nature' as limits upon reason, Fraser is clearly reiterating a key thought in the tradition of Scottish philosophy that emanated from Reid. From the more ambitious theoretical perspective of Hegelianism, as Fraser acknowledges, it will look like intellectual timidity. From his perspective, however, it expresses realistic intellectual humility. In his commemorative tribute to Fraser, published in the *Proceedings of the British Academy*, Seth summarises Fraser's own philosophical position by quoting from his very last publication, the introduction to his sixth edition of *Selections from Berkeley*. Berkeley endorsed, Fraser wrote, 'a Realism that is fundamentally Spiritual, although after a native rather than a German fashion' (Seth Pringle-Pattison 1915: 13). This neatly captures both the similarities and differences between the Scottish Hegelians and their critics. Viewed in this light, it is plausible to hold that Seth was led to modify the early enthusiasm for German Idealism revealed in the *Essays* in the light of a more 'native' style of philosophy, maintained and fostered over the larger part of a century by Fraser. Moreover, following in the footsteps of Fraser's *Philosophy of Theism*,[6] Seth gave it a greatly extended and yet more satisfactory articulation ten years later in his own Gifford Lectures.[7]

---

[6] For further discussion of Fraser see Chapter 9.
[7] For further discussion of Seth's lectures see Chapters 8 and 10.

7

Scottish Philosophy's Progress

I

In the Introduction to his *Treatise of Human Nature* (1739), Hume remarks that it does not take 'such profound knowledge to discover the present imperfect condition of the sciences ... The most trivial question escapes not our controversy, and in the most momentous we are not able to give any certain decision' (Hume 2007: 3). This state of things, he thinks, warrants a new and different approach.

> Here then is the only expedient, from which we can hope for success in our philosophical researches, to leave the tedious lingring method, which we have hitherto followed, and instead of taking now and then a castle or village on the frontier, to march up directly to the capital or centre of these sciences[1] to human nature itself, which being once masters of, we may every where else hope for an easy victory ... There is no question of importance, whose decision is not compriz'd in the science of man, and there is none which can be decided with any certainty, before we become acquainted with that science. (Hume 2007: 4)

The study of philosophy had been a marked feature of education in the Scottish universities for over 300 years before Hume wrote this. Nevertheless, with a striking military image, he set philosophy in Scotland in a new direction. His intellectual project, variously called the science of man, the science of human nature or

---

[1] He has previously listed these as 'Mathematics, Natural Philosophy, and Natural Religion' with 'Logic, Morals, Criticism and Politics'.

the science of mind, soon became the remit for philosophers in Aberdeen, Edinburgh and Glasgow, with St Andrews following at a rather greater distance in time.

Hume's *Treatise*, after a slow start, effectively shaped Scottish philosophy for almost 150 years. One enduring issue across this long period was the question of whether, as Hume hoped, this new approach to the topics that had been the mainstay of philosophy since ancient times could result in genuine intellectual advances. Did the science of human nature as it was pursued by the Scottish philosophers of the eighteenth and nineteenth centuries secure real progress, and if so, in what did that progress consist?

In seeking answers to these two questions, it is worth noting at the outset that for Hume and his contemporaries the terms 'science' and 'philosophy' were interchangeable. One important feature of the development of Hume's project over the century that followed his death was the gradual differentiation of these terms. Initially, there was no difference, but by the middle of the nineteenth century the difference came to matter, and in consequence a key topic was the nature of the relation between them. Was science the ally, or the rival, of philosophy?

A striking feature of Scottish philosophy from 1740 to 1890 is that each major figure claims to have made real progress, only to have that claim not merely questioned but vehemently rejected by the next. In the *Abstract* of the *Treatise* that Hume wrote (in the third person) with the hope of increasing interest in and sales of the original work, his concluding paragraph makes a very bold claim.

> Thro' this whole book, there are great pretensions to new discoveries in philosophy, but if anything can entitle the author to so glorious a name as that of *inventor*, 'tis the use he makes of the principle of the association of ideas . . . These principles of association are reduced to three, viz. *Resemblance*; . . . *Contiguity* [and] *Causation* . . . 'Twill be easy to conceive of what vast consequence these principles must be in the science of human nature, if we consider, that so far as regards the mind, these are the only links that bind the parts of the universe together . . . [T]hey really are to us the cement of the universe, and all the operations of the mind must, in great measure, depend on them. (Hume 2007: 416–17, emphasis original)

Like Hume, Thomas Reid uses 'science' and 'philosophy' interchangeably, and more than twenty years after the first appearance of the *Treatise*, he repeats Hume's assessment of the current state of the science of mind.

> That our philosophy concerning the mind and its faculties, is but in a very low state, may reasonably be conjectured, even by those who have never narrowly examined it. Are there any principles with regard to the mind, settled with that perspicuity and evidence, which attends the principles of mechanics, astronomy and optics? These are really sciences, built upon laws of nature which universally obtain. What is discovered in them is no longer matter of dispute: future ages may add to it, but till the course of nature be changed, what is already established can never be overturned. But when we turn our attention inward, and consider the phænomena of human thoughts, opinions and perceptions, and endeavour to trace them to the general laws and the first principles of our constitution, we are immediately involved in darkness and perplexity. (Reid 1997: 16)

By implication, since Reid knew Hume's *Treatise* well, he had not found it to be full of 'new discoveries'. While he makes no explicit reference to Hume at this point in the *Inquiry*, he does identify another factor at work in the poor state of the science of mind that may be taken to apply to Hume. Distaste for any 'lingring method' results in an unwillingness on the part of philosophers to make *slow* progress.

> It is genius, and not the want of it, that adulterates philosophy, and fills it with error and false theory. A creative imagination disdains the mean offices of digging for a foundation, of removing rubbish, and carrying materials; leaving these servile employments to the drudges in science, it plans a design, and raises a fabric. Invention supplies materials where they are wanting, and fancy adds colouring, and every befitting ornament. The work pleases the eye, and wants nothing but solidity and a good foundation. It seems even to vie with the works of nature, till some succeeding architect blows it into rubbish. (Reid 1997: 15)

Hume is expressly mentioned shortly after as, along with Berkeley, one of the most acute philosophers of 'the present age'. Yet in Reid's judgement, Hume's *Treatise*, far from making scientific progress, ultimately results in the precise opposite – self-contradictory sophistry.

[T]he author of the *Treatise* of human nature ... believed against his principles, that he should be read, and that he should retain his personal identity, till he reaped the honour and reputation due to his metaphysical acumen ... [But] [i]t is a bold philosophy that rejects, without ceremony, principles which irresistibly govern the belief and the conduct of all mankind in the common concerns of life ... Such philosophy ... can have no other tendency, than to shew the acuteness of the sophist, at the expense of disgracing reason and human nature, and making mankind Yahoos. (Reid 1997: 20–1)

With his own *Inquiry*, Reid aimed to pursue Hume's project, but avoid his sceptical conclusions. This was to be accomplished by replacing 'Principles of Association' with 'Principles of Common Sense'. For a time, his strategy was widely held to be most successful, so much so, indeed, that Scottish philosophy as a whole came to be identified with 'the School of Common Sense', despite the fact that major figures such as Hutcheson and Smith could scarcely be included in this classification.

The endorsement of Reid as the architect of a successful 'Scottish School of Common Sense' was widespread, though never universal it seems.[2] Dugald Stewart, who had studied briefly with Reid in Glasgow, became its most prestigious champion in Edinburgh. In his 'Life of Reid', Stewart quotes the passage from Hume about the 'hope for success in our philosophical researches', and connects it directly with Reid's *Inquiry*. '[B]y exemplifying, in an analysis of our most important intellectual and active principles, the only method of carrying out [Hume's project] successfully into execution, was the great object of

---

[2] According to Stephen Cowley, James Mylne, Reid's successor but one in the Glasgow Chair of Moral Philosophy, was a dissenter from the orthodoxy of Common Sense philosophy (see Stephen Cowley, *Rational Piety and Social Reform in Glasgow*, Eugene, OR: Wipf and Stock, 2015). Mylne occupied the Chair for almost forty years, but since in all this time he published nothing, the evidence for his own philosophical views is slender. Cowley bases his claim on student notes, and it does receive some confirmation from a brief reference, apparently to Mylne, by James McCosh, who was a student in Glasgow at the time (see *The Life of James McCosh: A Record Chiefly Autobiographical*, 1896). Alexander Campbell Fraser's *Biographia Philosophica* (1904) also lends some support to Cowley's contention.

Dr Reid, in all his various philosophical publications' (Stewart 1858: 275). Furthermore, by Stewart's reckoning,

> [Reid accomplished] what was still more essential at the time he wrote: he has exemplified, with the happiest success, that method of investigation by which alone any solid progress can be made; directing his inquiries to a subject which forms a necessary groundwork for the labours of his successors. (Stewart 1858: 274)

II

Not all of those successors, however, took the same view. Reid died in 1796. In 1810, Edinburgh Town Council was considering the election of a successor to Dugald Stewart, who had occupied the Chair of Moral Philosophy with great distinction since 1785. Once again, an emphasis was laid on scientific progress and the need to make an appointment that would contribute to it. In advance of the election, the Patrons appointed by the Council received a letter from Allan Maconochie, formerly Professor of Public Law and the Law of Nature and Nations and by then a judge in the Court of Session. The letter both underlines the importance of the appointment, and extols the merits of Thomas Brown.

> When the Honourable Patrons consider the high reputation to which that chair has been raised, and the eminence which, for the last seventy years, has belonged to Scotland in Metaphysical Science ... I beg leave to lay it down as certain, that only a mind of very singular powers, habits and accomplishments, is fitted to enter into the course of Moral Philosophy. It is not enough to have studied attentively the best writers ... and to be a person of judgment, worth, and literary talent and taste. There must be a peculiar aptitude of intellect, suited to the extreme subtilty of the subject ... Other sciences may well be taught by persons competent only to describe what is already known, though unable to add to the hoard of knowledge. But ... without a genius fitted to extend its boundaries ... no person ever gave a course of Moral Philosophy fitted to enlighten and animate the students ... [With] the appearance of Dr Thomas Brown as a candidate ... I shall look forward with the utmost confidence ... to a *real and effective progress* being achieved, in this fundamental science. (Quoted in Welsh 1825: 184, emphasis added)

Brown was duly appointed as the co-occupant of the Chair with Stewart, and his presumed successor.[3] According to his admiring biographer, David Welsh, Maconochie's confidence that intellectual progress would be made was amply vindicated. In concluding his account of Brown's *Lectures on the Philosophy of the Human Mind*, Welsh says:

> The great merit of Dr Brown consists in the clear and satisfactory analysis of what passes in our mind in the process of generalizing, by which he shows it is a threefold process – we perceive two or more objects – we are struck with their similarity in certain respects – we invent a common appellative to express the objects that agree in exciting the same relative feeling. This explanation corresponds so exactly with the phenomena, that it requires only to be stated in order to be admitted; and no difficulty remains to be explained, if it is not the fact, that the discovery of what appears so simple and obvious, should have been made at so late a period in the history of philosophy. The solution is, no doubt, to be found in the extraordinary powers of analysis that distinguished the ingenious discoverer; but in no small degree also in the mistaken doctrines that formerly prevailed ... Now, however, that the discovery of the process has been made, its truth and importance cannot fail to be duly appreciated; and it will in all future ages be considered as *one of the most important steps that was ever made in metaphysical science*. (Welsh 1825: 287–8, emphasis added)

And later, in his general summary, Welsh adds another accolade:

> Dr Brown has made a most important step in the principles of philosophising, perhaps the most important that has been made in metaphysics since the time of Descartes. (Welsh 1825: 316)

However, if Brown did make scientific progress, it was not, as Stewart had surmised, by relying on the 'necessary groundwork' that Reid had laid for the 'labours of his successors'. On the contrary, Brown only made real progress, as he and Welsh thought, by discounting Reid and returning, in part, to Hume.

> The genius of Dr Reid does not appear to me to have been very inventive, nor to have possessed much of that refined and subtle acuteness

---

[3] Brown's early death in 1820 prevented this succession, though it prompted Stewart's final resignation from the Chair.

which, – capable as it is of becoming abused, – is yet absolutely necessary to the perfection of metaphysical analysis. (Brown 1836: 267–8)

Welsh's estimate of Brown's post-Reidian accomplishment was published in 1825. Assuming it to be just, then thanks to Brown, Scottish philosophy had been making the progress Maconochie had anticipated, though this was only because its most honoured figure – Reid – had at last been displaced, and recognised as an unfortunate diversion. In line with Reid's own language, Brown was the 'succeeding architect blowing Reid's *Inquiry* 'into rubbish'.

However, just five years after Welsh published his assertion that Brown had secured 'one of the most important steps that was ever made' in metaphysics, it was emphatically rejected by Sir William Hamilton, subsequently appointed to the Chair of Logic and Metaphysics at the University of Edinburgh. In his *Edinburgh Review* essay on 'The Philosophy of Perception', Hamilton writes:

> Dr Brown's *Lectures on the Philosophy of the Mind* . . . afford evidence of how greatly talent has, of late, been withdrawn from the field of metaphysical discussion. This work has now been before the world for ten years . . . [and] while its admirers have exhausted hyperbole in its praise . . . the radical *inconsistencies* which [the lectures] involve, in every branch of their subject, remain undeveloped; their unacknowledged *appropriations* are still lauded as original; their endless *mistakes*, in the history of philosophy, stand yet uncorrected; and their frequent *misrepresentations* of other philosophers continue to mislead. (Hamilton 1853: 43–4, emphasis original)

Hamilton was not alone in this assessment of Brown. John Veitch, for instance, who was one of Hamilton's students and subsequently held Chairs of Logic in St Andrews and Glasgow, could hardly have differed more from Welsh's view in his estimation. In his volume on *Hamilton* for the *Blackwood's Philosophical Classics* series, Veitch writes:

> Dr Thomas Brown . . . was indebted largely to foreign sources for his opinions, but only to one school, the sensationalism of France . . . His writings and teachings form a sort of foreign episode in our philosophical literature. With a certain positive relation to Hume, he has no distinctive originality, and cannot be said to have had a permanent or continuous influence on the thought of the country. (Veitch 1882: 24)

Hamilton's own work aimed to remedy Brown's inconsistencies, mistakes and misrepresentations, and his philosophical endeavours in this direction were regarded by some of his contemporaries as notable advances in the subject. Veitch says, 'My own conviction is that Hamilton reached certain *results which are thoroughly stable and valid*' (Veitch 1883: 26, emphasis added).

Nevertheless, in due course Hamilton's philosophy was roundly condemned as profoundly mistaken. The attacks came from opposing sides. The most notable empiricist critic was John Stuart Mill. Having begun from an initially sympathetic position, Mill undertook a detailed scrutiny of Hamilton's philosophical writings. 'As I advanced in my task', he says, 'the damage to Sir W. Hamilton's reputation became greater than I first expected, through the incredible multitude of inconsistencies which showed themselves on comparing different passages with one another' (Mill 1971: 163). In the final chapter of the lengthy *Examination* of Hamilton that Mill published in 1865, he concludes, 'I can hardly point to anything he has done towards helping the more thorough understanding of the greater mental phaenomena' (Mill 1979: 490).

In the same year, equally severe criticism of Hamilton came from a quite different direction, James Hutchison Stirling's Hegelian-inspired Idealism. At the same time, Stirling was no less fierce in his criticism of Mill.

> From Hume in consequence of his queries in the *Treatise of Human Nature*, there have descended two lines of thinkers in Great Britain; one ironical, culminating in Mr Mill; one polemical, culminating in – shall we say? – Sir William Hamilton. But of both lines the efforts have been *nil*; both return exhausted to the queries of the *Treatise of Human Nature*; and as Hume left Philosophy in Great Britain, so in Great Britain Philosophy remains. (Quoted in A. M. Stirling 1912: 174)

In fact, Stirling was more scathing about the empiricists than about Hamilton – 'those four shallow, stiff, thin, conceited prigs – weak-heads or soft-heads or empty-heads or wrong-heads respectively – Mill, Bain, Buckle, Grote'[4] (A. M. Stirling 1912: 247) – and published a polemical essay explicitly attacking Alexander Bain at

---

[4] He is referring to George Grote, not John Grote, who was an Idealist of sorts.

the University of Aberdeen as the chief representative of empiricism in Scotland.[5] However, Stirling found no merits in either school. His principal contention was that in responding to the challenge set by Hume, the resources of Scottish philosophy had been exhausted, and the philosophical baton had passed to Germany. There true progress had been made in what he called the German 'philosophical succession'. Beginning with Kant, and making its way through Fichte and Schelling, this succession found its culmination in Hegel, the obscurity of whose philosophical language Stirling had set himself to penetrate. The result of eight years of intensive study was *The Secret of Hegel*, first published in 1865, to considerable acclaim. Subsequently, Stirling published *A Textbook to Kant*, which continued his mission of transforming philosophy in Scotland by importing the German succession. This book was received even more enthusiastically. A writer in the *British Quarterly Review* declared that 'Dr Stirling has contributed a permanent and precious possession to philosophical thought', and a review in *Mind* expressed the same opinion: 'Dr Stirling has done his work in such a way that it will never require to be done again' (A. M. Stirling 1912: 280–1).

Even if these accolades were warranted, the credit ultimately fell to German philosophy. Stirling's aim was not to persist with the 'succession' of Scottish philosophers from Hume to Hamilton, but to look elsewhere. By contrast, Bain, his almost exact contemporary and a close associate of Mill, had pursued the science of mind in a more strictly psychological fashion, and as a result was regarded in some quarters as progressing the project inaugurated by Hume and Reid in a more promising direction.[6] When it comes to advancing the scientific study of mind, John Grote told Bain in a letter 'you have done more' than 'our worthy Scotch predecessors' (Bain 1904: 254).

In the view of James McCosh, however, the 'more' that Bain had done had pushed things in the wrong direction. Though there is no mention of Bain in McCosh's *The Scottish Philosophy*, he is

---

[5] Both Stirling and Bain were friends of David Masson, the celebrated literary critic and, from 1865, occupant of the Chair of Rhetoric and English Literature at Edinburgh. So deep did Stirling think their philosophical differences ran that he declined Masson's invitation to dine with the Bains at his house.

[6] See Chapter 4.

identified in a later essay as a scientific counterpart to philosophical Idealists such as Stirling, and especially Edward Caird in the Chair of Moral Philosophy in Glasgow. In McCosh's estimation Bain's scientific materialism, no less than Caird's Idealism, did not amount to the advancement of Scottish philosophy, but its abandonment.

III

The conclusion to draw from all this, it would appear, is that 150 years on from the first appearance of the *Treatise*, Scottish philosophy had not advanced from the lamentable condition in which Hume claimed to have found it. Philosophers in Scotland were not themselves blind to this dispiriting conclusion. In October 1891, Henry Jones, the newly appointed Professor of Logic and Metaphysics at St Andrews, delivered his inaugural lecture. In it he gave eloquent expression to this very thought.

> At the present moment, as philosophers would themselves acknowledge, there is no theory that either obtains or deserves unquestioning confidence . . . Unprejudiced observers . . . who contrast the long catalogue of defeats sustained by the philosophers and the shattered condition of their ranks today, with the solid and advancing conquests of the natural sciences, have very naturally concluded that philosophy is seeking by a doubtful method an unattainable goal. (Jones 1893b: 160)

Jones reaches back into the history of Scottish philosophy well before Brown. 'The sad picture which Hume drew of philosophy in his day', he says, 'represents with much faithfulness its condition in our own.' He then quotes the passage from Hume's *Treatise* with which this chapter began.

> Principles taken upon trust, consequences lamely deduced from them, want of coherence in the parts, and of evidence in the whole – these are everywhere to be met with in the systems of the most eminent philosophers, and seem to have drawn disgrace upon philosophy itself. Nor is there required such profound knowledge to discover the present imperfect condition of the sciences, but even the rabble without doors may judge from the noise and clamour which they hear, that all goes not well within. (Hume 2007: 3)

Since, from the point of view of progress, Jones is identifying the time at which he was writing with the time at which Hume was writing, a negative conclusion seems inescapable. The eminence that Maconochie thought 'belonged to Scotland in Metaphysical Science' rested in large part on the intellectual progress that the philosophers of the Scottish Enlightenment were thought to have made and that was there to be built upon by succeeding generations. In reality, Reid's image of one generation of system builders being reduced to rubble by the next appears to be a more accurate account of the actual course of Scottish philosophy in which this process of building and wrecking occurred again and again.

Jones was not alone in bringing this issue into prominence. A few years later, he was succeeded in the Chair of Logic and Metaphysics at St Andrews by David G. Ritchie. Ritchie was one of the founding members of the Aristotelian Society and chose progress in philosophy for the subject of his 1898 Presidential address. 'Philosophy and the Study of Philosophers' begins with precisely the same observation as Jones's inaugural.

> Those who are engaged in the study of metaphysical philosophy often find themselves criticised by those who are working in the special sciences on the ground that, while the special sciences are continually adding to the sum of human knowledge and to man's power over nature, metaphysical philosophy makes no progress, but consists merely in a chaos of rival and contradictory speculations. (Ritchie 1899: 1)

Ritchie adds this further observation:

> Even those who are themselves busied with philosophical studies at times feel a certain doubt . . . The uncomfortable suspicion suggests itself that the great amount of writing and discussion actually going on . . . may be no real proof of vitality . . . for a very large part of it is concerned with the careful exposition and criticism of the great philosophers. Philosophy . . . appears to have become very largely the study of its own history. (Ritchie 1899: 2)

Yet a third Scottish philosopher of the same generation clearly regarded this subject as of the first importance also. In the very same month that Jones delivered his lecture, Andrew Seth, his predecessor at St Andrews, chose the same topic for his inaugural lecture in the Chair of Logic and Metaphysics at Edinburgh. The title of the lecture – 'The Present Position of the Philosophical Sciences' – is a little misleading, perhaps, because Seth effectively calls into question the conflation of 'philosophy' with 'science' that Hume, Reid, Brown and so on would have assumed. The main purpose of his lecture was to survey the range of subjects that fell within the responsibilities of the holder of the Chair – Logic, Psychology and Philosophy. About Logic he has relatively little to say, regarding it as 'comparable in some respects with the mental discipline of mathematics'. When he turns to psychology he notes that not so long before, the relation between psychology and philosophy was one of mutual hostility.

> The horror of the true-blue experientialist for what he calls 'metaphysics' was amply repaid by the tone of condescension and indifference which the idealists adopted towards 'empirical psychology'. Misled by a name, they visited upon the head of an unoffending science the inadequacies of Empiricism as a philosophical theory. Because the chief cultivators of psychology in England had been of the Empiricist persuasion, and had frequently confounded the limits of psychology and metaphysics, the transcendentalists tabooed the science as beneath the notice of a philosopher. Hence a state of unnatural division and mutual distrust – a distrust rooted in both cases largely in ignorance. (Seth Pringle-Pattison 1897a: 45–6)

'Today', Seth goes on to say, 'the situation is greatly changed.'

> Psychology has become more scientific, and has thereby become more conscious of her own aims, and, at the same time, of her necessary limitations. Ceasing to put herself forward as *philosophy*, she has entered upon a new period of development as a *science*. (Seth Pringle-Pattison 1897a: 46, emphasis added)

Seth expresses enthusiastic admiration for the 'marvellous activity displayed just at present in the department of psychology', and while much of this 'boom', he says, has resulted from recent work undertaken in Germany, France and America, he also observes that in Britain 'the study of psychology is a native growth', noting especially that 'Hume had brilliantly exemplified the national genius in that direction'. However, 'the British thinkers of the past were far from keeping their psychology unadulterated . . . they gave us, in general, psychology and philosophy inextricably mixed' (Seth Pringle-Pattison 1897a: 47). It is a gradual differentiation between the two subjects that has now mitigated their previous mutual hostility.

This differentiation, Seth thinks, can never be complete. 'Psychology, as the science of mental life, must always stand to philosophy in a more intimate relation than any of the other sciences can' (Seth Pringle-Pattison 1897a: 52), a contention that seems to be borne out by the huge twentieth-century enterprise of 'cognitive science'. Still, the key to understanding advances in philosophical thinking lies in distinguishing science and philosophy in the way that early proponents of 'the science of mind', such as Hume and Reid, did not.

IV

Probably few people would be inclined to dispute the importance of Seth's distinction now. But it remains to ask how, if at all, differentiating between philosophy and psychology could cast the history of Scottish philosophy in a better, or at any rate a different, light. Does the confusion between the two that reigned previously not simply confirm the dismissive attitude of non-philosophers who, in Jones's words, may now conclude that Scottish philosophy had all the time been seeking by a doubtful method an unattainable goal?

This was a matter of special interest to Seth on the occasion of his inaugural. 'It is by philosophy that this Chair and others like it in the Scottish universities must ultimately justify their existence; and it is to the inbred Scottish bent towards philosophy that the public interest felt in them is due' (Seth Pringle-Pattison 1897a: 53). We may wonder whether anything of that 'inbred bent' remains extant in Scotland, and it is certainly the case that the intense interest, and even passion, that surrounded some of the elections to philosophy Chairs in nineteenth-century Scotland has no counterpart in the twenty-first. Seth's context, however, had elements with continuing relevance for the present. He was speaking at the end of several decades that had been dominated by positivism.

> Comte promulgated his law of three stages, representing metaphysics as a disease of childhood, like measles, which the race was in the act of outgrowing. And since then, Comtian and other influences have undoubtedly produced in many quarters a positivistic or agnostic attitude of mind, which gives itself great airs of finality from time to time ... But metaphysics shows no inclination to die, by way of obliging these prophets of her decease. (Seth Pringle-Pattison 1897a: 53)

Comte stimulates little interest now, yet there remains a strongly scientific cast of mind that is antagonistic to metaphysics, and is still inclined to give itself a 'great air of finality'. This lends Seth's treatment of the subject more than historic interest. There are philosophical lessons to be learned.

Chief among these is the relevance of the science/philosophy distinction to the question of progress. Since Hume, Reid, Brown and Hamilton did not make this distinction, their hope of progress was modelled on the advances that Newton made in 'natural philosophy', which is to say, physics. The old nomenclature is misleading, however, because 'moral' as opposed to 'natural' philosophy is not an analogue of physics, but a quite different kind of inquiry. Seth focuses on three key features that reveal the distinguishing characteristics of philosophy. First, it differs from science because it is concerned with 'ultimate questions . . . the problems which lie beneath and behind all science' (Seth Pringle-Pattison 1897a: 54). Second, its role is 'to purge us of bad metaphysics . . . and there is no metaphysics so bad as the metaphysics of the physicist or biologist, when, in the strength of his own right arm, he makes a raid into philosophical territory' (Seth Pringle-Pattison 1897a: 55). Third, philosophical criticism of bad metaphysics is not restricted to illegitimate incursions on the part of science. It must be extended to the metaphysical systems of the past, so that the philosopher avoids superficial novelty and becomes a historian of thought 'with a wise admixture of sympathy and criticism'.

> But this critical, and to a certain extent negative work is not all. Philosophy must finally endeavour to be itself critically constructive . . . to be constructive without forgetting its own critical strictures . . . [C]riticism should seek to lead the learner, through the very consciousness of defects and inconsistencies in the systems examined, to a true statement of the problem, and a more adequate solution . . . And if, at the end, a completed system should still prove beyond our reach, the philosophical teacher will at least seek to indicate the general lines upon which an ultimately satisfactory theory must move. (Seth Pringle-Pattison 1897a: 56)

Effectively, Seth abandons the conception of 'progress' modelled on science in which previous Scottish philosophers had placed such faith, and offers instead a broader idea of conceptual development and intellectual enlargement. Conceived in this way, advancement consists in the gradual elimination of metaphysical error, in clearer formulations of the 'ultimate' questions, and in a more realistic acceptance of the inevitable limits of human acceptance. The true aim of philosophical reflection is an appreciation of the direction in which any reasonably hopeful attempt to resolve these ultimate questions must move.

Set against these criteria, the trajectory of Scottish philosophy can plausibly be argued to have undergone significant development. There are no 'discoveries' of the kind that Welsh attributed to Brown, but over time the narrowly psychological focus in the most celebrated works of Hume, Reid, Brown and Hamilton leads to the broader perspectives of Ferrier, Fraser, Caird and Seth himself. And it leads to them in part because philosophy, unlike the special sciences, has a special interest in its own history.

It is philosophy's relation to its own history that Ritchie explores at length in his Presidential address to the Aristotelian Society. Ritchie is acutely aware that the study of philosophy's history can come to displace philosophy itself. 'For we know how we lose sight of the forest for the trees and how . . . minute scholarship and antiquarian research are apt to be hostile to that looking at things as a whole which philosophy requires' (Ritchie 1899: 23). Yet it remains the case that 'the history of philosophy may often serve as a clue to guide us in the attempt to reach a philosophy of history' and on this point Ritchie quotes Hegel (in the *Encyclopaedia*) and endorses the view himself.

> Every philosophy, Hegel admits, has been refuted. The very fact that a philosophy was the philosophy of some past age proves that it cannot be the truest system for a succeeding age. But it is also true that no philosophy has ever been refuted. 'Every philosophy has been and still is necessary.' There is but one philosophy manifesting itself in the succession of philosophical systems. The history of philosophy is thus an integral part of philosophy itself. It is philosophy taking its time. (Ritchie 1899: 10)

Jones, in his St Andrews lecture, comes to a similar conclusion, and has some interesting thoughts to add. First, returning to the quotation from Hume, he rightly observes that Hume's memorable image – 'the rabble without doors may judge from the noise and clamour which they hear, that all goes not well within' – is not as plausible as it sounds.

> I concur with the rabble as to the noise and clamour, but I dissent from the conclusion it draws from them . . . The wise from the same premise will draw the opposite conclusion. They know that there is vigour of life in philosophy which excites the clamour of disputants. It is the philosophy which has sunk into silence that is dead. All truth is vocal and continues to clamour till it is purified from the discordant elements of error. Like virtue, and all *life*, spiritual and natural, truth is essentially combative in nature. (Jones 1893b: 160–1, emphasis original)

Focusing on the idea that philosophy is essentially activity, Jones invites us to consider it in the context of a different comparison.

> I believe that we may get a less prejudiced and perhaps truer answer [to the question about progress in philosophy] if we direct it against another form of activity, one whose high worth no one doubts even although it, like philosophy, is always turning back to the beginning. I refer to the Fine Arts. Their history, like that of philosophic systems, is a record of apparently abrupt phenomena. (Jones 1893b: 167)

This parallel with the arts is illuminating. If we consider the history of music, for instance, it is easy to see that there has been development. The Classical drew on, but also differed from, the Baroque, just as the Romantic built on the Classical, and the Modern on the Romantic. Each new phase started with what it had learned from previous eras, and at the same time experienced a certain dissatisfaction with it. Composers do not discount or discard their predecessors, but they nevertheless want to do better, and different. Unlike scientific progress, however, historical development of this kind does not render the past redundant. As scientific knowledge grows, critical experiments and innovative theories are regularly superseded. They lose their usefulness for practising scientists and become instead items of significant antiquarian interest to the historian of science. But the musical compositions of the past never become the sole province of historians of music. It is true that modern composers no longer write music in the style of the Baroque, and that if they did, it would quickly be recognised as pastiche. At the same time, the music of Bach and Handel is part of a living inheritance. It goes on being performed and listened to, and it continues to provide musical material for the successful induction of new generations of musicians and composers.

Philosophy is not Art, of course. Jones, interestingly, finds the difference in philosophy's special relation to science. The imagination of the artist, in whatever medium, can ignore the 'results' good science produces, but the philosopher cannot do so. Like Seth, Jones rejects any deep opposition (or indifference) between science and philosophy.

> Philosophy must be aware of the differences which Science reveals; it accepts with gratitude the sets of relations, the aspect of truth revealed by Science, and recombines them into a view of the world as a whole which is articulated and wherein the differences have free play.
>
> Philosophy seems to me to partake of the character both of the Sciences and of the Fine Arts; it combines the fundamental characteristics of both, viz., the analytic movement of Science and the synthetic impulse of Art. The sciences confessedly deal with aspects and phases only, and never with wholes. (Jones 1893b: 169)

It is the business of philosophy, on this conception, while taking full account of whatever the scientific pursuit of knowledge may reveal, to resist abstraction and seek to frame an explanation of experience *as a whole*. As Ritchie puts the same point:

> The thinking of experience as a whole remains the ideal for philosophy, an ideal which to different persons may seem more or less attainable; but the task which all philosophers must accept includes at least the criticism of the concepts used in the sciences and in ordinary thinking. (Ritchie 1899: 4)

This implies, of course, that experience is, ultimately, a unity, and thus raises a further question. On what basis does this possibility rest? Seth is clear on this issue. If the philosophical enterprise is to make any sense at all, it must acknowledge 'the necessity of a teleological view of the universe'.

> There is nothing of which I am more profoundly convinced than that philosophical truth lies with the teleological point of view. Any system which abandons this point of view lapses thereby from philosophy to science. The word teleology acts upon some people like a red rag upon a bull, from its association with certain old fashioned arguments which explained particular phenomena from their supposed

adaptation to external ends, more especially from their adaptation to the requirements and conveniences of man. This paltry mechanical teleology was never at any time convincing . . . and after being riddled by modern science, it may be held as finally beaten off the field . . . The philosophical teleology of which I speak concerns itself only with the End of the whole evolution. It concentrates itself upon the proof that there is an End, that there is an organic unity or purpose binding the whole process into one and making it intelligible. (Seth Pringle-Pattison 1897a: 57)

The debates of the twentieth century showed that 'paltry mechanical teleology' had not been 'finally beaten off the field', and this may explain why the 'philosophical teleology' embraced by Seth has few exponents now. In his own time, however, the claim that 'philosophical truth lies with the teleological point of view' could have expected a sympathetic hearing. Among major Scottish philosophers in the nineteenth century it is only Alexander Bain who consciously abandoned teleology entirely, and, interestingly, it is plausible to hold that as a result his 'system' did indeed 'lapse into' science, though Bain himself would not have spoken in this way. The Scottish Idealists, among whom Jones and Ritchie were numbered, formed the most obvious alternative to Bain's positivistic philosophy, and they would have wholeheartedly endorsed the idea of philosophy presupposing an 'organic unity or purpose' as the condition of intelligibility. Jones's first philosophical publication was an essay in a book of Idealist-inspired essays edited by Seth and R. B. Haldane.

Seth also contributed to the collection which was published in 1883. From that point on, however, he distanced himself from philosophical Idealism, and in due course revealed that the teleology he believed essential to philosophy was a version of theism. Theism was the subject he chose when invited to give two lectures at the inauguration of Princeton University in 1896, and he there distinguishes it from the Idealist's Absolute. In this respect, Seth was reverting to an earlier debate in Scottish philosophy where Hume's mechanistic conception of the 'science of mind' was confronted by Reid's implicitly teleological alternative. Seth was also resonating with a growing body of philosophical opinion within Scotland that had been greatly stimulated by the creation of the Gifford Lectures, to which many of the Scottish philosophers contributed. Thus, alongside the division between the empirical psychology of Bain and the Absolute Idealism of Caird, the reaffirmation of theism came to be regarded as the next step for Scottish philosophy to take. That reaffirmation, of course, could not ignore the advent of Darwinism or its relevance to the argument of Hume's *Dialogues Concerning Natural Religion*.

8

Religion, Evolution and Scottish Philosophy

I

The traditional teleological argument for the existence of God, commonly known as 'the design argument', aims to ground belief in God's existence in empirical evidence drawn from the world around us. The most telling items of evidence to which this argument appeals are biological organs that serve specific functions superbly well. The eye, to cite a frequently used example, serves the purpose of seeing so impressively, it seems impossible that it could have arisen by chance. Rather, it must have been brought into existence for that purpose by an intentional designer, which is to say, God.

David Hume's *Dialogues Concerning Natural Religion*, it is widely accepted, constitute an exhaustive and devastating critique of this argument. The characters engaged in dialogue debate a very modest version of the conclusion that the design argument might be held to sustain, namely, 'That the Author of Nature is somewhat similar to the mind of man'. Yet ultimately, even this very limited claim is found to be wanting. The design argument, which had widespread appeal in Hume's own day, is wholly lacking in cogency, it seems.

In the *Dialogues*, the character who articulates and defends the design argument is Cleanthes. The character who undermines it is Philo. Somewhat strangely, however, in the opening paragraphs of the final part of the work Philo, the sceptic, suddenly seems to endorse the very conclusion he has been attacking. He remarks to Cleanthes:

> [N]otwithstanding the freedom of my conversation, and my love of singular arguments, no one has a deeper sense of religion impressed

upon his mind . . . [by] the inexplicable contrivance and artifice of nature. A purpose, an intention, a design strikes everywhere the most careless, the most stupid thinker, and no man can be so hardened in absurd systems, as at all times to reject it. (Hume 1993: 116)

Is this really a volte-face? Is Philo in the end unpersuaded by the arguments he himself has made? The quoted passage has often been interpreted in this way, but there is at least one interpretation that makes the reversal a little less dramatic. Possibly, Philo is here giving voice to a lingering psychological doubt. The key lies in the word 'inexplicable' and in the phrase 'at all times'. Even if the criticisms he has brought against the design argument up to this point lead us to doubt the inference from natural world to supernatural designer, the 'contrivance and artifice of nature' remains very striking and we are left to wonder what explains it. In the absence of any other explanation, the inclination to think in terms of 'intention, purpose and design' is psychologically hard to resist.

Set in this context, it is easy to understand the dramatic impact of Darwin's theory of evolution, for it provides the missing explanation – chance mutation and natural selection. The power of this explanation derives in part from the vastly extended period of time over which Darwin thinks the natural world has evolved. Given the chronology calculated by Archbishop Ussher (1581–1656), who reckoned 23 October 4004 BC to be the first day of creation, it is implausible to suppose that the amazing 'contrivances' of nature could have come about by selection amongst chance mutations. But if 'chance' has had millions of years at its disposal, the plausibility of gradual evolution rises dramatically. In making natural selection the key mechanism, Darwin's theory gained still further plausibility since it appeals to a process that had long been familiar in the world of agriculture, namely selective breeding for the 'scientific' improvement of plants and animals. The theory of evolution simply extends the concept of selection to nature at large.

Thanks to Darwin's theory, then, the 'contrivance and artifice of nature' is no longer 'inexplicable'. Consequently, anyone with the same cast of mind as Philo, who is everywhere struck by the appearance of purpose, intention and design, can now see these as mere appearance. The 'contrivances' of nature are real, but not the product of intention. Rather they are the outcome of an enormously long period during which chance mutations have been naturally selected for the advantages they give the plants and animals that have them. There is no longer any need to entertain the hypothesis of supernatural design. The explanatory hiatus that leads the otherwise sceptical Philo to hesitate, then, is filled – by the theory of evolution. The result would appear to be that any lingering thought of a divine designer can now be abandoned.

II

The significance of such a conclusion goes beyond philosophical theology and touches Scottish philosophy more broadly. The mainstream Scottish philosophers who were widely regarded as having 'answered' Hume, notably Thomas Reid, George Campbell, Alexander Gerard, James Beattie and Lord Kames, were all Christian theists. They knew nothing of Darwin, of course, or even Hume's *Dialogues*, since the text only appeared after Hume's death. But they all expounded an essentially teleological philosophy that could, for a while, withstand the kind of criticism that the *Dialogues* present. With the advent of Darwinian biology, however, it seems that Hume's non-theistic naturalism must finally claim victory over its opponents. A similar point can be made about Scottish philosophers who were less explicitly theistic, notably Adam Smith and Adam Ferguson. Though their influential works never directly discuss arguments for the existence of God, and eschew metaphysical questions almost entirely, the philosophical theories they advance rest upon a broadly providential teleology. If Darwinian evolution eliminates any residual ground for a divine designer, by the same token, it renders the belief in Providence baseless.

The impact of Hume plus Darwin, however, cannot be confined to these particular eighteenth-century philosophers; it has profound implications for the tradition of Scottish philosophy as a whole. Though Scottish philosophy has often been identified with the eighteenth century, there is a continuity of teaching and debate that extends both before and after this period. Whether we locate its origins in the late seventeenth century, or even as far back as the foundation of the ancient Scottish universities two centuries before that, there is reason to hold that amidst all the variety of opinion over such a long period, the principal task of philosophy in Scotland was consistently conceived to be one of defending three fundamental positions, namely theism, metaphysical realism and libertarianism of the will. The stimulus that Hume's sceptical writings undoubtedly gave his philosophical contemporaries, and their 'Common Sense' response to him, is best understood as the Enlightenment phase of this continuing task.

Viewed in this light, the apparently powerful anti-theistic implications of Darwinian evolution in the decades that followed Hume were of great consequence. Accordingly, we might expect that the next generation of philosophers in Scotland who wanted to maintain their opposition to scepticism, materialism and determinism would respond in one of two ways. Either they would be compelled to abandon theism, or they would set about resisting Darwinism. It is perhaps surprising, then, that many of the philosophers who can be classified for this purpose as 'Scottish' took neither of these positions. Instead, they enthusiastically embraced Darwinian biology in their continuing defence of theism. Why should this be so?

Some illumination is cast on this question by considering in particular the writings of two prominent nineteenth-century Scottish philosophers – Henry Calderwood and Andrew Seth Pringle-Pattison. Both are easily located within the Scottish philosophical tradition. Calderwood was a student of Sir William Hamilton and an ordained Presbyterian minister. He held the Chair of Moral Philosophy at Edinburgh University from 1868 until his sudden death in 1897, when he was succeeded in the Chair by one of his students. Calderwood's background and training was in philosophy and theology, but he regarded the advent of Darwinian biology as the most significant intellectual event of his time. As a result, he undertook a serious study of biology spread over several years. The result was a substantial volume entitled *Evolution and Man's Place in Nature*, which was published in 1893. A second edition appeared in 1896, and the revisions Calderwood had made were so major that he describes it as 'virtually a new book'. These revisions were undertaken primarily in response to criticism by scientists and after more intense study, so that the revised volume is evidence of the remarkably detailed knowledge of contemporary biology and physiology that Calderwood had acquired. His last book was completed just before his death, but published posthumously. It was a biography of David Hume in the 'Famous Scots' series, and notable for the unusually sympathetic attitude that Calderwood, who never abandoned his Presbyterian commitments, brings to his subject.

Andrew Seth (latterly Pringle-Pattison) studied philosophy under Alexander Campbell Fraser, Calderwood's contemporary in the Chair of Logic and Metaphysics at Edinburgh. Fraser had been appointed Professor in succession to his teacher Sir William Hamilton, and in due course was succeeded by his student Andrew Seth.[1] Seth held the Edinburgh Chair from 1891 to 1919, having previously occupied the Chair of Logic and Metaphysics at the University of St Andrews. He was himself succeeded in the Edinburgh Chair by Norman Kemp Smith, who had been his student at St Andrews, and held a professorship at Princeton.

Seth's publications include two sets of Balfour Lectures, the first on *Scottish Philosophy* (1885) and the second on *Hegelianism and Personality* (1887) (with a third set – on Realism – published as a series of articles in the *Philosophical Review*). The first set was subtitled 'A Comparison of the Scottish and German Answers to Hume' and reveals a deep understanding of the philosophical tradition in which Seth was educated, with a no less sympathetic understanding of Kant, acquired during his postgraduate studies in Germany. The second lecture series articulates Seth's doubts about the Hegelianism that had recently become fashionable, and signals his intellectual differences with the Scottish Idealists among whom he had earlier been numbered.[2] A later collection of papers had a title similar to Calderwood's – *Man's Place in the Cosmos* (1897). The themes from all these books found their fullest treatment in his magnum opus, *The Idea of God in the Light of Recent Philosophy* (1917).[3] This volume comprises the revised texts of twenty Gifford Lectures he delivered at the University of Aberdeen in 1912 and 1913.

III

It is best to consider these two philosophers in reverse order and start with *The Idea of God in the Light of Recent Philosophy*. Its opening sentence describes Hume as 'the greatest Scotsman who ever applied himself to these subjects', and the first lecture undertakes an examination of the *Dialogues* that constitutes the background to the lectures that follow. This explicit and implicit praise of Hume is sincere. Seth's earlier criticism of Hegelianism

---

[1] Calderwood was succeeded in the Chair of Moral Philosophy by Seth's brother, James.
[2] See Chapter 6.
[3] See Chapter 10.

shows that he shares with Hume a subscription to empiricism, very broadly conceived, and to naturalism. That is to say, philosophy must be grounded in observation, and what it aims to understand and explain is the reality of the world of experience, in contrast, say, to either Platonic forms or abstract principles of Reason. In his lectures on *Scottish Philosophy*, Seth shows no sign of the somewhat partisan tendency on the part of Stewart and Hamilton to prefer Reid's 'answer' to Hume over Kant's. As Seth expressly acknowledges:

> The truth is, Reid's lack of form, and his frequent want of precision in statement, have militated fatally, from the first, against his being ranked as a philosophical classic . . . Though Kant's style is involved, his terminology often cumbrous and his works abounding in repetitions, yet he mingles no extraneous and strictly indifferent matter with his argument. In each of his great works there is the sense of a unity of aim . . . On the other hand, Reid's properly philosophical positions are imbedded in a mass of irrelevant psychological matter-of-fact, which obscures their bearing and impairs their force. (Seth Pringle-Pattison 1885: 124)

Nevertheless, in the end, Reid furnishes us with the basis of a more satisfactory answer to Humean scepticism than Kant can do.

> Having shown the baselessness of the accepted theory of ideas, which involved an illusory objectivity out of subjective units, Reid felt that he had broken down the middle wall of partition which cut us off from reality . . . Kant, on the other hand, having rashly accepted from Hume the principle or prejudice that mere sense is all that can come from the object, took a very different course. Instead of, like Reid, abandoning 'the ideal system,' he elaborately reconstructed it. (Seth Pringle-Pattison 1885: 144–5)

In responding to Humean scepticism, then, Seth's own subscription to empiricism and naturalism clearly aligns him with the 'Natural Realism' that underlay the arguments of Hume's Scottish critics.

But Hume was also an empiricist in epistemology and a naturalist in metaphysics. So where then did he differ from his Scottish critics? The answer is this: whereas Reid, Campbell, Smith, Ferguson and others thought that the underlying structure of the world revealed by empirical observation was teleological, Hume thought it was mechanistic. Nature for Hume is not, strictly speaking, *governed* by laws of nature. Rather what we call 'laws' are generalisations that simply describe the conjunctions between events that empirical observation reveals. Causality is nothing more than constant conjunction, and this is as true of the mind as it is of the body. Our perceptions 'cause' us to have the beliefs we do. For Reid, by contrast, the regularities uncovered by careful observation are law-like and purposeful. The mind is not merely a 'belief-forming' mechanism, as it is for Hume, but a rationally structured seeker after knowledge. Construing the mind in this way is not a conceptual option, but one of the fundamental first principles that cannot be seriously doubted.

> Another first principle is, That the natural faculties, by which we distinguish truth from error, are not fallacious. If any man should demand a proof of this, it is impossible to satisfy him. For suppose it should be mathematically demonstrated, this would signify nothing in this case; because, to judge of a demonstration, a man must trust his faculties, and take for granted the very thing in question. (Reid 2002b: 480)

The similarities between the two positions show that while Hume and Reid have much in common, the differences between them are nevertheless profound.

In terms of this disagreement, Seth, with reservations, sides with Reid. His fourth Gifford Lecture is entitled, significantly, 'The Liberating Influence of Biology'. Modern biology, he argues, liberates us from the narrow mechanistic conception of the world within which Hume, and Baconians more generally, have operated. Darwin's account of evolution has demonstrated both the existence and the importance of teleological explanation. Science cannot, as perhaps it could in Hume's day, rest content with efficient causation. The implications of this are considerable. Whereas a mechanistic conception explains phenomena in terms of their origins, a teleological conception explains phenomena in terms of the end that eventually emerges. So, for example, geological phenomena – mountains, valleys, river courses – are to be explained mechanistically; the prior action of wind and weather explains why the subsequent form of the landscape is as it is. Biological phenomena, by contrast, are explained by ends. It is the needs of the mature entity that explain the pattern of early development. Whereas physical objects are *subject to* causes, organisms *are themselves* causes. They act upon the world. Thus the change from egg to chicken is not an outcome of external forces, but the result of an internal impulse to a predetermined end, or telos. And the mature hen is not a receptacle into which wind and rain drive grubs and seeds, but a self-motivated organism that finds them and consumes them for its own maintenance.

The explanatory success of Newtonianism, understandably, gave the physical sciences great pre-eminence.

> In the case of biology, it was natural that the prestige of physics and the more recent advances of chemistry should lead, in the first instance, to the view that the processes which the biologist studies in the organism are only very complex examples of the mechanical and chemical processes which are observable in non-living bodies, and that the ideal of explanation in biology must therefore be a resolution of the biological fact into simple mechanical relations and movements of which, on this view, it is the combined result. (Seth Pringle-Pattison 1917: 68)

> But the concentrated biological research of the last fifty years, while it has extended our knowledge of the mechanics and the chemistry of organic processes, has strikingly failed to substantiate the mechanistic hypothesis from which most of the researchers started. Instead of coming nearer, the reduction of biological processes to terms of mechanism appears to recede, as knowledge deepens and becomes more intimate. (Seth Pringle-Pattison 1917: 71)

> Biology deals, not with transformations of matter and energy, but with the relations of organisms and their environment. Of course, the physical laws hold good throughout; it is easy, for example, to measure the amount of energy gained or lost in the course of vital activities. But the commerce of the organism and its environment can only be understood in terms of teleology or purpose. (Seth Pringle-Pattison 1917: 75)

So Hume, in the mouth of Philo, was right. 'A purpose, an intention, a design strikes everywhere the most careless, the most stupid thinker, and no man can be so hardened in absurd systems, as at all times to reject it.' The 'absurd system', it now turns out, is an insistence that everything is subject to the 'mechanistic' explanations of physics and chemistry – a view that Hume broadly endorsed, and that has persisted in some quarters.

Still, even if we accept that biological explanation is different, why should that defuse the arguments of the *Dialogues* or lead us to challenge their conclusion? Is there any reason to go beyond a *natural* teleology, and hypothesise some 'higher intelligence' that is revealed in and through our experience of the natural world?

IV

Hume's *Dialogues* show, it is widely held, the futility of any attempt to reason from 'world' to 'God' in the way that the design argument aims to do. The trajectory of thought that we find in Seth and Calderwood, especially Calderwood's *Evolution and Man's Place in Nature*, looks in the opposite direction, and might be expressed in this way. Taking the findings of modern biology seriously may require us to reason from God to world.

The teleology that modern biology vindicates against narrowly mechanistic views of the natural world is not new. Seth regards it, in fact, as simply the restoration of elements that are to be found in Aristotelian philosophy. What makes it important, however, is that this restoration has resulted from the most advanced, and most fruitful, pursuit of natural science. By the same token, modern science vindicates naturalism, which is to say, the belief that knowledge of reality is the knowledge of nature that science gives us. This endorsement of naturalism might appear to confirm the contention that the success of modern biology spells the demise of supernaturalism, and thus of theism. It is a contention that still figures prominently in contemporary science and religion debates. But such a conclusion only follows, Seth argues, if we wrongly interpret the natural/supernatural distinction in terms of metaphysical dualism. The naturalist holds, correctly, that the human mind is part of the natural world. The supernaturalist holds, again correctly, that the mental attributes of human beings elevate them far above all other creatures. As Locke expresses the point, 'The having of general ideas is that which puts a perfect distinction between man and brutes' (quoted in Seth Pringle-Pattison 1917: 100).

Some familiar forms of supernaturalism construe this 'perfect distinction' erroneously. They think of human beings as Platonic 'souls' that have been air-dropped, so to speak, into the world of nature from some other, higher, world. To this, Darwinian naturalists correctly reply that human beings are a species of evolved organism. This is what biology has shown. But then they commonly take the further step of supposing that 'evolved organism' is an exhaustive classification. Human beings, they insist, are not 'a little lower than the angels', as the Bible asserts, but rather just 'a little higher than the apes', as Darwin's investigations have often been taken to demonstrate.

Both parties to this dispute, Seth argues, are operating within a mistaken metaphysical dualism, one side affirming it, and the other denying it. The error will be avoided, he claims, if we embrace a 'higher naturalism' that can acknowledge both the ultimate unity of the physical and the mental, and the fact of major qualitative differences between them. These differences do not arise from a division between metaphysical substances, as Cartesians have held. But they are nonetheless immense. That is to say, while there is no metaphysical barrier between human beings and other creatures, any attempt on the part of biologists to diminish the evident mental differences between them (on the grounds that they are all products of evolution) flies in the face of the facts no less than the Cartesian metaphysician does. At this point, Darwinism becomes dogma, and is thus thoroughly unscientific. Seth puts the point memorably:

> Can anything be more futile than to ignore the qualitative distinction between the one range of mind and the other? When the dog develops a system of astronomy or the cow pauses on the hill-top to admire the view, we shall gladly welcome them to the logicians company of 'rational animals'; but, till then, the wise man will be content to recognize a difference which is real. (Seth Pringle-Pattison 1917: 103)

'Lower' naturalism sets its sights on reducing human beings from rational agents to biological organisms. Dualistic supernaturalism resists this by claiming that human beings are not biological organisms at all; they are immaterial souls that merely inhabit the bodies they animate. Seth's higher naturalism rejects both positions. While acknowledging that human beings are evolved biological organisms, it also asserts that the rational agency distinctive of human beings is a fact about their nature. In short, to all but the wilfully blind, any adequate description of 'nature' will include both rational and non-rational animals. To assert that all animal life is to be explained in the same way, or to deny that human beings are animals, is to discount the findings of dispassionate empirical observation.

Human beings, as rational animals, have a capacity for both reason and responsibility. That is to say, they can think logically or illogically, and they can act morally or immorally. These basic truths are known through observation and introspection, and universally acknowledged. (This is part of the 'Common Sense' to which Reid appeals.) They imply, of course, that human beings can apprehend norms to which they are subject. They can consider not only what they *do* believe, but what they *ought to* believe; not only what they are *inclined* to do, but what they are *obliged* to do. An important question arises as to the status of these norms. Do they in some sense have an independent existence, or are they human projections? Seth opens his second series of lectures with a summary of the first that makes his position on this question clear.

> From the side of the higher Naturalism, I sought to emphasize man's rootedness in nature, so that the rational intelligence which characterizes him appears as the culmination of a continuous process of immanent development. The organic point of view delivers us, I contended, from the difficulties which so sorely afflict modern philosophy as to the relativity or subjectivity or phenomenality of knowledge, and the impossibility of knowing things as they really are. These difficulties depend on the conception of the world as a finished fact independently existing, and an equally independent knower with a peculiar apparatus of faculties which inevitably colour and subjectify any fact on which they are brought to bear. Such a conception errs also, I insisted, by treating the function of intelligence as purely cognitive, in the sense of simply mirroring or duplicating external facts, whereas all knowledge is an experience of the soul, which, as such, has necessarily its feeling-value; and the existence of such living centres capable of feeling the grandeur and beauty of the universe and tasting its manifold qualities is what is alone really significant in the universe. All values are in this sense conscious values; and so it is that the sentient, and still more the rational, being appears as the goal towards which Nature is working, namely, the development of an organ by which she may become conscious of herself and enter into the joy of her own being. (Seth Pringle-Pattison 1917: 211)

As this passage reveals, Seth's 'higher naturalism' may be said to combine Lockean empiricism with Hegelian philosophy of history, and the remaining nine lectures build a case for theism on this foundation. Rather than following Seth, however, it will serve present purposes better to turn back to Hume, and thus be led on to Calderwood.

V

In a well-known passage from the *Treatise*, Hume remarks that 'the mind has a great propensity to spread itself on external objects, and to conjoin with them any internal impressions which they occasion' (Hume 2007: 112). The context in which he makes this remark is a discussion of causality. His claim is that we believe causes must have the effects they do, not because we have discovered necessary connections in the structure of the world, but because the constant conjunction that we experience of one type of event being followed by another results in a *psychological* compulsion. When we witness sunrise, for instance, an expectation inevitably arises within us that sunset will follow. This psychological compulsion 'spreads' itself on to the world, and leads us to believe, erroneously, that purely contingent connections between events are somehow 'necessary'.

The same phenomenon, Hume thinks, is to be found at work in morality.

> Take any action allow'd to be vicious: Wilful murder, for instance . . . The vice entirely escapes you, as long as you consider the object. You never can find it, till you turn your reflexion into your own breast, and find a sentiment of disapprobation, which arises in you, towards this action . . . [W]hen you pronounce any action or character to be vicious, you mean nothing, but that from the constitution of your nature you have a feeling or sentiment of blame from the contemplation of it. Vice and virtue . . . are not qualities in objects, but perceptions in the mind. (Hume 2007: 301)

Hume's claim has been hotly debated, but even if it is correct, it leaves something important unexplained. Why does 'the constitution of our nature' give rise to negative feelings about some actions and positive feelings about others? For Hume, the generality of these feelings among human beings is simply a fact, to be observed rather than explained. Here again, then, there appears to be a lacuna that evolutionary biology can be called upon to fill. Doesn't a strictly biological explanation of moral feelings mean they must have evolved in accordance with what promotes and what retards the survival of our species? Explanations of this kind have often been proffered and endorsed under the general label 'evolutionary ethics'. Their particular appeal is that they appear to combine the philosophical plausibility of Hume with the scientific authority of Darwin.

The key issue here is whether the rational and moral norms that govern human action – consistency, truthfulness, cost/benefit calculation, honesty, integrity and so on – can be explained in terms of evolutionary development.[4] Does human adherence to these norms emerge in the course of biological evolution? Darwin clearly thought that it did. Careful observation of other animals reveals a striking level of selective and purposeful behaviour, which is to say, behaviour that responds and adapts to context and circumstance. Birds, for instance, do not simply find nests as they do food; they make them. The purposeful behaviour of even quite lowly creatures can reach remarkable levels of sophistication. Ants labour meticulously in specific roles that together sustain and maintain an enormously complex social organisation. Since no one supposes that they accomplish this remarkable goal by intention and design, we can suppose they are moved and directed by instinct. It is plausible to think, therefore, as Darwin thought, that non-rational instinct is the biological basis from which rational behaviour eventually emerges.

Henry Calderwood's book *Evolution and Man's Place in Nature* is an exhaustive examination of this claim. As a Christian minister, Calderwood was of course an avowed theist, as well as a philosopher. He was also an admirer of Darwin, and, as previously noted, for the purposes of a revised edition of his book, he made himself impressively familiar with the most recent findings of biology. He had no doubt about the great importance of Darwin's contribution to the advancement of science, and thought its principal claim to be beyond dispute. Right at the start of the book, he makes this clear.

> I am satisfied that no reasonably successful account of life in the universe can be presented which does not accept the general conclusion of Darwin, along with the results of more recent research, at once sustaining and modifying his theoretic positions. It is no longer doubtful that a law of Evolution has had continual application in the world's history. (Calderwood 1896: 2)

---

[4] There are also aesthetic norms to be considered – visual beauty, musical harmony, literary imagery and so on. There have been many sustained attempts to explain these in evolutionary terms, but since they fall less obviously within the framework of *practical* rationality, which evolutionary success might more easily be called upon to explain, for present purposes they will be left aside.

But just how far does the application of evolution extend? Human beings are undoubtedly evolved organisms, but are all the phenomena of human life to be explained in this way? Calderwood thinks, on scientific grounds, that 'the reality of a spiritual life in man . . . in *Knowledge* and *Action*' cannot be so encompassed.

> Darwin's contention is that there is 'no fundamental difference between man and the higher animals in their mental faculties' (*Descent of Man*, p. 66). He relies on common observation for support of the position; but such observation, when analysed, shows his position to be untenable . . . We all remark the difference between rational and irrational conduct in man; we never charge a dog or a horse with acting irrationally, simply because we cannot expect either animal to act rationally, it being impossible for it to recognize principles of conduct which are essential to 'right action.' Men are thus agreed that there is a fundamental difference between the mental powers of men and those of the higher animals. Not only so, this fundamental difference is such as to place the two orders of life at vast distance from each other. This appears under every test that can be applied – emotional, industrial, literary, artistic. These facts show that the Evolution theory is inapplicable to Mind and thereby insufficient to afford a scientific view of its genesis. (Calderwood 1896: 160–1)

In the course of reaching this conclusion, Calderwood devotes a chapter to the topic of 'Animal Intelligence', also the title of a book by George Romanes, one of Darwin's most gifted exponents. Calderwood pays close attention to this book because it undertakes a sustained attempt to trace the emergence of human rationality from biological instinct. The presumption, of course, is that 'animal intelligence' is an intermediary stage between the two, and on the face of it this seems plausible. But, says Calderwood,

> Even after we have granted 'Animal Intelligence,' as established on conclusive evidence, and so have admitted that the genesis of intelligence is a problem raised by the powers of the higher animals, we cannot compare the higher mammals with man in respect of Intelligence, without granting a fundamental difference, completely separating these animals from participation in the rational power belonging to man. The consequence of Darwin's theory is well indicated in his own words, when considering how to uphold man's 'descent from some

lower form' of life: 'If no organic being, excepting man, had possessed any mental power, or if his powers had been of a wholly different nature from those of the lower animals, then we should never have been able to convince ourselves that our high faculties had been gradually developed' (*Descent of Man*, p. 65). (Calderwood 1896: 161)

But our rational powers *are* of a wholly different nature. Human intelligence as exhibited in 'industrial, literary, [and] artistic' life has nothing comparable amongst other animals. So by Darwin's own lights, it is implausible to suggest that these manifestations of intelligence have developed gradually out of instinct via the lower intelligence other animals exhibit.

It is important to note that in rejecting the evolutionary explanation of human reason, Calderwood makes no appeal to theological doctrine or biblical revelation. It does not matter, in this connection, what the Bible says, since as Calderwood puts it: 'prima facie *evidence* is against the hypothesis that human Intelligence illustrates evolution from a lower to a higher phase of Intelligence' (Calderwood 1896: 98, emphasis added).

VI

From whence then did it come? Earlier in the book Calderwood makes some interesting observations relevant to this question, and though he does not expand upon them very much, they give us an indication of one way in which a theistic metaphysics might emerge from evolutionary biology. Although there was in his time, as there is still, a tendency to assume that the highest instances of animal intelligence are to be found among the primates, Calderwood points out that the most striking instances of animal intelligence are not to be found in apes, but in dogs and horses trained to perform specific tasks. This kind of intelligence is not native wit, so to speak, but a learned response to commands and directions. When we consider this phenomenon carefully, he thinks, we will notice a crucial difference between the innate intelligence of the dog, and the intelligence that is exhibited when the dog is trained to perform some new skill.

> That Animal Intelligence reappears in successive generations is certain; for such intelligence is the possession of the species e.g., of the whole race of dogs ... But the genesis of this new power cannot be

> found within organic inheritance . . . As in human history we depend on education for the development of Intelligence, so it is with the training of the dog. The animal's intelligence cannot be cultivated by good feeding, but only by good training. This fact places the dog in relation with man, in a manner impossible to lower orders of life. (Calderwood 1896: 100)

While it is true that the effectiveness of the training depends upon the natural intelligence of the dog, the purposeful work it is trained to do – rounding up sheep, fetching game, guarding premises and so on – depends upon a higher intelligence, namely the human intelligence that conceives, directs and reflects upon educating the dog. It is easy to be misled by the fact that all this thought and effort would be futile if the dog were not capable of being trained, into supposing that this capacity for intelligent behaviour explains the sophisticated things it learns to do. It is evident, however, that the ultimate source is the higher human intelligence which 'places the dog in relation with man'.

Calderwood's main point is this. Darwinian biology has shown convincingly that the organic structures of mammals, including human beings, have evolved. Some non-human animals have evolved to a point at which they can engage with, and learn from, a higher level of intelligence, namely human beings. What then are we to think about the yet higher intelligence of human beings? In this case too, presumably, organic evolution generates a capacity to engage with and learn from a higher level of intelligence. If this line of reasoning is cogent, then it appears that accepting the theory of evolution opens up a new way of thinking. Philo was right. We cannot reason from world to God by way of analogy with, for instance, watch and watchmaker, as the traditional design argument seeks to do, not least because the world contains organisms such as vegetables as well as mechanical 'contrivances'. On the other hand, it turns out that evolutionary biology, despite the huge advance in scientific understanding that it constitutes, does not have the resources to frame an adequate understanding of all the facts that confront us. The facts about humanity's mental and moral life have to be *explained*, and cannot, as many Darwinians have thought, be *explained away*. Any attempt to do so, indeed, is quite contrary to the major scientific advance that evolutionary biology made.

Calderwood's argument is a notably specific one. He identifies a particular question for the Darwinian account, namely how the gap between instinct and intelligence is to be bridged (an issue that Darwin himself held to be essential), and then makes a sustained, largely biological case for thinking that the gap cannot be bridged in evolutionary terms. By implication and admission, of course, this is primarily of interest for its much larger claim that evolutionary biology cannot encompass 'the reality of a spiritual life in man'. In making this claim, Calderwood was endorsing a position more explicitly advanced by Darwin's great contemporary A. R. Wallace, also a celebrated biologist who, it is widely acknowledged, developed the concept of natural selection independently of Darwin.

Wallace's book on *Darwinism*, published in 1889, also seeks to place limits on the explanatory scope of natural selection, and claims that it cannot explain the exercise of human faculties in morality, music, mathematics or metaphysics since these are not useful for survival and are found most strikingly in only a very small proportion of human beings. Wallace's contentions came under very critical scrutiny in an extended essay in the *Westminster Review* by David G. Ritchie, Calderwood's contemporary in the Chair of Logic and Metaphysics at St Andrews. In 'Natural Selection and the Spiritual World' Ritchie singularly fails to be impressed by Wallace's arguments. This is not just because he thinks they are demonstrably weak, but because they are wrong headed.

> The spiritual world need not be summoned as a mysterious counterpart to the material world, intruding itself into the latter, wherever the scientific investigator finds a difficulty at first sight, or the person who is afraid of science finds a convenient place of refuge for threatened beliefs. If a spiritual principle is recognized in the universe, it must be recognized not in the exceptional, not in holes and corners, like those intramundane species in which Epicurus stowed away the gods; but a spiritual principle must be recognized everywhere, as the condition of our knowing a system of nature ... Not in an exceptional origin of certain rare human qualities, but in the nature of human thought, however originated, is to be found the true spiritual greatness of man; and in the achievements of the human spirit in the institutions of society, in art, in religion, in science, and in philosophy is to be read, if anywhere, the little we can read about the ultimate meaning of the universe. (Ritchie 1890: 469)

In another paper, delivered to the Aristotelian Society, and entitled 'Darwin and Hegel', Ritchie expresses his impatience with any 'God of the gaps' argument in biology.

> If we may judge by past experience all attempts on the part of 'Intuitionists' [in which he includes philosophers and theologians who appeal to 'Common Sense'] to meet Evolutionists on questions of 'origins' are doomed to failure: one untenable position has to be surrendered after another. The Idealist makes no such attempt. He only insists that, after we have had as complete a history as can be given of how things have come to be what they are, we are justified in looking back from our vantage ground and seeing in the past evolution the gradual 'unrolling' of the meaning that we only fully understand at the end of the process. The process is not completed; and therefore this attempt has to be renewed for each generation. But at every stage it is in the highest that we know we must seek the key to the philosophical interpretation of nature and of man. (Ritchie 1891: 74)

This passage is not directed against Calderwood, nor could it be, since Ritchie's essay had appeared some years before Calderwood's book was published. In any case, the point it makes cannot be said to apply to Calderwood, who was neither 'afraid of science' nor in search of 'a convenient place of refuge for threatened beliefs'. Calderwood does think, or at any rate suggests, that human rationality must have an origin that is 'exceptional' from the point of view of natural selection. It is not exceptional, however, from the perspective of a spiritual principle that 'must be recognized everywhere'. And indeed, his allusion (rather than explicit invocation) to an 'extra-human' origin is wholly consonant with a suitably modest sense of 'the little we can read about the ultimate meaning of the universe'.

It is this move from origin to meaning that is crucial, and in yet another paper on the subject, this time entitled 'Origin and Validity' and published in *Mind*, Ritchie endorses something very like the gap between impulse and intelligence that Calderwood aims to argue for. Let us suppose, contrary perhaps to Calderwood's contention, that natural selection for survival can explain why human beings have come to exercise 'higher' intelligence in adopting and pursuing courses of action. Ritchie thinks this still leaves unexplained the rational basis for their doing so, their recognition that they *ought* to do so.

The old Intuitionist Ethics comes into direct conflict with scientific investigations into the origin of moral ideas. The theory of Idealism for which I am contending, only maintains that all accounts of the evolution of morality are inadequate to supply a complete theory of Ethics, unless the presence of *an* ideal to all human effort be recognized as involved in the presence of the eternal Self which any account of knowledge or conduct supposes . . . The ideal must vary, else progress would be impossible. But there must be an ideal, a judgment of 'ought,' else morality would be impossible. (Ritchie 1888a: 77, emphasis original)

Now whether or not Calderwood commits the mistake that Ritchie attributes to the 'Intuitionists', it seems precisely this sensitivity to ideals or norms that marks off the 'higher' intelligence of the trainer from the 'lower' intelligence of the dog. A very intelligent dog exhibits its intelligence by doing brilliantly what it has been trained to do. But it has no awareness of any higher purposefulness served by its obedience, any sense of what makes the things it is trained to do interesting and valuable. By contrast, it is just such an awareness that trainers possess, and it is their sensitivity to an ideal that enables them to devise ever better training methods and routines. It seems, though, that the 'explanation' of their sensibility cannot reasonably be thought to have biological origins, at least in the way that the instincts underlying training have. That is because, even at the most advanced stage of evolution, human beings can acknowledge the requirements of truth, goodness, beauty and so on, and yet be indifferent and even hostile to them. Vandals, for example, must recognise beauty in order to destroy it. It follows that the source of these norms, and their authority – in this case, what makes the beautiful worth promoting and preserving – must in some sense lie outside the realm of impulses that have emerged from a process of natural selection.

Seth, Calderwood and Ritchie all seem to agree about this. So where then does the difference between them lie? Seth rejects Hume's mechanistic version of naturalism, and hence the 'argument from design' that rests upon it and which the *Dialogues* demolish. Calderwood thinks that even a thoroughly biological or organic version of naturalism reveals a deficiency waiting to be supplied by the divine agency that the design argument tried, but failed, to establish. Ritchie has recourse to 'the eternal Self' which, at any point in time, is to be identified with 'the highest that we know'. It is here that we can see a difference open up within

Scottish philosophy, between those such as Seth and Calderwood who persisted with something like the theism of Reid, and those such as Ritchie who looked instead to Hegel. The issue lies at the heart of the vigorous debate that took place between the Scottish Hegelians and their critics in the closing decade of the nineteenth century.[5]

---

[5] See Chapter 6.

9

The Gifford Lectures and the Re-affirmation of Theism: Alexander Campbell Fraser

I

In 1855, at the unusually early age of thirty-one, John Tulloch was appointed Principal of St Mary's College, the Divinity Faculty of the University of St Andrews. In the same year, he was awarded the Burnet Prize for an essay entitled 'Theism: The Witness of Reason and Nature to an All-Wise and Beneficent Creator', published as a book shortly afterwards by William Blackwood and Sons. Tulloch's essay was interesting in at least two respects. At St Andrews, as well as Principal, he occupied the Chair of Systematic Theology and Apologetics, and his essay signalled a move away from the doctrinaire and rather narrow Calvinistic theology of his predecessors towards a more liberal 'rational theology'. This more liberal theology lay at the heart of Tulloch's influential contribution both to the Church of Scotland as it emerged from the trauma of the 'Disruption' in 1843, and to the study of theology in the Scottish universities. On the other hand, Tulloch's liberalism in theology conceded nothing to recent trends in philosophy. His defence of theism had the rising tide of Positivism in its sights no less than dogmatic Calvinism. Auguste Comte's six-volume *Course on Positive Philosophy* had been published between 1830 and 1842, and enthusiastically welcomed by John Stuart Mill, who tells us that while the main elements of his *System of Logic* were formulated by the time he read Comte, 'his book was of essential service to me in some of the parts that still remained to be thought out' (Mill 1971: 126). Mill regarded Comte's subsequent *Treatise on Sociology, Instituting the Religion of Humanity* (1851–4, four volumes) with considerably less favour, though he did pick up on the expression 'religion of humanity' in his posthumously published essay 'The

Utility of Religion'. In Scotland, Alexander Bain became the standard bearer of a version of positivism when, with Mill's support, he was appointed Regius Professor of Logic in Aberdeen in 1860.

Tulloch was Principal of St Mary's for over thirty years. It was a period that witnessed the publication of a number of remarkably influential books. Most notable was Darwin's *On the Origin of Species by Means of Natural Selection*, published in 1859, and followed in 1871 by *The Descent of Man, and Selection in Relation to Sex*. Darwin himself was hesitant to explore or enlarge on the implications of his work for religion and ethics, but both books provided a huge stimulus for others to do so. Thomas Huxley, who famously described himself as 'Darwin's bulldog', was one, and Herbert Spencer another. Huxley became Professor of Natural History at the Royal School of Mines in the same year that Tulloch assumed the Principalship of St Mary's, and held the post for much the same period of time. It was Huxley who coined the term 'agnosticism', and though principally a biologist and anthropologist, he wrote and lectured extensively on the implications of evolutionary biology for philosophy, religion and ethics. His book *Evidence as to Man's Place in Nature*, published in 1863, became a key text in the debate about science and religion. Spencer, though described by some as 'the philosopher of the half-educated',[1] was author of a scarcely less influential book written in the light of Darwin's *Origin of Species*, namely *Principles of Biology*, published in 1864, the source of the expression 'survival of the fittest'. Less directly connected with Darwin and science, but no less influential in debates about religion, was Matthew Arnold's book about the Bible, *Literature and Dogma*, published in 1875.

During his Principalship, Tulloch published a series of lengthy review articles, eventually collected into a single volume, with some new material. Entitled *Modern Theories in Philosophy and Religion*, this volume appeared in 1884, just two years before he died. Comte, Mill, Huxley, Spencer and Arnold all figure in these essays and their works and influence comprise much of the background to Tulloch's

---

[1] W. J. Mander's assessment is even more damning. Spencer, he says, dealt 'very swiftly and dogmatically with matters that the history of metaphysical speculation has proven to be extremely subtle, complex and contestable. Blind to the depth of the questions with which they are concerned, his undergraduate-level arguments are as self-confident as they are superficial' (Mander 2020: 67).

reviews. In many cases, however, the more immediate objects of his attention are once prominent figures whose names are now largely forgotten – Frederick Harrison, G. H. Lewes, William Smith, John Tyndall, John Robert Seeley (the anonymous author of *Ecce Homo*) and James Sully. This is not a matter of any great moment, however, because, as Tulloch makes clear in the preface, the writers whose works he critically reviews are interesting chiefly – perhaps only – because they give contemporary expression to perpetually recurring themes in religion and metaphysics.

> These Essays have a common object ... The question with which they deal in diverse application is the great question of contemporary thought ... Is there a spiritual world? Is there a metaphysical as well as a physical basis of life? ... All the naturalistic systems of thought so prevalent at the present time assume a negative answer to these questions. They speak of mind or spirit or consciousness – they cannot help doing so; but they mean by such language merely a phenomenon – a phase of natural being – never a spiritual entity or reality, distinct by itself, and essentially belonging to another and a higher state of being. Metaphysics is flouted as mere verbalism. Religion is discarded along with Metaphysic, or at least religion in the old sense.
>
> This is the drift of the modern spirit – the 'Zeitgeist,' as it is called. It has penetrated philosophy, literature, religion itself; men and women, in numbers, are trying everywhere to satisfy themselves with theories spun out of the naturalistic web supposed not merely to confine life, but to constitute it. One might use the words of Bishop Butler with reference to the allied but very different state of thought in his own time, and say, 'It has come, I know not how, to be taken for granted by many persons, that Christianity is not so much a subject of inquiry, but that it is now at length discovered to be fictitious' – at least 'among all people of discernment'. (Tulloch 1884: v–vi)

Tulloch's reference to Butler, whose *Analogy of Religion, Natural and Revealed* was published 150 years previously, implicitly acknowledges that the rejection of metaphysical religion was not the exclusive province of the nineteenth-century Zeitgeist. With Comte and his followers in mind, Tulloch says,

> It is the pretention of Positivism to reduce all knowledge to the form of science. It affirms not only that the inductive or scientific method is applicable to the whole range of phenomena or events which come

under our observation, but that there is nothing beyond the application of this method. What we cannot observe, classify, and generalize are not realities. (Tulloch 1884: 53)

While Tulloch's primary concern was to address the philosophical climate of his own times, he knew that the Positivism he strove to oppose had a longer history. The modern version was little different to the doctrine that made the eighteenth-century Deists sceptical of miracles, and close to the mentality of the 'cultured despisers of religion' to whom Schleiermacher addressed his *Speeches on Religion* of 1799. The essays in *Modern Theories* are replete with names and publications that have long since ceased to have much currency, but they remain interesting and valuable because the underlying topics with which they are concerned are of recurring significance in many periods, including the present. Tulloch, in fact, finds that modern Positivism echoes the ancient world. His essay on 'Modern Scientific Materialism' begins with this observation.

> It would seem as if the human mind, with all its restless activity, were destined to revolve in an endless circle . . . Nature and all its secrets become better known, and the powers of Nature are brought more under human control; but the sources of Nature and life and thought – all the ultimate problems of being – never become more clearly intelligible. Not only so, but the last efforts of human reasoning on these subjects are even as the first. Differing in form . . . they are in substance the same. (Tulloch 1884: 125)

And in a later essay on 'Pessimism' he offers this illustration of the point.

> The widespread scientific materialism, for example, at which the present race of Oxford and Cambridge and Scotch students have caught, as if it were a new revelation by the grace of Professor Tyndale and others, is really nothing but the old atomism of Democritus. (Tulloch 1884: 171)

The consequence is that Tulloch's thoughts on the books he reviews contain important insights of continuing relevance to the topics of philosophical scepticism, philosophical pessimism, the place of mind in nature, the metaphysical basis of morality, the possibility of religion without supernaturalism, and the epistemological status of science. Moreover, though a theologian and churchman by profession, his style of argument is a combination of historical exposition and philosophical analysis, the same style that marks his magnum opus, *Rational Theology and Christian Philosophy*, a two-volume study of the Cambridge Platonists that, it is plausible to hold, has never been surpassed.

In claiming that the 'drift of the modern spirit' is 'naturalistic', however, Tulloch, even by his own lights, somewhat overstates the case. The last two essays in the book are focused on strictly philosophical writers. The first of these is a review of James Frederick Ferrier's posthumously published collected papers and lectures on Greek philosophy, an essay that also serves as an admiring tribute to Ferrier by a friend and colleague. The final essay is a review of no fewer than eight books on Immanuel Kant, including several by Scottish-educated philosophers – Edward Caird, Robert Adamson, John Watson, William Wallace and James Hutchison Stirling. In concluding the essay on Ferrier, Tulloch says that Ferrier, far from being a materialist, 'was possessed of a lofty faith in the divine dignity of human reason and the reality of a Truth transcending that of the senses' (Tulloch 1884: 374). Then, in the course of the essay on Kant, and somewhat contrary to his earlier reference to the 'Scotch' students attracted to scientific materialism, he attributes a similar view much more widely when he remarks that in Scotland 'spiritual philosophy has never lost its ascendancy'.

> The country of Hume is proud of him, as it has good reason to be. He really is the intellectual progenitor of all that is strong in materialism. To him both the Mills, father and son, and Dr Bain . . . owe the essential breadth of their thought. Great, however, as is the admiration for Hume's genius in his native country, he never carried before him the drift of speculation there as in England. His limits have been understood in Scotland as in Germany; and, acknowledged to be impregnably strong on his own ground, the measure of this ground has yet been noted and pointed out. We make no pretensions, on the part of the Scottish school of philosophy, of having given an effective rational reply to Hume . . . Such a question is beyond our present purpose, and is not meant to be raised here. But, at any rate . . . the Scottish universities have never been swept by the wave of materialism which overspread Oxford [in the mid 1850s]. (Tulloch 1884: 438)

Instead of framing a 'Scottish' reply to Hume after the manner of Reid and Common Sense, many of the authors whose work Tulloch is reviewing had turned to Kant and Idealism instead. The result was a philosophy even more 'spiritual' and anti-materialist than anything the writings of Reid, Stewart or Hamilton might have stimulated. In Tulloch's estimation, James Hutchison Stirling, Scotland's most prominent Hegelian and the author of *Textbook of Kant*, had 'smitten the sophisms of scientific materialism with crushing force' (Tulloch 1884: 440), while the Scottish Idealists in general had taken their cue from Kant himself. For while Kant set the realities of morality and religion 'outside the sphere of cognition in the scientific sense, [he] did not, with our modern Agnostics, relegate them to the mere domain of imaginative fiction'. Rather, 'he held fast, however inconsequently, to the great facts of God, and moral freedom, and immortality' (Tulloch 1884: 443).

II

Tulloch's remark that finding an answer to Hume 'on the part of the Scottish school of philosophy . . . is beyond our present purpose, and is not meant to be raised here' suggests, though it does not say so, that while the Scottish Kantians had chosen a different path, there still remained the possibility of formulating such an answer. Whether he had this in mind or not, it is a fact that very soon after, just such a possibility opened up, and in the end, even, eventually uncovered common cause between Common Sense and Idealism. Two developments proved to be especially important. First, in the same year that Tulloch's book appeared, Andrew Seth gave the Balfour Philosophical Lectures at the University of Edinburgh and chose for his subject 'Scottish Philosophy: A Comparison of the Scottish and German Answers to Hume'. Seth did not attempt to revitalise the Scottish answer to Hume, but he set out with new clarity the philosophical strategy Reid had adopted, the principal reasons for its failure, and the elements of a possible rapprochement between Reid and Kant. Second, in 1885, the same year that Seth's lectures were published, Lord Adam Gifford, an Edinburgh lawyer who had made a considerable fortune in the course of his commercial practice, left £80,000 in his will, to be distributed between the four universities of Scotland in specified amounts.

By the standards of the time – indeed, of any time – Gifford's bequest was very large,[2] but if the generosity of the bequest was

---

[2] There are several different ways in which the contemporary value of Gifford's bequest might be calculated. Comparative purchasing power is the most conservative, but even this produces a figure well over £8 million/$11 million.

unusual, even more unusual, perhaps, was its purpose. Unlike most other smaller gifts and bequests, its aim was not to finance some part of the universities' established activities, or provide additional teaching posts, scholarships and prizes, but to enable the four universities to give the general public access to the thinking of the very best academic minds. '[S]aid sums are to be paid in trust only for the ... purpose of establishing in each of the four cities ... a Lectureship or Popular Chair for Promoting, Advancing, Teaching and Diffusing the study of Natural Theology, in the widest sense of that term' (Jaki 1995: 98). The lectures should be 'public and popular', the will goes on to say, and accessible to 'the whole community without matriculation', that is, Scottish society beyond the universities.

Lord Gifford's will professed to leave 'all the details and arrangements' of each lectureship in the hands, and at the discretion, of 'patrons' appointed from within the individual universities. At the same time, he included in it a lengthy enunciation of nine principles that the universities would have to follow. While most of these principles concerned the administration of the lectures and financial management of the funds, two of them touched on important matters of substance. The fourth principle laid it down that the lecturers would not be subject to a religious test of any kind. They could be of 'any religion or way of thinking', and even 'sceptics or agnostics or freethinkers', provided only that they would be 'true thinkers, lovers of and earnest inquirers after truth'. The fifth principle placed a constraint upon the approach that the lecturer must take. The lectures must 'treat their subject as a strictly natural science' (Jaki 1995: 100).

The first sets of lectures took place in 1888–9 – at Edinburgh, Glasgow and St Andrews – just three years after Lord Gifford made his will, with the lectures in Aberdeen beginning in 1889. Somewhat oddly, most of the early lectures did not really fit Gifford's express intent, since they focused on the scientific study of religion rather than natural theology treated scientifically. Max Müller, Professor of Comparative Philology at Oxford, inaugurated the lectures at Glasgow with an anthropological treatment of primitive religious practices leading to a comparison of aspects of Hinduism and Islam. Andrew Lang, whose expertise lay in folklore, lectured on the history of religion at St Andrews, and E. B. Tylor, another distinguished anthropologist, gave the first lectures in Aberdeen. In Edinburgh, James Hutchison Stirling lectured under the more promising title of 'Philosophy and Theology', but his lectures were not so much an exploration in natural theology as an extended treatment of what natural theology might be. The first lectures, in fact, to take Gifford's remit properly to heart were those given in 1892–4 by Alexander Campbell Fraser at the University of Edinburgh, from which he had recently retired as Professor of Logic and Metaphysics.

In his *Biographia Philosophica*, Fraser records his resolve to lecture more fully in accordance with Gifford's intention.

> I was surprised one morning by an announcement that I had been chosen by my own university as their Gifford lecturer on Natural Theology . . . Whilst I was grateful for the unexpected honour, I was at first indisposed to undertake an office which, if interpreted by the example of preceding Gifford lecturers in Edinburgh and the other Scottish universities, was concerned with the historical Science of religion or of theism . . . But after carefully examining the Deed under which those remarkable lectureships were lately founded in the Scottish universities . . . I found that a Gifford lecturer was expressly invited to discuss fundamental questions about the constitution of the universe, and man's relation to its Supreme Power, which had haunted me in youth, and during my tenure of the Chair of Hamilton . . . These I thought were questions about which I might have something to say [since] my thought had been leading up to them for the greater part of my life. There was, indeed, little time for more thinking, or for penetrating more deeply into the enormous literature on the subject . . . But something, it seemed, might emerge from a sincere attempt to present the philosophical faith to which I had made my way, and the foundation in reason on which it rested. (Fraser 1904: 291–3)

The outcome was the *Philosophy of Theism*, published by Blackwood's in 1896, and appearing in a substantially amended second edition in 1899.

Fraser's reference to his long professorship at Edinburgh as occupancy of 'the Chair of Hamilton' is both striking and significant. Unlike John Veitch, his contemporary and counterpart in the Logic Chair at Glasgow, Fraser was not an exponent of the philosophy of Sir William Hamilton, nor did he join those who leapt to Hamilton's defence against the attacks of Mill and Stirling. Nonetheless, in his *Biographia Philosophica* he gladly acknowledges his debt to Hamilton, and thereby the Scottish philosophical tradition. This quiet allegiance was a key factor in the fiercely disputed competition for Hamilton's successor, when Fraser won out against James Frederick Ferrier. His appointment caused some surprise since, from many points of view, Ferrier was the better qualified candidate. Already a Professor at St Andrews, Ferrier had published a series of essays on *The Philosophy of Consciousness*, running to over 250 pages, and a major work, the *Institutes of Metaphysics*. Fraser, by contrast, was Professor at the fledgling Free Church New College and had published very little, just six essays in the *North British Review*, and an introductory textbook for students entitled *Rational Philosophy in History and in System*. Nevertheless, Fraser was appointed, and this was because the Town Council patrons had been persuaded by John Cairns's pamphlets and Victor Cousin's testimonial that Fraser would be a more reliable exponent of 'the Scottish philosophy'.[3]

Fraser occupied 'the Chair of Hamilton' for more than thirty-five years. During that time, he was the revered teacher of some of the most gifted Scottish philosophers, and gave exemplary service to the University of Edinburgh as Dean of the Faculty of Arts. He undertook distinguished editorial work for Oxford University Press on editions of Berkeley and Locke, and wrote philosophical biographies of both of them for the *Blackwood's Philosophical Classics for English Readers* series. However, by the time he retired in 1891, he had not produced much original philosophical work of his own. Notably, he did not contribute anything to the often technical and sometimes impassioned debates between the traditionalists, empirical psychologists and philosophical Idealists that were so prominent a part of Scottish philosophy in the later nineteenth century. The invitation to deliver Gifford Lectures changed that, and provided Fraser in his retirement with an opportunity to formulate at length the conclusions at which he had arrived after many decades of teaching and study. Two years after his lectures appeared in print, Fraser then published another philosophical biography, this time of Thomas Reid. Reid does not appear in the index of *Philosophy of Theism*, but the purpose of the biography, Fraser tells us in the preface, is 'to present Reid in a fresh light, and in his relations to present-day thought'. In this connection he expressly mentions both McCosh's and Seth's books on Scottish philosophy.

> In the concluding chapter I have looked at the philosophical appeal to inspired data of Common Sense, in the wider light of the theistic philosophy of the universe, and not merely as part of the inductive science of the human mind. This connects the theistic postulate of spiritual

[3] For a full account of this competition see Chapter 3.

reason, as the foundation of human experience, with Reid's appeal to the ultimate but often dormant necessities of human nature, a subject treated more fully in my *Philosophy of Theism*. (Fraser 1898: 5)

Taken together, then, for present purposes these late publications have special interest. In Fraser's own words, they offer an articulation and defence of 'the Scottish chapter in that enduring alternation between agnostic despair and endeavour after perfect insight' taking Thomas Reid to be 'the national representative, in the eighteenth century, of the *via media* between these extremes' (ibid.). Fraser's reaffirmation of theism is presented as a renewed, and substantially enhanced, continuation of 'the Scottish answer to Hume'.

III

The conception of philosophy that underlies the *Philosophy of Theism* is one that had gained a general currency in the late nineteenth century. The proper aim of philosophy, it was widely held, was to arrive at a unified understanding of human experience as a whole, and this marked it off from science, which was concerned with the empirical observation and law-like explanation of specific phenomena. Such a distinction was unknown to the eighteenth century, and accordingly Fraser's endeavour stands in considerable contrast to Reid's, whose *Inquiry* contentedly accepts 'servile employment in science' by undertaking 'the mean offices of digging for a foundation, of moving rubbish, and carrying materials', and eschews any grander aspiration that 'plans a design, and raises a fabric' only to have 'some succeeding architect' demolish it (Reid 1997: 15).

The detail and care with which Fraser constructs his argument would hardly fit with the description 'grand design or fabric'. At the same time, it is undoubtedly very different in character to Reid's, much more an engagement in metaphysical speculation than psychological observation. It is this gap, ultimately, that Fraser aims to bridge. In this he is assisted by the fact that if the style is different, the starting place is the same – Hume. Like Reid, Fraser praises Hume as a brilliant philosopher – 'the most intrepid theological and philosophical thinker that Scotland has produced' – whose ingenious arguments, nonetheless, are wholly unpersuasive. Given that the topic in hand is theism, it is inevitable that Fraser should make mention of the *Dialogues* (as well as the *Natural History of Religion*), but it is in Hume's perplexity at the end of Book 1 of the *Treatise* that he finds the questions his lectures are intended to address. In Lecture 5 he expressly quotes Hume, but initially he asks these questions for himself and in his own words. 'In what sort of universe – divine, or diabolic, or indifferent – and for what purpose, if any, am I existing consciously? What is the deepest and truest meaning of this ever-changing universe in which I am now struggling? What the origin and the outcome of this endless flux?' (Fraser 1899: 4–5). His method of answering these questions, like that of Hume and Reid, is to appeal to the facts of experience, but he does so at a very high level of generality. The 'three primary data' he cites are these. A material world exists; we are self-conscious agents; we are aware that the existence of people and things is contingent and depends upon some conditioning force or 'Universal Power'. These are facts that common sense affirms, and that it is near impossible to deny. No one, Fraser thinks, has ever seriously doubted that we are self-conscious beings, aware of and able to act upon a world beyond ourselves, yet subject to and dependent upon a force or forces that we neither control nor fully understand.

How are these facts related? In framing a unified philosophical understanding of human experience, a common strategy has been to treat one of them as fundamental and seek to explain the others in terms of it. Fraser explores three such 'monisms' to which he gives the labels Universal Materialism, Panegoism and Pantheism. Universal Materialism takes the material world to be self-subsisting and explains self-consciousness as a sophisticated product of matter in motion. Panegoism takes conscious experience to be fundamental and explains the material world as a projection whose existence depends upon the 'universal power' that is mind. Pantheism, at least as Spinoza elaborates it, makes 'mind' and 'body' modes of one underlying 'substance' – God or Nature – which is eternal, infinite and unchanging. Fraser elaborates these three monisms with insight and sympathy, but he identifies a deep flaw in each of them.

Consider first the full implications of Universal Materialism.

> Natural sequence – not Purpose, benevolent or malevolent – is the final solvent of the problem of the universe. Deeper than this the human line cannot go . . . Man and his material organism are absolutely identified

> in this final interpretation of the universe . . . Good and evil, right and wrong, merit and demerit, self-satisfaction or remorse, are scientifically discovered to be words which have acquired their misleading meaning at an inferior era in this world's history . . . Yet . . . where is the universal materialist to stop in what he attributes to Matter, if he may attribute to it the rational acts, and moral experience of a human body? The thinking and observing processes themselves – those processes through which the materialist finds that conscious mind, in all its states, is virtually molecules in motion – are only part of a molecular process. Its verified inferences, as well as its unproved hypotheses, are all alike transitory illusions . . . thus Monism, at least in the form of Universal Materialism, itself disappears, along with conscious intelligence, in the abyss of Universal Nescience. (Fraser 1899: 57–61)

In short, 'The key which pretended to open the secret of reality has been taken away in the very act of using it. Universal Materialism is intellectual suicide' (Fraser 1899: 67). Since Panegoism is essentially an immaterial conception, it seems to begin at an advantage over the self-destructive nature of materialism. Panegoism draws upon the inescapable fact that 'an extended thing without secondary qualities cannot be imagined as an outward or material thing at all' (Fraser 1899: 72). Without mind, there is no matter. Nevertheless, in the end egoistic monism does not fare any better than its materialistic rival.

> One who looks upon the universe at the panegoistic point of view sees in the whole material world . . . only inward experiences . . . Instead of an external flux of variously qualified things, in orderly motion in space, the universe becomes a flux of orderly ideas and feelings, in the history of my conscious ego. In this transformation scene my conscious life is the final supposition . . . Nothing now appears in the universe of existence but conscious mind; and the only mind of which I am conscious is my own . . . the universe is born and dies with the person who experiences it; and the only person of whose existence I am conscious is myself. Matter and God are absorbed and lost in Me. The solitary Ego, as the only datum, reduces human experience to absurdity, if not to contradiction. (Fraser 1899: 72–4)

Fraser thinks that Panegoism has never had any serious exponents in the history of philosophy. 'But its exaggerations at least help to illustrate the subordinate office of Matter in the universe of existence' so that its merit is 'chiefly as an aid to reflection upon the absurdity of dominant Materialism' (Fraser 1899: 75).

With this dispatch of both Materialism and Panegoism we come to Pantheism. 'May the final intellectual and moral satisfaction desired by the philosopher be found when God is assumed as the only reality, and when we think of Matter and Ego as only illusory modes of God?' (ibid.). Fraser observes that in sharp contrast to Panegoism, 'Pantheism, in one or other of its many protean forms, is a way of thinking about the universe that has proved its influence over millions of human minds . . . [and] governed the religious and philosophical thought of India for ages' (Fraser 1899: 80). But it is Spinoza who may be regarded as 'the prince of pantheists'. His system of thought, however, has proved hard to interpret. 'In the age that followed his life Spinoza was regarded as an atheist and a blasphemer. In the nineteenth century he receives homage as a saint . . . Once anathematised by Jews and Christians, this proclaimed atheist is now described as a god-intoxicated mystic' (Fraser 1899: 90). It is 'the characteristic elasticity of pantheism' that explains this radical diversity of interpretation, Fraser suggests, because 'the pantheist conception is susceptible of either a materialist or an idealist development'. At its heart, though, there is this deep flaw. The unity of experience that Pantheism seeks in the infinite and eternal is purchased at the price of necessity, and thus the elimination of contingency.

> The universe of reality must be eternally necessary, as otherwise we are involved in the contradiction that Nature might be different to what it must be. What we call contingency and change is the issue of an imperfect comprehension of infinite reality, under the delusive form of sense or imagination. What really exists cannot be contingent: it seems so only because it is viewed in the light of deficient knowledge. (Fraser 1899: 98)

However:

> A dilemma confronts this pantheistic unity and necessity. Either we reduce individual things and persons to vain shadows, and then the undetermined Substance [becomes] a featureless unity; or we must assume that the data and rational implicates of our experience are real – so far as they go – and that God is incompletely yet really revealed in our physical and spiritual experience . . . It is by means

of *monads*, says Leibniz, that Spinoza is refuted: Spinoza would be right if there were no *monads* . . . Let us substitute persons or moral agents for *monads*, and say that if there were no inspired self-acting persons, a necessitated physical universe would be the only revelation of God. For our moral experience of remorse and responsibility is an insurmountable obstruction to unity. Logical pantheism is inconsistent with human ideals of moral goodness, and with real evil. God must be perfect; therefore whatever and whoever exists must be perfect. Nero and Borgia, Socrates and Jesus, are alike and equally divine. Now if we find something existing which ought not to exist, and which has come into existence by no divine necessity, we find what disturbs Spinoza's theory. But the existence of this disturbance is witnessed to by remorse, which is as much a necessity of moral reason as physical causality is of scientific reason; and neither reason can be proved inconsistent with the other. We find in the universe that of which the Universal Power cannot be the origin. (Fraser 1899: 100-1)

It seems impossible under the conditions of human experience and understanding to connect in philosophic imagination Infinite with finite; temporal succession with the Eternal Now. It is impossible under human conditions, for scientific understanding to conquer an Infinite which refuses to enter as a rounded object into experience. It is impossible to see All as All is visible at the divine centre. The alternatives for man are *Homo mensura* or *Nulla mensura* [either 'man is the measure' or nothing is]. (Fraser 1899: 103)

IV

With this conclusion, Fraser returns to Hume and the questions by which Hume declares himself 'confounded'. 'Where am I, or what am I? From what cause do I derive my existence, and to what condition shall I return? Whose favour shall I court, and whose anger must I dread? What beings surround me? And on whom have I any influence, or who have any influence on me?' (*Treatise* 1.4.7, quoted in Fraser 1899: 113). Philosophical thinking has left Hume 'invironed with the deepest darkness'. Since, as he thinks, 'reason is incapable of dispelling these clouds', we must accept that there is no rationally defensible response to even the most radical scepticism.

> Hume [says Fraser] is the prime leader of modern agnosticism. It is thus formulated by Hume 'When you go one step beyond the *mundane* system, you only excite an inquisitive humour, which it is impossible

The Gifford Lectures and the Re-affirmation of Theism 181

> ever to satisfy'. But Hume sees that this agnosticism, when fully thought out, involves total nescience, not merely theological ignorance. (Fraser 1899: 112)

In other words, in thinking about the ultimate questions of our existence and experience, we are driven to scepticism about even the 'mundane' world that daily surrounds us. This is evident in Hume's reworking of themes from the *Treatise* in the first *Enquiry*. Section 4 sets out 'Sceptical Doubts about the Understanding' and Section 5 then offers a 'Sceptical Solution of these Doubts'. This 'solution', however, is not founded in reason. We can uncover no rational principle for supposing that our invariable association of one phenomenon with another is the reflection of a real relationship between them. If we are not to be 'confounded', the best we can do is invoke a quite different kind of principle.

> This principle is CUSTOM or HABIT. For wherever the repetition of any particular act or operation produces a propensity to renew the same act or operation, without being impelled by any reasoning or process of the understanding, we always say, that this propensity is the effect of Custom. By employing that word, we pretend not to have given the ultimate reason of such a propensity. We only point out a principle of human nature. (Hume 1999: 121)

A little later he offers this example from everyday life.

> When I throw a piece of dry wood into a fire, my mind is immediately carried to conceive, that it augments, not extinguishes the flame. This transition of thought from the cause to the effect proceeds not from reason. It derives its origin altogether from custom and experience . . . Here then is a kind of pre-established harmony between the course of nature and the succession of our ideas, and though the powers and forces, by which the former is governed, be wholly unknown to us; yet our thoughts and conceptions have still, we find, gone on in the same train with the other works of nature. Custom is that principle, by which this correspondence has been effected; so necessary to the subsistence of our species, and the regulation of our conduct, in every circumstance and occurrence of human life. (Hume 1999: 129)

But any parallel we may seem to see between 'the course of nature' and 'the succession of our ideas' is not a 'harmony', still less a pre-established one. It is entirely fortuitous, if indeed there is any parallel at all. As Hume observes elsewhere, the mind has a tendency to 'spread itself upon the world', as, for instance, when we see faces in clouds. No one supposes that this succession of ideas reflects or is in harmony with the course of nature, or that it has anything to do with 'the powers and forces' by which the formation of clouds is governed. It is, rather, the result of fanciful imagining. Our belief that the log is fuel for the fire, however, seems of a different order, and not to be dismissed as the outcome of imagination.

It is precisely on this point that Fraser quotes a letter in which Hume himself appears to acknowledge the inadequacy of mere psychological propensity. The propensity to believe in our senses, he says, has to be 'somewhat different from our inclination to find our own figures in the clouds, our faces in the moon, our passions and sentiments even in inanimate matter. For these last may and ought to be controlled, and can never be legitimate ground of assent, or foundations of reasoning' (letter to Gilbert Elliot, March 1751, quoted in Fraser 1899: 119). But what is to 'control' our attributing happiness to the sun or sadness to the moon, if it is not real knowledge of astronomy? The 'principle' of custom and habit of the mind legitimates *whatever* it is we find ourselves believing.

Hume's manner of reasoning, then, results in what Fraser calls 'final scepticism' or 'total nescience'. Of course, as he goes on to observe:

> The scientific agnostic is ready to take the inductive 'leap in the dark' with faith in a natural order assumed to be present in his sense surroundings, not the conclusion of a logical reasoning emptied of all trust and sense of mystery . . . [E]very step in the physical interpretation of the world . . . involves the substitution of indemonstrable trust for complete insight . . . The incoherent agnosticism that retains physical science is not really a protest against faith; it is only an arrest of faith at the point at which faith advances from a narrower to a larger interpretation of life and the universe. (Fraser 1899: 120)

Fraser's reference to 'faith' as trust makes his account of the matter crucially different to a common conception of faith construed as blind belief about the unknowable. The point is not that agnostic scientists have beliefs that they cannot prove or ground in evidence. Rather, they place their trust in the methods of inquiry they use as potentially fruitful in the formulation and testing of hypotheses about the natural world. But by the same token, the scientific materialist must concede that metaphysical inquiry, which requires a similar trust in the intelligibility of the universe, is not blind belief about the unknowable either. Both the scientist and the metaphysician must accept that either '*Homo mensura* or *Nulla mensura*'. What this means is that human knowledge is conditioned by human abilities; we cannot know what we do not have the faculties to know. There may well be angelic beings in the universe, Fraser speculates, who have many more senses than we do. Yet if all their senses are different to our five, what they can know about the universe will not be what we can know, and vice versa. This truth about the conditionality of knowledge, however, gives us no grounds for supposing that neither angels nor humans know anything at all. What this thought experiment shows, and all it shows, is that conditioned knowledge necessarily falls short of omniscience.

It is on this important point that Fraser concludes the first part of his *Philosophy of Theism*. Philosophical Monism seeks the omniscience of 'perfect insight' into the universe, and when inevitably the search fails, the result is a retreat to sceptical agnosticism. Sceptics, we might say, are disappointed Monists. Neither party is willing to embrace human science on the grounds that it is not divine omniscience, unwilling, that is to say, to substitute 'indemonstrable trust' for 'complete insight'. In the remainder of the book, Fraser offers 'the religious conception of the universe, gradually developed in Theistic Faith . . . instead of either Monist speculation or Agnostic despair' (Fraser 1899: 120).

V

The second and third parts of *Philosophy of Theism* undertake this task with the same rigour, care and insight that mark the first part. A key to the argument is the existence of human beings as moral agents, and in the end, philosophical theism is recommended as the only metaphysical conception of the universe that allows us to view our lives as meaningful, and our moral agency with optimism. The argument is cogent, but certainly not conclusive. Fraser does not overestimate its strength, though his final contention is a bold one: 'The extinction of theistic faith is the extinction of reason in man' (Fraser 1899: 331).

For present purposes, however, it is not the force of his argument that is of primary interest, but its relation to the trajectory of Scottish philosophy. Fraser's reaffirmation of philosophical theism constitutes a further 'Scottish chapter in that enduring alternation between agnostic despair and endeavour after perfect insight'. This phrase, quoted earlier, appears in Fraser's biography of Reid. The final chapter of that book charts the place of Reid in relation to nineteenth-century Scottish philosophy, and it does so with a view to answering this question: 'What has modern thought, as developed at the end of the nineteenth century, to say to a Scottish eighteenth century inquiry into human mind that finds its root in a postulated sense of reality, which must be taken as finally authoritative when it is recognised in its genuine integrity?' (Fraser 1898: 144).

This chapter is, to my knowledge, unique in the literature on Reid, perhaps because Fraser was uniquely well placed to write it. He undertook to write the book almost exactly 100 years after the death of Reid, and he had himself lived through seventy-five of those years. Dugald Stewart and Thomas Brown were still alive when Fraser was born; Sir William Hamilton was his teacher and mentor. It was Victor Cousin who first directed his attention to Reid. James Frederick Ferrier was his rival to succeed Hamilton, and though the competition was fierce they remained on familiar terms with each other. James Hutchison Stirling, the author of *The Secret of Hegel*, was a personal friend, and Edward Caird was a respected contemporary in the Chair of Moral Philosophy at Glasgow. All these philosophers are mentioned in Fraser's Scottish retrospective on Reid. It was Stewart who kept Common Sense philosophy in the forefront after Reid's death, until Brown inaugurated a 'revolt against Reid' in the spirit of Hume's associationist psychology. It was Cousin who, in the 1820s, gave Reid new prominence in France, while in Scotland 'the magnificent intellect of Hamilton raised deep questions among us that lay dormant in Reid' (Fraser 1898: 150). Ferrier then raised a second 'revolt' against Reid, this time in the interests of abstract metaphysics. He did so, though, to less effect than Stirling and Caird, whose turn to Hegelianism reflected their dissatisfaction with Reid's psychological inquiry as far too limited an approach to the mysteries of existence that are the proper province of philosophy. It is Fraser's intimate knowledge of philosophy in Scotland over this extended period that enables him to see a connection between the philosophy of Enlightenment Scotland and the varieties of thought that marked nineteenth-century Scottish philosophy. This further enables him to see how the position he articulates and defends in his Gifford Lectures can throw fresh light on Reid.

The Gifford Lectures and the Re-affirmation of Theism

> If Reid's mission was to call attention to our direct mental grasp of outward realities, by exploding a theory which seemed to paralyse that grasp, it would have been his corresponding mission now to justify, in name of the moral and spiritual elements of the common sense, the religious interpretation of the universe, which finds in the facts of matter and man a continuous self-revelation of omnipotent love and mercy. (Fraser 1898: 145)

The times had changed, of course.

> Instead of philosophy at war with common sense, common sense is now alleged as at war with the finally moral and religious conception of the universe, which Reid accepted as conclusive under the premises of an old-fashioned natural theology. Now universal natural law is supposed to exclude God. (Fraser 1898: 145)

Reid's subscription to 'old-fashioned natural theology' is evident from the surviving student notes of the lectures he gave on the subject. In his published works, however, though he invokes God from time to time, he never expressly addresses the question of God's existence, nor makes it a formal part of his argument. Nor is belief in God listed among the principles of Common Sense, and it does not figure in his disagreements with Hume. It is indeed evident that a theistic framework of thought is implicit in the *Inquiry* and *Essays*, but Reid himself thinks that its relevance is indirect. He expressly says so in Essay 2 of the *Intellectual Powers*.

> Shall we say then that this belief [in the creditworthiness of immediate sense experience] is the inspiration of the Almighty? I think this may be said in a good sense; for I take it to be the immediate effect of our constitution, which is the work of the Almighty. But if inspiration be understood to imply a persuasion of its coming from God, our belief of the objects of sense is not inspiration; for a man would believe his senses though he had no notion of a Deity. He who is persuaded that he is the workmanship of God, and that it is a part of his constitution to believe his sense, may think that a good reason to confirm his belief. But he had the belief before he could give this or any other reason for it. (Reid 2002b: 231–2)

Two comments are especially worth making about this passage. First, this is one of the clearest occasions on which Reid eschews metaphysical questions in favour of confining himself to psychological analysis, and the deficiency that nineteenth-century Scottish philosophers came to see in him was precisely this. Second, as Thomas Brown correctly observed, by confining himself in this way, Reid could not ultimately resolve his disagreement with Hume. Hume does not deny that people believe in the creditworthiness of their senses. Indeed, he affirms it. But, as the passage from the first *Enquiry* quoted earlier makes plain, he holds that the principle underlying this is not a principle of reason. It is a purely psychological principle generated by repeated experience and reinforced by custom and habit. It is open to Reid to *assert*, of course, that the creditworthiness of the senses is a *rational* principle, but his claim on this score is not any better grounded than Hume's.

Would a more explicitly theistic metaphysics on Reid's part make a difference? Fraser thinks so, and it is relatively easy to see how this would work. Hume's picture of the mind is essentially mechanical. Impressions cause ideas, and ideas become associated through, for example, conjunction and contiguity. It is in this way that the mind comes to have the beliefs it does. Thus conceived, the mind is simply a belief-forming mechanism. Happily, though fortuitously, beliefs formed in this way often serve the practical interests of the person who holds the belief. Less happily, there is no ground for supposing that beliefs thus formed, even if they sustain successful agency, convey any knowledge of the external world. This is why Hume's conception of the mind seems unable to offer any rational defence against scepticism.

By contrast, Reid's conception of human psychology is essentially teleological. The mind is not merely a mechanism acted upon by causes, but an active device with its own proper function, namely arriving at *true* beliefs about the world and making rational judgements. As a truth-seeking device, the principles in accordance with which the mind acts are productive not merely of beliefs, but of knowledge, and while like any instrument it can malfunction from time to time, 'Truth has an affinity with the human understanding which error hath not' (Reid 2010: 189). When human understanding is functioning properly its success is assured. Why? Because minds are 'the workmanship of God', and have a distinctive 'constitution' that fits them for the world in which they have been placed. If theism is true, there really is a 'pre-established harmony' between mind and world, because both are parts of a universe created and directed by divine purpose.

Between 1796, when Reid died, and 1896, when Fraser published the first edition of his Gifford Lectures, Scottish philosophy had undergone changes so great that Reid's 'Philosophy of Common Sense' (unlike Hume's empiricism) was widely regarded as at best a historical curiosity of little enduring value. This was the view especially of Hegelians such as James Hutchison Stirling, Edward Caird and David Ritchie. Yet Fraser concludes his biography of Reid as follows.

> Of the magnificent Hegelian constructions [Reid] would probably have said what he says of Samuel Clarke's theological demonstration – 'These are the speculations of men of superior genius. But whether they be as solid as they are sublime, or whether they be wanderings of imagination in a region beyond the limit of human understanding, I am unable to determine' . . . Yet Reid, if he were now among us, might find the common sense not superseded but idealised, in the more articulate response of reason in man to the all-pervading active Reason which the later philosopher identifies as his own . . . If we recognise in the Common Sense, and in its underlying Theistic Faith, that without which all our knowledge must dissolve in ignorance, then the faith must be accepted as in reason the final ground of the knowledge . . . In this way a humanised Hegelianism, which seeks to restore or retain the often dormant faith in a perfectly good God, and thus the future of man, may even be taken as in line with Reid, under the altered intellectual conditions at the end of the nineteenth century. (Fraser 1898: 155–9)

The breadth of Fraser's familiarity with the Scottish philosophical tradition, and his decades-long inclination to pursue and sustain it, thus enables him to give a definitive account of the tradition's ultimate integrity. His philosophical biography of Reid reveals that the reaffirmation of philosophical theism contained in his Gifford Lectures is a revitalisation of 'the Scottish answer to Hume' which, at the same time, is able to find common cause between the proponents of Common Sense and the Scottish disciples of Kant and Hegel. By any reckoning, this is no mean achievement.

10

The Culmination of Scottish Philosophy: A. S. Pringle-Pattison

I

Andrew Seth (latterly Seth Pringle-Pattison[1]) occupied the Chair of Logic and Metaphysics at the University of Edinburgh from 1891 to 1919. The Chair itself had a distinguished history. Seth succeeded his teacher Alexander Campbell Fraser, who had himself succeeded his teacher Sir William Hamilton. Together the tenure of these three philosophers in the Edinburgh Logic Chair extended over more than eighty years, and all of them were held in high esteem by their philosophical contemporaries and their students. None of them, however, has attracted much attention in the history of modern philosophy. Even their contribution to the history of philosophy in Scotland is largely overshadowed by the towering figures of the previous century. Alexander Broadie's *History of Scottish Philosophy* (2009) is uniquely comprehensive, yet while his discussion of Hume, Smith and Reid extends to 175 pages, his discussion of Hamilton and Pringle-Pattison is confined to twelve. Fraser (who figured so prominently in the previous chapter) is merely mentioned.

Though Broadie's treatment is modest, wider-ranging histories of philosophy, as could be expected, invariably give these figures even less attention, often none at all. When Hamilton does figure, it is largely as a historical curiosity, notable chiefly as the subject of J. S. Mill's devastating *Examination*, and a figure whose own

---

[1] In 1898 he added Pringle-Pattison to his name as a condition of inheriting a country estate from a distant cousin. For the sake of simplicity I shall ignore this name change in mid-career and generally refer to him in this chapter as Pringle-Pattison. In the bibliography his publications are listed under Seth Pringle-Pattison, including those published before the name change.

work no longer has any interest for contemporary philosophy. The case of Pringle-Pattison is a little different because in several places he has been accorded special status as a forerunner in the development of 'personalism'. The *Stanford Encyclopedia of Philosophy* tells us that in the first half of the twentieth century 'personalism' came to designate a variety of philosophical schools that grew out of a reaction to the de-personalising elements in Enlightenment rationalism, Hegelian Idealism, and materialist psychology. Personalist philosophical systems are so called because they focus on 'the person' as the most fundamental explanatory principle of reality, and the leading representative of British idealistic personalism, the entry goes on to note, was Andrew Seth Pringle-Pattison.[2] This claim is elaborated at slightly greater length in the *Oxford Handbook of British Philosophy in the Nineteenth Century*, where, under the heading of 'Personal Idealism', Pringle-Pattison is allocated a section in the chapter on 'British Idealist Philosophy of Religion'. Broadie is more emphatic. 'Seth was the first of the Scottish, indeed the British, idealists to provide a detailed statement of personalism, and many followed him' (Broadie 2009: 321). David Boucher, in his edited volume *The Scottish Idealists: Selected Philosophical Writings*, takes a slightly modified line. Seth's philosophical contribution to the Scottish Idealists, he says, lay in his exposition of a '[p]ersonal Idealism [that] defended the metaphysical autonomy of personality against both naturalism, which made personality the outcome of nature, and Absolute Idealism, which made personality an "adjective" of the Absolute itself' (Boucher 2004: 77). Similarly, Cairns Craig in his contribution to the *History of Scottish Theology* finds a connection between Pringle-Pattison's 'personal idealism' and the Canadian theologian Lily Dougal (Craig 2019: 199). In *The Unknowable* W. J. Mander says categorically that Pringle-Pattison was 'a vital figure in the development of the Idealist tradition' and 'highly significant as the chief theorist of the Personal Idealists' (Mander 2020: 268–9).

Such unanimity of opinion is impressive, and all these writers can call on good evidence in support of their identifying Pringle-Pattison as a 'personal idealist' if we follow the *Stanford Encyclopedia*'s characterisation. His differences with Enlightenment rationalism, Hegelian Idealism and materialist psychology are

---

[2] See <https://plato.stanford.edu/entries/personalism>.

easily documented. The first receives careful criticism in *Scottish Philosophy* (1885), the second in *Hegelianism and Personality* (1887), and the third in a lengthy essay in *Man's Place in the Cosmos* (1897). However, though these books undoubtedly form an important part of Pringle-Pattison's work, they are by no means all of it. Nor are they properly considered in isolation. His record of publication stretches over almost fifty years from 1883, when he was an Assistant to the Professor of Logic at Edinburgh through his occupancy of Chairs of Logic and Metaphysics first in Wales, then at St Andrews, and finally in Edinburgh. He continued to lecture and write in retirement, and his last book, partly based on the Gifford Lectures he gave in 1923, was published in 1930, just a year before he died. It was only at the start of this long career that Pringle-Pattison could be said to have any great allegiance to Idealism. The earlier works should all be seen as steps in the gradual development of a philosophical position that finds its most extended treatment in his magnum opus, *The Idea of God in the Light of Recent Philosophy* (1917), an earlier set of Gifford Lectures he delivered at the University of Aberdeen and published in 1917. In this major work Pringle-Pattison does comment explicitly on Personal Idealism. But he does so very briefly, only in connection with Pragmatism, and in a tone of detachment. None of the names listed by the *Stanford Encyclopedia* as major figures in the development of Personalism appears in the index.

There is good reason, then, to question the widespread consensus about Pringle-Pattison among the few historians of philosophy who have considered him. In any case, even if there is a historical influence to be traced from Personal Idealism to Personalism more broadly, his role in this narrative must be highly contingent and very limited compared to, say, the French philosopher Charles Renouvier (1815–1903), who coined the term *'personnalisme'*, or Borden Parker Bowne (1884–1953), the founding figure in what became known as 'Boston Personalism'. At most, Pringle-Pattison was a minor causal antecedent of a development that did not mature until almost all his work was complete. Consequently, his contribution to the emergence of personalism, even if of some significance, could not possibly be the reason for the high regard his philosophical work attracted during his lifetime. Since his contemporaries knew nothing of a philosophical trend that had yet to manifest itself, they could hardly praise him for anticipating it. If we are to explain the regard in which Pringle-Pattison's work was held, it must be in terms of his own times, not the times that came after. It is with respect to the philosophical world of which he was a part that a retrospective understanding of his historical importance is to be found.

Where then does his significance lie? G. F. Barbour asks this question in a memoir included in Pringle-Pattison's *Balfour Lectures on Realism*, posthumously published by Blackwood's in 1933. Somewhat tentatively, Barbour offers an assessment that does not mention personalism.

> It is too soon . . . to assess the rank which the books of Pringle-Pattison may finally hold among the philosophical writings of his time. He himself assuredly made no claim to rank among the *di majores* of philosophy . . . Yet the value of his work will assuredly extend beyond his own generation, and even that of those who learned from him. It summarized, *and in some sense brought to a close*, a development of two centuries in Scottish philosophy. (Seth Pringle-Pattison 1933: 157–8, emphasis added)

The purpose of this chapter is to demonstrate, in accordance with this assessment, that placing Pringle-Pattison in the context of two centuries of Scottish philosophy is both more accurate and more illuminating than classifying him among the ranks of early Personalists. As I shall try to show in what follows, there is indeed a sense in which Pringle-Pattison brought Scottish philosophy to a close.

II

Pringle-Pattison's first significant publication appeared in a volume entitled *Essays in Philosophical Criticism* that he edited with R. B. Haldane, and to which he contributed the opening essay – 'Philosophy as Criticism of Categories'. This essay is a detailed examination, and criticism, of Kant. Some features of it will be returned to, but at this point it is sufficient to note that Pringle-Pattison sees in Kant a brilliant philosophical development that enables us to escape the metaphysical captivity of both idealist and materialist dualism. Nevertheless, it is a development that is incomplete as it stands. The essay does not mention Hegel, who for Edward Caird and others provided the materials for this completion, but it does end with an affirmation that has a decidedly Hegelian ring. 'True metaphysics lies, as we have tried to show, in that criticism of experience which aims at developing out of the material of science and of life the completed notion of experience itself' (Seth Pringle-Pattison and Haldane 1883: 40).

Four years later, in *Hegelianism and Personality*, his second set of Balfour Lectures, Pringle-Pattison made clear his reservations about Hegelian or Absolute Idealism, and in effect removed himself from the group of young Scottish Idealist philosophers whose enthusiasm for Hegel had given rise to *Essays in Philosophical Criticism*. This group included D. G. Ritchie, latterly Professor of Logic and Metaphysics at St Andrews, and Ritchie tellingly began his review of *Hegelianism and Personality* (in the journal *Mind*) with the words *Et tu, Brute!* He goes on:

> The kindly rehabilitation of Reid in Prof. Seth's first series of Balfour Lectures and the suggestions in their concluding paragraph of problems unsatisfactorily treated by Hegelianism had hardly prepared us for the fierce blows here bestowed upon the 'Neo-Kantians'. But, though at first one is apt to think this attack by a friend of Idealism 'the most unkindest cut of all,' yet undoubtedly the most valuable of criticisms is that made by someone who has himself seen from inside the position he is criticising. Not only does Prof. Seth express in the strongest terms his own 'great personal obligations to Hegel' (p. 229), but he has in an eloquent passage (p. 59) spoken of the feelings experienced by those who have lived through the phase of thought represented by the Idealism of Fichte or of the late Prof. Green ... Seth rejects Kant's own retention of 'things-in-themselves,' as unknowable [but] neither will he now accept the system of idealism reared upon Kant's foundation. (Ritchie 1888b: 256)

Ritchie's reference to Seth's 'kindly rehabilitation of Reid' is notable. Thomas Reid's three major works were published between 1764 and 1788 and were hugely influential for a time, constituting a sort of philosophical orthodoxy in the Scottish universities. Almost sixty years after the last of the three was published, they were gathered together in a collected edition, edited, and heavily annotated, by Sir William Hamilton. If Hamilton meant his editorial labours to secure a renewed and enduring place for Reid in the world of philosophy, he was too late. By 1846, when Hamilton's edition was published, Reid's star was no longer in the philosophical firmament. Following the death of Thomas Brown in 1820, Scottish philosophy was quite widely regarded as moribund, and Hamilton himself had been hailed as the great force that brought it back to life.³ This was not because of his devotion to Reid, however. Indeed, some thought that for a man with his gifts, Hamilton's labours on Reid were largely wasted. This view was stated more or less explicitly by James Ferrier, who began his very lengthy review of the newly published *Collected Works* with a decidedly backhanded compliment.

> Although Dr Reid does not stand in the very highest rank of philosophers, this incomparable edition of his works goes far to redress his deficiencies . . . It is probable that the book derives much of its excellence from the very imperfections of its textual author. Had Reid been a more learned man he might have failed to elicit the unparalleled erudition of his editor; had he been a clearer and closer thinker, Sir William Hamilton's vigorous logic and speculative acuteness would probably have found a narrower field for their display. (Ferrier 1883: 407)

In the remainder of the review Hamilton's 'speculative acuteness' is left aside. Ferrier's focus is on the philosophical destruction of Reid, and his very negative estimate, together with the language in which it is expressed, outraged some people, as his unsuccessful candidature to succeed Hamilton in the Edinburgh Chair of Logic and Metaphysics showed.⁴ However, the rejection of Reid, and of Dugald Stewart, had begun much earlier and at the hands of Stewart's successor Thomas Brown. So while Ferrier may have stated the case against Reid with unusual forcefulness, he was in fact giving expression to a philosophical assessment that was quite widely held. By the 1840s, the appeal to 'Common Sense' as an argument against scepticism and atheism had lost any of the sophistication with which Reid may have made it, and become closely identified with the 'vulgar' version endorsed by an anti-intellectual mindset that was closed to philosophy. In a chapter entitled 'Philosophy before Ferrier's Day', his biographer Elizabeth Haldane voices this widely held belief when she describes the appeal to Common Sense as a 'relapse into a self-satisfied indolence of mind'.

> What, then, was the work which Ferrier placed before himself when he commenced to write and teach philosophy? He was thoroughly and entirely dissatisfied with the old point of view, the point of view of the 'common-sense' school of metaphysicians . . . 'Common-sense' – an attribute with which we all believe we are in some measure

---

³ See Chapter 2.
⁴ See Chapter 3.

endowed – explains everything if we simply exercise it, and that is open to us all ... We are all acquainted with this talk in speculative regions of knowledge, but we most of us know how disastrous it is to any true advancement in such directions. What happens now is just what happened in the eighteenth century. Men relapse into a self-satisfied indolence of mind: in religion they are content with believing in a sort of general divine beneficence which will somehow make matters straight; and in philosophy they are guided by their instincts, which teach them that what they wish to believe is true. (E. Haldane 1899: 49)

If Haldane has properly captured the degree to which the philosophy of Reid and 'common-sense' was dismissed by Ferrier's time, and which subsequently led Scotland's philosophers to embrace the Idealism of Kant and Hegel, then Pringle-Pattison's 'rehabilitation of Reid' was courageously swimming against the philosophical tide. Moreover, the subtitle that he gave his first set of Balfour Lectures – 'A Comparison of the Scottish and German Answers to Hume' – signalled a rehabilitation not just of Reid, but of Scottish philosophy more broadly. Even without the criticisms voiced in *Hegelianism and Personality*, then, placing the Scottish answer to Hume alongside the German immediately puts an important distance between Pringle-Pattison and the Scottish Idealists with whom he has generally been classified. For them, there was no Scottish answer to Hume. Germany has left Reid and his proponents behind. That explains why, according to his students, the leading Idealist, Edward Caird, never made reference to any Scottish philosophical name later than David Hume. For Caird, Reid and 'Common Sense' held no philosophical interest whatsoever.

Pringle-Pattison's rehabilitation of Reid swims against this tide, but he explicitly separates Reid's account of the essential principles of knowledge from 'the nomenclature he adopts'.

[I]t may be admitted from the outset, that the name 'Principles of Common Sense' is unfortunate on account of its misleading associations – associations which have been strengthened rather than weakened by the unguarded utterances of its champions. The term is misleading because it confounds philosophy and life ... So far as a philosophy ... abolishes distinctions and principles that are actually present in life – we must agree with Reid that such a system is 'at war with the common-sense of mankind.' We must conclude that it is an inadequate, one-sided, and therefore fallacious system. But though philosophy is thus ultimately to be judged by its accordance with life, the two must always remain essentially separate. They move on different plains. Life, whether knowing or doing, is a direct process . . . Philosophy is a reflection upon life – a process wholly secondary and indirect . . . We may do without philosophy, if we will; but we cannot make common-sense, in the ordinary acceptation of the term, take its place and do its work. (Seth Pringle-Pattison 1885: 106–7)

Pringle-Pattison, unlike Ferrier, is able to look beyond the terminology of 'common-sense' and find a deeper and more properly philosophical element in Reid. He thereby distinguishes between Scottish philosophy, as inaugurated by Reid, and 'the philosophy of common-sense', as expounded by Reid's misguided followers. Even with this distinction in mind, however, he has criticisms that accord in part with Ferrier. 'Reid's properly philosophical positions', he observes, are nevertheless 'imbedded in a mass of irrelevant psychological matter-of-fact' and this 'obscures their bearing and impairs their force' (Pringle-Pattison 1885: 124). Still, in the end, Reid's response to Hume, though unsatisfactory, is superior to Kant's because, for all its unclarity, it resists what Reid calls 'the way of ideas', and what became known more generally as 'representationalism', the presumption that the mind's apprehension of reality is mediated by mental representations. For all his innovative brilliance, according to Pringle-Pattison, Kant ultimately failed to escape the presumption of representationalism. His first *Critique* is impressive in its abstraction and its scope. Nevertheless, it continues to operate within the dualism of Hume's 'impressions' and 'ideas'. So, if by the Scottish 'answer' to Hume we mean Reid, and if by the German 'answer' we mean Kant, then a satisfactory answer to Hume is still awaited. In the case of Germany, Kant's philosophical endeavours had found an influential successor – Hegel. It was to Hegel that the Scottish Idealists appealed, so it was natural for Pringle-Pattison to turn his attention there in the second set of Balfour Lectures.

III

Thanks to his postgraduate studies in Germany, Pringle-Pattison was fluent in German and had an extensive knowledge of German philosophy (and psychology). This enabled him to trace Hegel's origins in Kant, through the neo-Kantianism of Fichte and Schelling.

He finds, and endorses, certain key insights in Hegel. First, as he argued in the early essay on 'Philosophy as Criticism of Categories', the purpose of philosophy is to undertake 'a systematic survey of our conceptions [that] enables us to estimate the significance of each single conception aright, and prevents us from putting it to work for which it is inadequate or unfit . . . the "truer" categories . . . give a more adequate account of the ultimate reality of things' (Seth Pringle-Pattison 1887: 86). Second, 'nothing is more essential than to be on our guard against the seductive simplification of facts which consists in their reduction to simpler categories . . . The explanation by reduction to simpler categories is . . . an abstract account [that is] true so far as it goes, but not the whole truth, and consequently false if put forward as such' (Seth Pringle-Pattison 1887: 87–8). Thirdly, and most importantly, 'Nothing can be more certain than that all philosophical explanation must be explanation of the lower by the higher, and not vice versa; and if self-consciousness is the highest fact we know, then we are justified in using the conception of self-consciousness as our best key to the ultimate nature of existence as a whole' (Seth Pringle-Pattison 1887: 89).

Hegel himself, Pringle-Pattison claims, goes far beyond what his key insights warrant. In particular, he suppresses the role of experience in the interests of presenting his philosophy as a deductive system in which logic takes the place of experience. But, though Hegel presents everything as a grand logical synthesis within which (in accordance with his famous slogan) the reality of things is supposedly grounded in their rationality, the truth is that the elements that are systematised must have first been obtained 'by an ordinary process of reflection upon the facts which are the common property of every thinker' (Seth Pringle-Pattison 1887: 90). This emphasis upon the facts of experience, and the tendency of Absolute Idealism to suppress them in the name of 'Logic', is what leads Pringle-Pattison to his disagreement with the British Idealists.

> The radical error both of Hegelianism and of the allied English doctrine I take to be the identification of the human and the divine self-consciousness, or, to put it more broadly, the unification of consciousness in a single Self. This identification or unification depends throughout . . . upon the tendency to take a mere form for a real being – to take an identity of type for a unity of existence. Each of us is a Self . . . We are not mere objects existing only for others, but as it were, subject

and object in one. Selfhood may also be said to imply that, in one aspect of my existence, I am universal, seeing that I distinguish my individual existence from that of other beings, while embracing both within a common world ... There could be no interaction between individuals, unless they were all embraced within one reality; still less could there be any knowledge by one individual of others if they did not all form parts of one system of things. But it is a great step further to say that this universal attitude of the Self, as such, is due to the fact that it is one universal Self that thinks in all so-called thinkers. This is, to say the least, an extremely unfortunate way of stating the necessities of the case ... [T]hough selfhood involves a duality in unity, it is nonetheless true that each Self is a unique existence which is perfectly *impervious* ... The unity of things (which is not denied) cannot be properly expressed by making it depend upon a unity of the Self in all thinkers; for the very characteristic of a self is its exclusiveness. (Seth Pringle-Pattison 1887: 215–17, emphasis original)

Read together, *Scottish Philosophy* and *Hegelianism and Personality* set the parameters for Pringle-Pattison's subsequent philosophical writings. These parameters may be stated as follows. First, philosophical understanding seeks a unified explanation of experience. Consequently, any form of metaphysical dualism constitutes failure. Second, philosophical explanation must avoid any form of reductionism; explaining *away* is not explaining. Consequently, an explanation must be capable of accommodating every fact of experience if it is to be considered satisfactory. Thirdly, reductionist explanation results from every attempt to explain the 'higher' in terms of the 'lower'. Consequently, the proper order of explanation must be the other way around.

Given these parameters, it is easy to understand the general direction of Pringle-Pattison's subsequent writings and to place many of them within the philosophical programme he was pursuing. Thus, in *Man's Place in the Cosmos*,[5] the very lengthy essay on 'The "New" Psychology and Automatism' seeks at one and the same time to acknowledge the significant advances made within the sphere of experimental psychology, and to identify the categorial boundaries that these advances have tempted its proponents to

---

[5] It is on the second edition of this collection that the name Pringle-Pattison first appears.

exceed. It is as much a mistake on the part of the 'new' psychology as of the old to reduce the phenomenon of 'will' to that of 'feeling' in order to secure a theoretical unity, since this flies in the face of fact. The equally lengthy essay that follows, a review of Bradley's *Appearance and Reality* entitled 'A New Theory of the Absolute', resists the elimination of experience in the name of the 'intellectual necessities of all-inclusiveness and internal harmony'. 'Our idea of what the Absolute must be', Pringle-Pattison concludes, 'must be founded on the ideal necessities which our nature compels us to acknowledge.' These are 'not merely intellectual; they are aesthetical, ethical and religious as well' (Seth Pringle-Pattison 1897a: 225).

These two essays reveal Pringle-Pattison's extensive knowledge of and facility in both empirical psychology, especially the innovative work being done in Germany, and the Idealism dominant in British philosophy. But they also show the independence of his thought from either of these, as he sought a philosophical position that would do what Ferrier and others thought could not be done – combine the results of psychology and conclusions of metaphysics in a unified understanding of human existence and experience. He explicitly sets out the necessity of this in 'The Present Position of the Philosophical Sciences' (reprinted in *Man's Place in the Cosmos*), the inaugural lecture he gave on assuming the Chair of Logic and Metaphysics at Edinburgh in succession to Alexander Campbell Fraser. Having observed that the philosophical systems of the past should be taught and criticised in such a way that they 'become so many stepping-stones on which we rise to fuller and clearer insight', he identifies two features that 'a true philosophy' must have. 'The first is the necessity of a teleological view of the universe' as against a reductive materialism. The second is to rank human agency as the highest form of existence, not as a Hegelian 'world-spirit' or 'the abstraction of the race', but in the individual, and thus to regard 'love and self-denial, purity and stainless honour' as both having 'a root in the nature of things' and at the same time giving us 'our nearest glimpse into the nature of the divine' (Seth Pringle-Pattison 1897a: 60–3).

Using the history of philosophy as a source of 'stepping-stones', resolutely adopting a teleological perspective, and treating the highest forms of human endeavour and experience as a 'glimpse into the nature of the divine' is precisely what he aimed to do in *The Idea of God in the Light of Recent Philosophy*, his first set of Gifford Lectures, delivered at the University of Aberdeen in 1912–13, and published in 1917.

IV

As might be expected from the outcome of over thirty years' reflection, Pringle-Pattison's *The Idea of God in the Light of Recent Philosophy* is an exceptionally rich work, and though it has been out of print for many years, it bears close reading and rereading. For present purposes, however, it is sufficient to highlight some of its leading themes and features. The book begins with Hume, proceeds to Kant and then considers the century-long duel between the philosophical naturalism to which Hume gives influential expression and the philosophical Idealism that springs from Kant. Into this debate, Pringle-Pattison introduces what he describes as 'the liberating influence of biology'. The importance of this liberation is twofold. First, it shows that the most advanced and careful empirical inquiry, while undoubtedly conducted in the spirit of Hume, results in a vindication of teleological explanation. It thus shows how improper any ambition to explain all natural phenomena mechanistically is, which is to say, explanation confined to efficient causes or 'matter in motion'. Secondly, empirical biology opens the way to the formulation of a 'higher' naturalism, one that takes full account of the spiritual dimension of human agency and experience without any questionable recourse to a metaphysical 'supernatural' realm distinct from and opposed to the 'natural'.

This 'higher naturalism' presents the best prospect of arriving at a coherent, comprehensive and inclusive philosophy within which 'reality' is not an abstraction from experience, as so-called 'scientific' conceptions generally are. Rather, thinking in terms of 'higher naturalism' offers an intellectual understanding that integrates all the facts of human experience, not merely perceptual, but cognitive, emotional and volitional, and combines them with a full acknowledgement of our organic being as evolved creatures within the natural world. Hitherto, philosophical systems have tended to invoke an opposition between 'mind' and 'nature'. The materialist takes nature to be fundamental, and so construes 'the mental' as an epiphenomenal by-product of physical and biological processes. The mentalist takes 'mind' to be fundamental, and so construes the physical world to be a projection of 'ideas'. Neither can ultimately explain or justify the preference it gives to one side of the nature/mind dichotomy; neither can do justice to the facts of human experience; and neither can accommodate the huge scientific advance that Darwinian biology has made.

Against this background, which is set out in the first six lectures, Pringle-Pattison goes on to examine a number of philosophical distinctions – between positivism and agnosticism, idealism and pan-psychism, idealism and mentalism, the absolute and the finite. His aim again and again is to overcome false dualities by resisting reductionism in one form or another. It leads him, in due course, to consider certain religious concepts more directly, and ultimately, of course, given the intention of the Gifford Lectures and the title of the book, the idea of God.

It is not the purpose of this chapter to trace the steps of his argument or assess its merits, though this would be an interesting and probably profitable task. Rather, it remains to ask about his relationship to Scottish philosophy and whether Barbour, his biographer, was right is surmising that Pringle-Pattison 'summarized, and in some sense brought to a close, a development of two centuries in Scottish philosophy'. In terms of summary, we might start with the observation that many of the philosophers who figured prominently in the debates of the Scottish philosophers – Aristotle, Berkeley, Locke, Hume, Reid, Hamilton, Ferrier, Kant, Hegel, Mill – are to be found in the index of *The Idea of God*, with multiple entries in several cases. Some Scottish names are notable for their absence – Hutcheson, Kames, Smith and Ferguson, for instance. But despite the close connection between metaphysics and moral philosophy that was a prominent feature of Scottish philosophy, none of these figures contributed much to the philosophical debates with which Pringle-Pattison was principally concerned. The question of summarising, though, extends beyond this. More substantial support for Barbour's contention is to be found in the sustained way in which Pringle-Pattison draws on what he finds to be strengths and insights on opposing sides of the debates that had taken place within Scotland (and further afield), and he does so by uncovering and pursuing the philosophical issues that had animated those debates. Anyone reading *The Idea of God* who was ignorant of the history of Scottish philosophy since Hume would, knowingly or not, have remedied that ignorance by the end of the book. So we may safely conclude, I think, that Pringle-Pattison did effectively summarise two centuries of Scottish philosophical debate.

The question of bringing Scottish philosophy to a close is more complex. What exactly would this mean? It obviously cannot mean that the problems with which the Scottish philosophers had been concerned over a long time were settled, in the sense that no further discussion was needed or even possible. Philosophical problems are not of this nature, as Pringle-Pattison himself points out on several occasions. They are perennial, and must occur to human beings whenever they begin to reflect on the nature and meaning of existence, at any historical point or geographical location. Nor can it mean that, as a matter of history, philosophical conversation in Scotland drew to a close, since this is obviously false. Nevertheless, in order to make sense of the idea of a tradition of philosophical thought culminating, we must identify something of both these elements; culmination implies both fulfilment *and* termination. The question is not whether it is possible to identify a point at which debate and inquiry stop, but whether, within continuing debate and inquiry, one line of thought that has had a long innings is acknowledged as, somehow, having reached a point at which it has said all that it has to say. Accordingly, to say that Scottish philosophy culminated in Pringle-Pattison is to say that in *The Idea of God* he developed the line of philosophical thought that sprang from Reid as far as it could be developed. To argue this convincingly, however, more needs to be said about the philosophical tradition which drew to a close with his reflections. Forty years before Pringle-Pattison's magnum opus was published, James McCosh had lamented the end of 'The Scottish Philosophy' in his book of that name. For McCosh, the distinguishing marks of Scottish philosophy were these. It was inductive. That is to say, it relied on observations arising from experience, and not on self-evident logical principles such as the law of non-contradiction, from which all metaphysical truths might be derived. Further, though it laid special emphasis on the observations of self-consciousness, it was open to obtaining relevant material from the investigations of the natural sciences. Finally, and most importantly, its philosophical conclusions rested on principles which, while obtained through experience, were properly thought of as metaphysical, because without them that experience would be unintelligible.

McCosh thought that the mediating ground Reidian Scottish philosophy strove to occupy had gradually been eroded by a radical division between the philosophers of Scotland. On the one side were those, like Bain, for whom empirical observation and experiment was separate from and a necessary preliminary to any worthwhile metaphysics. On the other were those, like Ferrier, for whom metaphysics was an entirely a priori 'science', indifferent to whatever facts experimental psychology might reveal. In his inaugural lecture, Pringle-Pattison remarks on the division that McCosh highlights.

> It is not so long since contempt for Psychology was current in the leading idealistic school of this country. The horror of the true-blue experimentalist for what he calls 'metaphysics' was amply repaid by the tone of condescension and indifference which the idealists adopted towards 'empirical psychology.' Misled by a name, they visited upon the head of an unoffending science the inadequacies of Empiricism as a philosophical theory. Because the chief cultivators of psychology in England had been of the Empiricist persuasion, and had frequently confounded the limits of psychology and metaphysics, the transcendentalists tabooed the science as beneath the notice of a philosopher. Hence a state of unnatural division and mutual distrust – a distrust rooted in both cases largely in ignorance. (Seth Pringle-Pattison 1897a: 45–6)

Pringle-Pattison's concept of 'higher naturalism' is expressly intended to transcend that 'unnatural division and mutual distrust' by articulating an informed and reflective rejection of both these alternatives as 'one-sided'. It may thus be said to recover the mediating ground that McCosh thought had been lost. Somewhat surprisingly, Pringle-Pattison, who must have known of McCosh, does not reference him in any of his writings, not even in the two lectures on theism that he delivered at the inauguration of Princeton University, an event widely regarded as the ultimate (though posthumous) fruit of McCosh's twenty-year presidency of the College of New Jersey.[6] Nevertheless, his mature philosophical position meets all the criteria McCosh specifies as those of 'the Scottish philosophy'. Pringle-Pattison is thus more successful than his Scottish predecessors in his attempt to frame a philosophical explanation of experience, but unlike his Scottish contemporaries he has persisted along the same lines rather than turning in a quite different direction.

---

[6] McCosh, no less oddly, makes no mention of Pringle-Pattison (whom he could only have known as 'Andrew Seth'). When he identifies continuing representatives of Scottish philosophy, he names Seth's Edinburgh contemporaries Henry Calderwood and Robert Flint but he does not mention Seth himself.

But why should this bring things to a close? Since nothing in philosophy is ever finally settled, why should Pringle-Pattison's accomplishment, however impressive, not become another of the 'many stepping-stones on which we rise to fuller and clearer insight'? The answer is that there is no logical barrier against the possibility of someone treating it in this way. It simply is the fact that no one did. That contingency is ultimately what warrants the claim that Pringle-Pattison's mature thought was the culmination of Scottish philosophy; it brought to it a new level of philosophical sophistication while at the same time bringing it to a close.

Any further explanation must appeal to cultural and institutional factors. When commenting in his inaugural lecture on the division and distrust that had hitherto soured relations between psychology and metaphysics, Pringle-Pattison added immediately, 'Today the situation is greatly changed.' Perhaps that was true as far as the distrust was concerned, yet a still deeper division between empirical study and philosophical inquiry took hold in Scottish universities. This was true not only with respect to the study of mind, but in the pursuit of other subject areas that had hitherto been the province of moral philosophy. Over time the universities created separate Chairs and Departments of political science, economics, sociology, anthropology and literary criticism. The beginnings of this wider development can be found long before the period to which Pringle-Pattison is referring. Literary criticism began as the study of 'rhetoric', a responsibility of the Professor of Logic in most places, but led to the creation of a separate Chair as early as 1762.[7] The social sciences had their origins in Hume, Smith and Adam Ferguson. When Dugald Stewart succeeded Ferguson in the Chair of Moral Philosophy at Edinburgh, he began the teaching of political economy. Chalmers introduced political economy at St Andrews in the 1820s and Ferrier continued it.

Developments beyond the Scottish universities were also significant in bringing Scottish philosophy to an end. Improved travel and communication broke down the relative isolation of Scotland's educational institutions. As the number and size of universities in England and Wales expanded rapidly, the universities of Scotland became part of a much larger academic network, and a series of

---

[7] See Chapter 5.

reforming Acts brought them more into line with the widespread changes that were taking place. These changes included the intentional advancement of natural sciences as university subjects. The result of the expansion of institutions and more highly differentiated subject areas was that the acknowledged scope of metaphysics and the philosophy of mind narrowed. Philosophy in the universities gradually lost the centrality it had previously enjoyed and became just one subject among many.

One further change was of great importance. Scottish philosophy's most brilliant graduates were often compelled to find teaching positions outside Scotland. Some did return to Scotland, but they brought with them a much expanded academic perspective. Pringle-Pattison himself took a position in Wales until one opened up in Scotland. His brother James Seth taught in the United States for several years before returning to Edinburgh, as did Norman Kemp Smith. A. A. Bowman was a colleague of Kemp Smith's in Princeton before returning to Glasgow. D. G. Ritchie spent many years in Oxford before the Chair of Logic and Metaphysics at St Andrews became vacant. The movement went the other way as well, and A. D. Lindsay followed the familiar path from Glasgow to Balliol before returning to Glasgow as Professor of Moral Philosophy. But he only held the Chair for two years before returning to Oxford. W. R. Sorley followed a similar path. On the strength of his undergraduate performance at Edinburgh, he won the Shaw Philosophical Fellowship available to Scottish graduates and went to Trinity College, Cambridge. Having succeeded Andrew Seth as Professor of Logic and Philosophy at Cardiff, he then returned to Scotland as Regius Professor of Moral Philosophy at the University of Aberdeen. Just six years later, however, he went back to Cambridge as Knightbridge Professor in succession to Henry Sidgwick. This 'flow' of the next generation of leading philosophical thinkers set them far apart from the relatively circumscribed university world of, for instance, Hamilton, Ferrier, Bain, Tulloch, Calderwood and Veitch.

Around the turn of the twentieth century, there was a notable shift in British philosophical fashion. The Idealism that had been in the ascendant was displaced by logical empiricism. Against the background of university reform and integration and the 'flow' of academics, it seems impossible that the Scottish universities should have remained immune to this change. At any event, Pringle-Pattison's project of framing a philosophical theory of existence within the parameters that Scottish philosophy had hitherto observed simply found no new protagonists. On the strength of his arguments in *The Idea of God*, we may say that he brought new cogency to Scottish philosophy, if by that we mean the approach to philosophical problems inherited from Hume and Reid. But on purely historical grounds, we may also say that his work marked the end of a distinctive Scottish philosophy and thus brought its history to a close.

11

John Macmurray and the Self as Agent

I

Chapter 10 concluded with the claim that Andrew Seth Pringle-Pattison brought the Scottish philosophical tradition to a close. This contention is not universally accepted. Though there has been little discussion of the issue, a few commentators have extended the tradition considerably past this point by identifying John Macmurray (1891–1976) as a representative of Scottish philosophy. All the philosophers considered in previous chapters, even those who lived into the twentieth century, were essentially products of nineteenth-century Scotland. Macmurray, by contrast, was a philosopher of the twentieth century. What he does have in common with, for example, Hamilton, Bain, Ferrier and Caird is the fact that, having been acclaimed in his own time, his copious publications have been remarkably neglected by both contemporary philosophical discussion and the history of philosophy. Accordingly, this final chapter has a twofold purpose. First, in light of the conclusion of the previous chapter, it will aim to identify Macmurray's relation to the Scottish philosophical tradition. Second, in the course of doing so, it will try to recover something of his significance as a thinker.

According to Alexander Broadie in *A History of Scottish Philosophy*, it is a mistake to confuse the Scottish philosophical tradition with the 'Scottish School of Common Sense'.

> Scottish philosophy is a good deal wider than the school of common sense philosophy. I am speaking here of a long tradition of philosophizing traceable back to the thirteenth century ... As regards the Scottish philosophical tradition the first major thinker was Duns Scotus ... His philosophical successors of the Pre-Reformation period, especially John Mair, were philosophically very close to him ... and ... it may reasonably be supposed that when Mair taught at Glasgow ... and St Andrews ... his interest in Scotus's philosophy was on display. Mair's persistent reference to Scotus as *conterraneus*, my fellow countryman,

indicates his sense of closeness to the earlier man . . . [W]ith the arrival in Scotland of the Reformation and renaissance humanism, philosophy in Scotland, as elsewhere in Europe, went through a process of renewal . . . The brilliant philosophy contributed by Scots [during the eighteenth century] to the great western philosophical project did not come from nowhere, appearing in Scotland as if by miracle, but on the contrary was a continuation of a long tradition of Scottish philosophizing. (Broadie 2009: 4–5)

The continuation of this tradition did not cease at the Enlightenment, Broadie thinks, but extended well into the nineteenth century, and beyond. His treatment of the nineteenth century, however, is rather less surefooted than that of the medieval and Enlightenment periods. With the exception of James Ferrier and Andrew Seth Pringle-Pattison, most of the prominent figures in later nineteenth-century Scottish philosophy are barely mentioned. Alexander Bain receives a page, there are two brief references to Alexander Campbell Fraser, Edward Caird, the doyen of the Scottish Idealists, is just one in a list of names, and John Veitch, James Hutchison Stirling and Henry Calderwood do not appear in the index. Yet, despite this significant hiatus, Broadie continues the history of Scottish philosophy into the twentieth century, and concludes with John Macmurray, Professor of Moral Philosophy at the University of Edinburgh from 1945 to 1961. Indeed, he devotes more pages to Macmurray than he does to Ferrier and Pringle-Pattison combined.

This calls for some explanation because it sits rather ill with the facts. In the final decades of the nineteenth century, philosophy in Scotland, both in the universities and among the public at large, was exceptionally vibrant. Alexander Bain established the highly successful journal *Mind*, and a stream of philosophical books were authored by philosophers in Scotland, many of them issued by Scottish publishers, notably William Blackwood and Sons in Edinburgh and James MacLehose and Sons in Glasgow. Early in the new century, however, things seemed to falter. The entry on 'Scottish Philosophy' in the *Oxford Companion to Philosophy* concurs with Broadie in reaching back to Scotus and Mair, but it shares James McCosh's view that, thanks to 'the poisonous seeds of idealism' imported from Germany in the late nineteenth century, the tradition of Scottish philosophy could only 'linger' for a short time as the new century unfolded (Honderich 1995: 815). If this is true,

John Macmurray, who left Scotland in 1913 and did not return for more than thirty years, can hardly be seen to be continuing a tradition of philosophising that had more or less died out.

On the other hand, it should be said, Broadie's contention is not an eccentric one. Cairns Craig, in the opening editorial of the *Journal of Scottish Thought*, describes Macmurray as a thinker 'steeped in Scottish traditions' (Craig 2007: ii), and explains the fact that the journal's first issue devotes half its pages to Macmurray in terms of the 'continuities within Scottish thought' (xix) which it was the new journal's founding purpose to promote. Since the time of Macmurray's death in 1976, however, only a very modest secondary literature has been generated. There is no entry for Macmurray in the *Stanford Encyclopedia of Philosophy*, his name never appears in contemporary philosophy journals, and the number of books devoted to him is tiny. Nevertheless, most of the little that has been published agrees with Broadie and Craig in identifying him as a 'Scottish philosopher'. That is how Wikipedia categorises him, and there is indeed a historical basis for this identification. Macmurray was born and raised in Scotland. He graduated from the University of Glasgow, and joined the long line of Snell Exhibitioners (including Adam Smith and Edward Caird) who went from Glasgow to study at Balliol College, Oxford. There his tutor was another Scottish-born and Scottish-educated philosopher, A. D. Lindsay, subsequently Professor of Moral Philosophy at Glasgow. After holding academic positions in South Africa and London, Macmurray was appointed Professor of Moral Philosophy at Edinburgh, a post that he held from 1945 to 1961. In 1953–4 he joined the company of many Scottish philosophers when he delivered two sets of Gifford Lectures at the University of Glasgow, and he duly published carefully revised versions of these lectures in 1957 and 1961. In addition to this substantial biographical connection with philosophy in Scotland, some emphasis has been laid on the fact that, during his time in Edinburgh, he was regarded as pursuing a strand of philosophical thought quite different to the analytic school focused on logic and language that came to dominate philosophy in Britain at that time.

Are these facts enough to warrant the classification 'Scottish philosopher'? Do they secure him a place in the Scottish philosophical tradition as Broadie and Craig depict it? In addressing these questions Esther McIntosh expresses some ambivalence.

> Insofar as Macmurray's philosophy strives to explain the human condition and the means to live well, it is entirely consonant with the

> Scottish philosophy that preceded him ... Nevertheless, it is also the case that Macmurray comes after and does not engage directly with the most famous tension in Scottish philosophy; namely, the Enlightenment debate between Hume's scepticism and Reid's 'School of Common Sense' ... [I]t is reaction against this debate that sees the rise of Scottish Idealism, which, through Caird, promotes the educational role of moral philosophy that informs Macmurray's ideas on the subject ... Consequently, in an effort to maintain the Scottish conception of humane philosophy, Macmurray attempts to hold out against linguistic philosophy. (McIntosh 2015: 300)

Viewed in this way, Macmurray's relationship to Scottish philosophy, it seems fair to say, is somewhat tangential. Moreover, it is also purely functional. McIntosh's contention speaks only to the educational role that Macmurray attributed to philosophy. It has nothing to do with the content of his philosophy, or how the arguments he used and the views he expressed and defended related to philosophical debates in Scotland at an earlier period.

In support of McIntosh's contention, there is the fact that across Macmurray's extensive writings there are just a few scattered references to Hume, and none at all to Reid, Smith, Brown, Ferrier or Bain. Yet, though this seems to count decisively against Craig's description of him as a thinker 'steeped in Scottish traditions', it is possible to find a deeper connection than McIntosh detects between the content of Macmurray's philosophy and the debates in Scottish philosophy that preceded him. Whether or not he was consciously aware of the connection, Macmurray's major works do indeed engage philosophically with 'the most famous tension in Scottish philosophy'. Moreover, a case can be made for regarding this engagement as constituting a highly innovative step in the resolution of the tension. If this is true, as I hope to show, then whether or not to classify Macmurray as a 'Scottish philosopher' seems a secondary matter. It is certainly of less interest than this question: in what way, if any, does Macmurray's 'personalism' bear on the issues that animated Scottish philosophy in the eighteenth and nineteenth centuries?

II

There is no doubt that Macmurray's major philosophical work is to be found in the two volumes of Gifford Lectures that he published under the title *The Form of the Personal*. It is generally agreed that, for those already familiar with his writings, the lectures contained no great novelties. Nevertheless, they constitute the most sustained and mature version of views that he had previously expressed in his many publications, in addition to radio broadcasts that attracted large audiences for over a decade.

The first of these volumes is *The Self as Agent*, and its opening chapter is entitled 'The Crisis of the Personal'. Whether or not Macmurray knew it, this title invites comparison with James Ferrier's essay 'The Crisis of Modern Speculation', published a little over 100 years before. This is not simply because the titles are similar, but because Ferrier's essay articulates precisely the philosophical background against which the force of Macmurray's key contention is best appreciated.

According to Ferrier, writing in 1845, metaphysical speculation had reached an impasse. In the longstanding philosophical task of understanding the relation between the human mind and the external world, three distinct positions had emerged – Hypothetical Realism, Idealism and Scepticism. None was satisfactory, but the crisis arose from the fact that these three, mutually exclusive positions also appeared to exhaust all logical possibilities. Hypothetical Realism (the amended version of Reid effectively endorsed by Sir William Hamilton) 'admitted that an outward world could not be immediately known . . . but must be postulated in order to account for impressions'. In this way it aimed 'to reconcile common sense with philosophy' (Ferrier 2001c: 266). Idealism, on the other hand, 'did not care to conciliate commonsense' and thought that it would be simpler to explain perceptions as being in 'conformity with the original laws of our constitution'. It could thereby dispense with the 'unnecessary encumbrance' of the 'external world called into existence by hypothetical Realism' (Ferrier 2001c: 267). Scepticism, Ferrier says, 'has assumed various modifications, but the chief guise in which it sought to outrage the convictions of mankind' was with the claim that 'our perceptions could not possibly be true and faithful representatives' of a mind-independent world, so that the universe 'must be something very different' from what we naturally take it to be (Ferrier 2001c: 268).

The principal purpose of Ferrier's essay, however, is not simply to analyse the 'crisis' but to reveal its resolution in a completely new approach to the problem. Without attributing any specific authorship, he expounds 'a great change which the question regarding man's intercourse with the external world has undergone'

(Ferrier 2001c: 269). This great change accepts the distinction between 'perception' and 'outward objects', but lends it 'only a relative validity'.

> If by one principle of our nature we are continually forced to make this separation, we are just as continually forced, by another principle of our nature, to repair it . . . Our intercourse with the external universe was the given whole with which we had to deal. The older philosophies divided this given whole into the external universe on the one hand, and our perceptions of it on the other; but they were never able to show how these two, the objective and the subjective, could again be understood to coalesce . . . The new philosophy . . . shows that the question respecting perception answers itself in this way, that there is no occasion for thought to explain how that may be united into one, which no effort of thought is able to put asunder into two. (Ferrier 2001c: 270–80)

The key idea is this. The distinction between Subject and Object is integral to any account of knowledge. That is why we cannot avoid making it. However, just as 'convex' and 'concave' are geometrically distinct but not separable, so Subject and Object are conceptually distinct, but metaphysically inseparable. The crisis of speculation arises from the false supposition that things which are conceptually distinct are thereby ontologically independent. The crisis is overcome once we acknowledge the necessary metaphysical unity of Subject and Object. This is, in Ferrier's estimation, a huge advance, and he concludes his essay by 'heralding the sunrise of a new era of science, the era of genuine speculation' (Ferrier 2001c: 288).

It is not germane for present purposes to ask whether Ferrier's claim to a wholly new 'discovery' in metaphysics is cogent. It is sufficient to observe that a 'new era of science, the era of genuine speculation' did not in fact arise, at least within Scottish philosophy. Old divisions remained, exemplified in the philosophical gulf between, for instance, Edward Caird and John Veitch at Glasgow. Caird, who held the Chair of Moral Philosophy and subsequently became Master of Balliol, was the leading exponent of Kant and Hegel, and identified closely with German Idealism. Veitch, who held the Chair of Logic and Rhetoric at the same time, persisted in maintaining the Common Sense Realism of Reid and Hamilton, and never failed to fulminate against Hegel and his 'meaningless jargon', according to Henry Jones, who was a student there at the time (Jones 1922: 139). Veitch had, in fact, been a colleague of Ferrier's at St Andrews.[1] But by this time – 1874 – though a new edition of Ferrier's *Collected Works* was in preparation, the philosophical development in which 'The Crisis of Modern Speculation' placed such hopes was largely ignored, or forgotten. The sun had not risen on a new era of science and philosophy, or at least not yet.

III

In itself, of course, this does not show Ferrier's analysis to be mistaken. Perhaps his successors were wrong in failing to pursue the implications of the conclusion at which he had arrived. Still, another possibility is that Ferrier's 'new' philosophy was not as new as he supposed, and continued to rest upon an even more basic assumption which he shared with both sides of the division that he aimed to transcend. That would explain why, ultimately, he failed to transcend it. In 'The Crisis of Modern Speculation', Ferrier inadvertently makes clear what this still more fundamental assumption is.

> Perception, the perception of an external universe, is the groundwork and condition of all other mental phenomena. It is the basis of the reality of mind. It is this reality itself. Through it, mind is what it is, and without it, mind could not be conceived to exist. Since, therefore, perception is the very life of man, when we use the word *mind* in this discussion we shall understand thereby the percipient being, or the perceiver. (Ferrier 2001c: 263)

This presupposition – that perception is 'the basis of the reality of mind' – is shared by Locke and Berkeley, who by Ferrier's account ought to be found on opposite sides of the debate he aims to overcome. For Berkeley, famously, *esse est percipe* – to be is to be perceived – and though there are important differences, Locke states essentially the same presupposition very plainly in the *Essay*.

---

[1] Ferrier had opposed Veitch's appointment and, somewhat oddly, given his view of the irrelevance of psychology to philosophy, had supported Alexander Bain's unsuccessful application.

John Macmurray and the Self as Agent 213

> Let us suppose the Mind to be, as we say, white Paper, void of all Characters, without any *Ideas*; How comes it to be furnished? Whence comes it by that vast store, which the busy and boundless Fancy of Man has painted on it, with an almost endless variety? Whence has it all the materials of Reason and Knowledge? To this I answer, in one word, From *Experience*. In that all our knowledge is founded; and from that it ultimately derives it self. Our Observation employ'd either about *external, sensible Objects; or about the internal Operations of our Minds, perceived and reflected on by ourselves, is that, which supplies our Understanding with all the materials of thinking.* (Locke 1975: 104, emphasis and capitalisation original)

The centrality that this passage lends to 'observation' lies at the heart of Hume's empiricism, and by extension is a key strand in the Scottish philosophical tradition. This undoubtedly sets Macmurray apart. He makes only one brief reference to Locke, not many more to Hume, and in general pays very little attention to empiricism. The term makes no appearance in the index of either volume of lectures. Instead, he focuses most of his attention on Kant, but interestingly this is for a reason that strengthens his connection with Ferrier. Ferrier does not claim to be the originator of the novel approach he elaborates in 'The Crisis of Modern Speculation'. While elsewhere he denies any Hegelian influence, it seems very plausible to read his heralding of a 'new' philosophy as an implicit acknowledgement of Kant, whose 'Critical Philosophy' was becoming better known in Scotland around that time. Macmurray too hails Kant's Critical Philosophy as a 'break with tradition' and the first step on the path to a more adequate philosophical understanding of human experience.

Macmurray thinks, as Ferrier does, that the key to this break lies in its assertion of the necessary interdependence of subject and object, mind and world. But the greatness of Kant, he holds, is not shown by the success of his system, but by the fact that 'all subsequent philosophies have been built out of the ruins of the Critical philosophy' (Macmurray 1957: 39). None of these subsequent philosophies (especially that of Hegel) has achieved adequacy either, however. They all cling to some favoured subset of the elements of the Critical Philosophy, and as a result do not penetrate the difficulty that lies at its heart.

> [E]very significant movement in philosophy since Kant can be derived from the Critical philosophy by rejecting parts of it; and by reasserting

> what any of them has rejected, the premises for its refutation can also be found. Modern philosophies have often gained in coherence by this selectiveness; they have invariably gained this greater consistency at the expense of adequacy. (Macmurray 1957: 39–40)

> If Kant's solution fails, then another solution must be found if philosophical adequacy is to be achieved. For it is essential to philosophy that a means should be discovered of thinking coherently the unity of experience as a whole. (Macmurray 1957: 66)

Philosophy as 'thinking coherently the unity of experience as a whole' is an intellectual ideal Macmurray shares with almost all the late-nineteenth-century Scottish philosophers, especially, but not only, those drawn to Idealism. Philosophy's principal task, accordingly, is to overcome any and all forms of dualism. This same ambition underlies Ferrier's attack on the division of experience into the subjective and the objective, a division that, he thinks, persists in Hypothetical Realism, Idealism and Scepticism. Yet, arguably Ferrier's own presupposition – that 'the perception of an external universe is the groundwork and condition of all other mental phenomena' – introduces an even more fundamental dualism. The perceiver is not a separated Subject, and the perceived is not a separated Object, but the experience of perceiving is nonetheless radically distinct from the thing that is perceived. If, despite his best efforts, Ferrier's account remains fundamentally dualistic, this serves to confirm Macmurray's contention that a 'radical modification of our philosophical tradition is [still] demanded' (Macmurray 1957: 38).

The crucial step in articulating this radical modification is to grasp both the contradiction in Kant's thought and, at the same time, the direction in which it tellingly pushes us. The contradiction, it has widely been held, lies in the fact that Kant has to postulate an unknowable 'thing-in-itself' at the core of what is intended as a theory of knowledge. Macmurray, however, focuses attention on a less familiar aspect, a fracture in Kant's account of reason.

> The Critical philosophy . . . is an argument whose conclusion contradicts its major premiss. This premiss is the pre-supposition that reason is primarily theoretical. The conclusion is that reason is primarily practical. This is the general formal incoherence which comes to a head in the attempt to solve the antinomy of freedom . . . [T]he form

in which Kant seeks to resolve the antinomy depends upon assuming the primacy of the theoretical standpoint. It is this which makes it necessary to conceive the problem as a relation between two possible objects of knowledge – two worlds – one of which *is*, and the other *is not* determinable through our modes of cognition. It is not surprising, therefore – indeed it is inevitable – that the attempt should bring to light the underlying inconsistency and produce a palpable incoherence ... In this general inconsistency, this failure to decide between the primacy of the theoretical and the practical the Critical Philosophy points beyond itself. (Macmurray 1957: 67–8, emphasis original)

Macmurray is here emphasising a difficulty in Kant's treatment of the 'antinomy of freedom' that many commentators have acknowledged, namely his inability to make causality and agency compatible. Since Kant is unable to show at a theoretical level that we are free beings, he has to make freedom a necessary postulate of practical reason. The *Critique of Pure Reason* cannot accommodate the rationality of action, with the result that a *Critique of Practical Reason* is necessitated. But practical reason, it turns out, is not cognitive at all. It is self-command resting ultimately on hope, not on knowledge. Thus reason operates quite differently in theory and in practice. Theoretical reason is reflective, and productive of knowledge, but cannot guide action. Practical reason guides action, but not in virtue of knowledge. The truth of a hypothetical imperative – 'If you want X, do Y' – never tells you what to do.

Here then is a new dualism, not Descartes's ontological dualism of mind and body, nor the Lockean empiricist's experientialist dualism of object and subject, but a dualism nonetheless. The dualism with which Kant ends up is not within reality, but within reason itself. How is it to be overcome? Macmurray's solution adopts the essentially Kantian framework, but reverses the relationship of theory and practice. If theoretical reason uncovers a deterministic world that cannot accommodate action, then we must make practical reason our starting point and see how to derive causality from agency. The Critical Philosophy thus drives us to 'the primacy of the practical' and leads ultimately to the abandonment of Kant's conception of the Self as reflective being, as well as Ferrier's affirmation of the mind as a perceiver. The Self must be reconceived as an agent, an active doer who, *amongst many other activities*, engages in theoretical reflection. Macmurray is quick to point out, however, that this move does not constitute a retreat from philosophy. It is not a capitulation to the commonly expressed demand for 'practicality' which results from a utilitarian insistence on 'relevance' for action, the attitude instinctively adopted by those ignorant of, and not infrequently ill-disposed towards, philosophy.

> [T]o start from the primacy of the practical does not mean that we should aim at a practical rather than a theoretical philosophy . . . What it does mean is that we should think from the standpoint of action. Philosophy is necessarily theoretical, and must aim at theoretical strictness. It does not follow that we must theorize from the standpoint of theory. (Macmurray 1957: 85)

To philosophise 'from the standpoint of action' requires a sustained opposition to a conception of mind that has long been dominant in philosophy and to which Ferrier, for all his supposed radicalism, gives expression when he says that perception of an external universe is the basis of the reality of mind.

> The traditional point of view [says Macmurray] is both theoretical and egocentric. It is theoretical in that it proceeds as though the Self were a pure subject for whom the world is object. This means that the point of view adopted by our philosophy is that of the Self in its moment of reflection, when its activity is directed towards the acquirement of knowledge. Since the Self in reflection is withdrawn from action, withdrawn into itself, withdrawn from participation in the life of the world into contemplation, this point of view is also egocentric. The Self in reflection is self isolated from the world which it knows. (Macmurray 1957: 11)

For Macmurray, the false dualism of 'mind' and 'matter' is in large part a result of conceding to Descartes that the most fundamental and incontrovertible truth is a proposition 'cogito, ergo sum' – 'I think, therefore I am'. This grounds reason in reflective apprehension, not deliberative action. The analysis holds equally well against Locke's and Hume's contention that it is observation of external, sensible objects and internal operations of our minds that provide 'all the materials of thinking'. That, too, makes reason essentially reflective. One of Macmurray's most important insights is that the 'experience' which Locke and Hume take as their starting point seems plausible chiefly because visual experience is erroneously taken to be paradigmatic of perception in general.

> If we construe the Subject as the observer, then in knowledge the Self, as subject, 'stands over against' the object, which it knows, and any activities involved in this knowing must be purely subjective, or mental; that is to say, they make no difference to, or have no causal effect upon, the object. The influence of the visual model is very clear in this. In visual perception we do stand over against the object we see; it is set before us, and our seeing it has no causal effect upon it. Seeing it is *prima facie* a pure receptivity; to exercise it attentively, we withdraw from action altogether. We stop to look. In consequence, the visual model tends to instigate a strong contrast between knowing and acting, which in abstract theory passes easily into a conceptual dualism. (Macmurray 1957: 106)

It is true that in one sense the things we *see* are 'external', and this is the truth that lends an initial plausibility to Hume's and Locke's assertion that all perceptions are internal 'copies' of the appearance of external objects. But this would only hold if what is true of vision were true of all the senses, and this further assertion seems quite implausible. What does the smell of cheese 'copy', and what is the external 'object' when I hear someone play a chord? It might be tempting to reply that smells and sounds give us *indirect* acquaintance with an object, whereas sight gives us *direct* acquaintance. But the immediacy of sight is an illusion. Time (albeit in most cases a very short time) must elapse before we receive the light rays that objects reflect, which means that connecting what we see with our seeing it requires more than visual apparatus. It requires memory. Touch, as Macmurray points out, is a much more truly immediate mode of sense perception. When I touch something, I am directly in contact with it. Importantly, though, the internal/external dichotomy cannot be applied to touch, because I am *at one and the same time* aware of the nature of the thing I touch and of my felt experience of it. Softness and hardness in an object are not the same as the feeling of softness and hardness that I experience. Yet, both are present, and inseparable, in the act of touching. Here, in contrast to vision, we have a single experience in which perceiver and perceived are conjoined.

This concomitant apprehension of 'Self' and 'Other' is key to understanding the unity of reality and experience. 'The Self does not first know itself and determine an objective; and then discover the other in carrying out its intention. The distinction of Self and Other is the awareness of both; the *existence* of both is the fact that their opposition is a practical, and not a theoretical opposition' (Macmurray 1957: 109, emphasis original). Experience, then, exhibits the unity of subject and object. Only an erroneous understanding of mind and matter could lead us falsely to separate them.

IV

False dualism can be avoided, Macmurray contends, once we grasp that 'reason is primarily not cognitive but practical' (Macmurray 1957: 63). It is essential to understand this contention properly. The point is not to prefer acting *over* thinking, or to make action more foundational than thought, but rather, to assert two propositions. First, and contrary to a prejudice to which philosophers are prone, thought is no less fully involved in practical deliberation over courses of action than it is in intellectual theorising and the acquisition of knowledge.

> The question which underlies any philosophical inquiry into action is, How can I do what is right? It is not, How can we know what it is right to do? ... The belief that we can only do what is right by first knowing what it is right to do and then doing it is an assumption. It implies the very principle which Kant was so rightly concerned to deny. (Macmurray 1957: 140)

> In some sense, 'ought' implies 'can'. In some sense, therefore, if we can act rightly, it must be without prior theoretical determination of what it is right to do. The discrimination of right and wrong in action must be prior to and not dependent upon the theoretical discrimination of the truth or falsity of a judgment. (Macmurray 1957: 141)

Second, if we hold fast to the concept of the Self as Agent, we can see that 'mind' and 'body' are not themselves realities, but (often useful) abstractions *from* reality.

> When we distinguish between persons and material things, the characteristics we attribute to things are a selection from the characteristics we attribute to a person. He is a material object, though that is not a complete nor a sufficient characterization. When I say then that our knowledge of the physical world, however scientific, is anthropomorphic, I mean that unless I had fallen downstairs, or otherwise lost

control of my movements, I could not understand what was meant by 'a body falling freely through space'. We can state this generally. The concept of 'a person' is inclusive of the concept of 'an organism', as the concept of 'an organism' is inclusive of that of 'a material body'. The included concepts can be derived from the concept of 'a person' by abstractions; by excluding from attention those characters which belong to the higher category alone. The empirical ground for these distinctions is found in practical experience. We cannot deal with organisms successfully in the same way that we can with material objects, or with persons. The form of their resistance – in opposition or in support – necessitates a difference in our own behaviour. The empirical genesis of 'mind' and 'matter' dualism lies in this, that having abstracted a 'material' object [the body] from the concept of a person . . . we then illegitimately form a concept, on the negative analogy of the 'material', by thinking a unity of what has been excluded. This is the concept of the 'non-material' or 'the mind', or of consciousness as an independently existing entity. (Macmurray 1957: 117–18)

In this way the 'mind' or 'soul' comes to be conceived as a thing, to be studied and manipulated in the way that bodies are. That is why a 'Crisis of the Personal' arises for modern ways of thinking. The embodied Person becomes a disembodied mind. Both body and mind become subjects of scientific study. There are benefits to be gained by such study, but the danger is that the Person, which is fundamental, is inadvertently eliminated, or becomes epiphenomenal, a product of the 'physical' or the 'mental' alone.

V

It is at this point, contrary to McIntosh's contention, that Macmurray's argument, implicitly though not explicitly, engages directly and profitably with 'the Enlightenment debate between Hume's skepticism and Reid's "School of Common Sense"'. At the end of Book 1 of the *Treatise*, Hume gives powerful expression to the radical duality of thought and activity when he acknowledges the anomie and paralysis to which his 'very refin'd and metaphysical' reasonings have led him.

> Where am I, or what? From what causes do I derive my existence, and to what condition shall I return? Whose favour shall I court, and whose anger must I dread? What beings surround me? And on

whom have I any influence, or who have any influence on me? I am confounded with all these questions, and begin to fancy myself in the most deplorable condition imaginable, inviron'd with the deepest darkness, and utterly deprived of the use of every member and faculty. (Hume 2007: 175)

Ironically, given his starting point, Hume finds a way out of 'the deepest darkness' in activity, which is to say, agency.

> Most fortunately it happens, that since reason is incapable of dispelling these clouds, nature herself suffices to that purpose, and cures me of this philosophical melancholy and delirium, either by relaxing this bent of mind, or by some avocation, and lively impression of my senses which obliterate all these chimeras. I dine, I play a game of back-gammon. I converse, and am merry with my friends; and when after three or four hours' amusement, I wou'd return to these speculations, they appear so cold and strained, and ridiculous, that I cannot find in my heart to enter into them any further. (Hume 2007: 175)

It is 'nature', not 'reason', that makes such diversions attractive and gives simple sense experience its special appeal. Hume does not seem to see that games and conversation also involve an exercise of reason. How could I play backgammon without thinking about rules and strategy? How could I prepare dinner without thinking about the right menu, the best ingredients and the most effective method?[2] It is not reasoning as such, but only reason *in the form of philosophical theorising*, that cannot dispel the clouds.

Hume is an impressively systematic thinker and his claim that 'moral distinctions are not deriv'd from reason' follows from his system; they are not so derived, because they cannot be. It follows that morality must be a matter of feeling. If there are any facts relevant to morality, they are facts about how we feel. Immoral people are those who, in the face of, say, dishonesty, incest or parricide (to use Hume's own examples), lack the feelings of approval and disapproval that most people have. Here, as in dispelling metaphysical clouds, 'nature' generally, and happily, kicks in.

Reid argues against Hume's reduction of morality to feeling on linguistic grounds. If 'This is wrong' really did mean 'I disapprove

---

[2] Hume himself was an enthusiastic cook.

of this', that is what I could and would have said. Hume's account renders the customary language of morality redundant. Yet people go on speaking in this objective mode. Why would they do so when they have expressive language available to them? Reid builds on this thought in Part 3 of the *Essays on the Active Powers of Man*, where he observes that reason has long been held to have two functions, 'to regulate our belief, and to regulate our actions and conduct' (Reid 2010: 152). He takes issue with Hume's claim in the *Treatise* that 'reason is no principle of action'. Yet in the elaboration of his alternative, he nevertheless acknowledges a difference with theoretical or speculative reason.

> To judge of what is true or false in speculative points, is the office of speculative reason; and to judge of what is good or ill for us upon the whole, is the office of practical reason. Of true and false there are no degrees; but of good and ill there are many degrees, and many kinds; and men are very apt to form erroneous opinions concerning them; misled by their passions, by the authority of the multitude, and by other causes. (Reid 2010: 157)

It is on the basis of this observation that Reid draws his distinction between the 'theory of morals' and 'practical ethics'.

> By the theory of morals is meant a just account of the structure of our moral powers; that is, of those powers of the mind by which we have our moral conceptions, and distinguish right from wrong in human actions. This is indeed an intricate subject, and there have been various theories and much controversy about it in ancient and in modern times. But it has little connection with the knowledge of our duty; and those who differ most in the theory of our moral powers, agree in the practical rules of morals which they dictate. (Reid 2010: 282–3)

In illustration of his point Reid offers us an analogy.

> A good ear in music may be much improved by attention and practice in that art; but very little by studying the anatomy of the ear, and the theory of sound. In order to acquire a good eye or a good ear in the arts that require them, the theory of vision and the theory of sound, are by no means necessary, and indeed of very little use. Of as little necessity or use is what we call the theory of morals, in order to improve our moral judgment. (Reid 2010: 283)

This rigorous division between the theoretical and the practical, however, is not one that he does or can sustain. Even his analogy contains a qualification. The theory of vision and sound are not declared wholly irrelevant to practical ends, but 'by no means necessary, and . . . of very little use'. In the case of 'theories of morals' Reid positively holds that mistaken theories (such as Hume's) can have very deleterious effects. It is true that they do not logically imply any specific actions or principles, but they can nonetheless confuse and obfuscate moral agents by undermining the confidence with which moral judgements would otherwise be made. Someone persuaded by Hume that morality is essentially a matter of feeling is unlikely to engage in protracted deliberation, still less lay great emphasis on the need for it. When Hume uses the same anatomical analogy, he accepts, contrary to his assertions in the *Treatise*, that 'an artist must be better qualified to succeed . . . who besides a delicate taste and a quick apprehension, possesses an accurate knowledge of the internal fabric . . . The anatomist presents to the eye the most hideous and disagreeable objects, but his science is useful to the painter' (Hume 1999: 90). Similarly, Reid is compelled to acknowledge that sound moral judgement is not as impervious to the theory of morals as in some places he appears to allege.

Reid's response to Hume, then, falls short in much the same way as Kant's. In their attempts to overcome scepticism, they fracture human reason into two, the theoretical discovery of truth and the practical guidance of action. As a result, neither can offer a truly unified account of human experience of the kind to which, Macmurray thinks, philosophy must aspire. There is this difference, however. Kant's philosophy, whatever its inadequacies, still constitutes a 'radical break' with traditional thinking. Reid's philosophy constitutes no such break, and remains largely in the camp of Locke and Hume. This is made apparent by another analogy Hume and Reid both use. In the *Natural History of Religion*, Hume writes: 'We are placed in this world, as in a great theatre, where the true springs and causes of every event are entirely concealed from us' (Hume 1993: 140). In Essay 5 of the *Active Powers*, an essay principally concerned to engage with Hume, Reid writes: 'The earth is a great theatre, furnished by the Almighty, for the entertainment and employment of all mankind. Here every man has a right to accommodate himself as a spectator, and to perform his part as an actor' (Reid 2010: 316). The shared analogy makes clear the difference in their positions. For Hume, the world is a theatre and human beings are the audience. For Reid, the world is a theatre and human beings are, variously, both audience and actors. This is, of course, a more accurate representation of experience. It is a fact that we do not simply watch plays, but also act in them. Still, Reid's use of the image does not radically change Hume's. He merely amends its application. Human beings are indeed spectators. However, they are also agents.

VI

Set against this background, we can appreciate the relevance of Macmurray's Gifford Lectures to the long trajectory of Scottish philosophical debate. By displacing the Self as the subject of sense experience, and replacing it with the Self as agent, Macmurray in effect completes the partial move that Reid made in response to Hume. Human beings do watch plays, but they also act in them. This is a fact, but to avoid any false metaphysical division to which we might be led – that audience and actors are in some sense ontologically or metaphysically distinct – we must operate with a conception of human beings that incorporates the activities of watching and performing within a broader category. Agency is just such a conception. Both practical deliberation and intellectual reflection fall within it.

> The Self that reflects and the Self that acts is the same Self; action and thought are contrasted modes of its activity. But it does not follow that they have an equal status in the being of the Self. In thinking the mind alone is active. In acting the body is indeed active, but also the mind. (Macmurray 1957: 86)

To conceive of the Self as agent, rather than a Cartesian thinker or a Lockean perceiver, is not to denigrate 'Reason'. Rather it is to affirm that rational agency – deliberative action – lies at the foundation of our nature. We are first and foremost 'doers', and that means that the things we believe, and the theories we advance, are as dependent on deliberative action as the clothes we make and the meals we prepare. Macmurray's insistence that we conceive the Self as agent puts our existence as human beings first and in effect replaces 'I think, therefore I am' with 'I am, that is why I think'.

Human thinkers must be born into the world, but obviously they do not think from the moment they are born; they must first learn how to do so, just as they must learn how to walk, feed themselves, speak, play games, make friends and do all the other things that make them human. From this affirmation, we may draw a further critically important implication. This is the topic that Macmurray takes up in his second volume of lectures – *Persons in Relation* – and his observations on this score are especially insightful. Human beings are biological organisms. This is undeniable and an indispensable idea lying at the heart of evolutionary biology's success, and a premise of much philosophy since Aristotle. Yet it is a profound mistake to regard our organic nature as fundamental.

> We start where all human life starts, with infancy; at the stage of human existence where, if at all, we might expect to find a biological conception adequate. If it is not adequate to explain the behaviour of a new-born child, then *a fortiori* it must be completely inadequate as an account of human life in its maturity. The most obvious fact about the human infant is his total helplessness. He has no power of locomotion, nor even of co-ordinated movement. The random movements of limbs and trunk and head of which he is capable do not even suggest an unconscious purposiveness . . . he has no power of behaviour; he cannot respond to any external stimulus by a reaction which would help to defend him from danger or maintain his own existence. In this total helplessness . . . the baby differs from the young of all animals. Even the birds are not helpless in this sense. (Macmurray 1961: 47)

In the light of these observations, it is of the first importance to observe that while as organisms human babies are totally helpless, they are nonetheless persons and as such aided in community. 'The activities of an infant, taken as a whole, have a personal and not an organic form. They are not merely motivated, but their motivation is governed by intention.' How can this be? The answer is:

> The intention is the mother's, necessarily; the motives, just as necessarily, are the baby's own. The infant is active; if his activities were unmotivated, he would be without any consciousness, and could not even develop a capacity to see or hear. But if he is hungry, he does not begin to feed or go in search of food. His feeding occurs at regular intervals, as part of a planned routine, just as an adult's does. The satisfaction of his motives is governed by the mother's intention. It is part of the routine of family life. (Macmurray 1961: 51)

Here we are enabled to see how understanding the Self as agent, rather than passive spectator or reflective thinker, allows us to conceive of human experience as fundamentally unitary. Contrary to a long tradition of philosophical thought reaching back to Aristotle, Macmurray thinks that we 'can dismiss at once any notion that we are born with a set of 'animal' impulses which later take on a rational form. There is no empirical evidence for anything like this, and it is inherently improbable' (Macmurray 1961: 52). Human beings are indeed biological organisms and thus material objects. But they are more fundamentally persons because their lives are governed by rational agency from the moment of birth.

> So far as concerns behaviour which is adapted to a natural environment, the human infant does not behave at all. Their movements are conspicuously random ... The movements gradually lose their random character and acquire direction and form. But the character of this development is quite unlike that observable even in the highest animals. It does not rapidly produce a capacity to adapt itself to the environment. In the early stages, at least, it does not seem to tend in this direction at all. It is quite a long time before the baby learns to walk or stand or even to crawl; and his early locomotion, so far from making him more capable of looking after himself, increases the dangers of his existence, and the need for constant parental care and watchfulness. Nature leaves the provision for his physiological needs and his well being to the mother for many years, until indeed he has learned to form his own intentions, and acquired the skill to execute them and the knowledge and foresight which will enable him to act responsibly as a member of a personal community. (Macmurray 1961: 52–3)

Suppose we accept Hume's and Reid's analogy of the world as 'a great theatre'. Theatres abound in all sorts of activities. As well as audiences and actors, there are technicians, managers, attendants, stage crew, cleaners and so on. To pick out the audience, or the actors, or even some combination of the two, as key to the life of the theatre is to abstract in a way that falsifies the reality. To think of it as an interrelated world of persons with intentions, acquired skills, knowledge and foresight enabling them to engage effectively as members of a community is to see the world of the theatre as a unified whole. Similarly, to characterise human beings as perceivers, or doers, or even some combination of the two, is to abstract from the reality of which they are a part. Looking at things, performing practical tasks, organising and directing group activity, studying the human body scientifically, reflecting philosophically on human experience – these are all things that people do. Taking one of them as basic, as Hume and Ferrier take perception to be, or two, as Kant and Reid take thought and action to be, abstracts from reality and inevitably renders a unified account of experience impossible.

VII

The great philosophical innovation to be found in Macmurray, then, is the incorporation of theoretical reason within practical reason, and the consequent conception of the Self as agent. This reconceptualisation offers a way of overcoming the problems of solipsism and scepticism that arise from Cartesian and quasi-Cartesian conceptions of the Self as a thinking subject looking out on to the external world, and moved to action by a separate faculty of desire. Construing the Self as an agent has the further advantage of enabling a unified account of what it is to be a human being. Rather than having to find some 'connection' between mind and body, the material, the organic and the rational aspects of human nature are integrated. The 'person' is neither a 'higher' spiritual or mental entity somehow attached to the body, nor an emergent supervenient product of organic existence. Rather, the human being as 'person' is the reality, from which 'organism' and 'material entity' are abstractions made for theoretical purposes. If the philosophical move that Macmurray makes and develops at length in his Gifford Lectures is successful, this gives him a claim to be a philosopher of considerable consequence. And even if it fails, he remains a philosopher of striking originality.

Macmurray intended his reorientation of thought from the theoretical to the practical to bear chiefly on the ancient debate between Realists and Idealists, and this is what relates his thinking to Scottish philosophy in the eighteenth and nineteenth centuries. However, it also throws some light on his differences with the twentieth-century 'linguistic' philosophy of his day.

In 1901, on the initiative of William Knight, Professor of Moral Philosophy at St Andrews, the professors of philosophy came together in a professional association called the Scots Philosophical Club. Fifty years later, a successor of Knight's at St Andrews,

Malcolm Knox, took the lead in establishing a new journal, *The Philosophical Quarterly*. At Knox's invitation, Macmurray, along with several of his professorial colleagues, contributed a paper to the first volume. He chose 'Some Reflections on the Analysis of Language' as his topic, and it is one of the few places where he engages directly with the debates in the philosophy of logic and language that were then current.

Macmurray thinks that the shift of attention from 'thought' to 'language' characteristic of the new 'linguistic' movement in philosophy is a step in the right direction, but only partially so.

> Properly understood, this new approach constitutes an important advance in philosophy. Unfortunately, it does not seem to have been properly understood by the protagonists for its adoption. There is nothing surprising in this. It is a common occurrence in the history of philosophy, and easily comprehensible. The pioneer remains entangled in the assumptions of the system of thought which his own originality is undermining. The full implications of his discovery take time, and often a long time, to become apparent. He tends to use them, therefore, as weapons in a controversy which they have robbed of significance. (Macmurray 1951: 326)

The controversy that has been robbed of its significance is that between Idealism and Realism, and the important point about that controversy is that it rests on a common basis, namely operating within a 'Subject-Object frame of reference'.

> Idealists and realists are proponents of 'subjective' and 'objective' solutions respectively. Historically, the substitution of language for thought emerges as a realist move to achieve a complete objectivity, by banishing the Subject. To put it crudely, if in the context of the idealist-realist controversy, I say, as a realist: 'But thinking is only talking', I seem to be arguing for a 'physical' and against a 'mental' interpretation of thinking. If I take my statement seriously, I shall proceed to show that all the characteristics and functions of thought can be accounted for without referring to the Subject and its supposedly 'subjective' doings. Yet in doing so I shall still be using the subject-object dichotomy as my frame of reference. I shall be in a position similar to Berkeley's when he denied the existence of matter. The denial depends upon the distinction between 'mind' and 'matter' and is comprehensible only in terms of it. (Macmurray 1951: 326)

To make real headway, Macmurray thinks, we need to acknowledge a threefold relation.

> The general formula which expresses the full language-situation is: 'I say S to You about O', where O stands for Object and S for what is said about it, the statement. The significant implications of this formula are as follows:—
>
> Any instance of language (S) is in virtue of a three-fold relation, to an 'I', to a 'You' and to an Object.
>
> Any analysis of language which fails to take account of all three terms, 'I', 'You' and 'O', to which every S is related must be inadequate.
>
> The fact that there is an S presupposes, though it does not express, a determinate set of relations between 'I', 'You' and 'O' such that 'I' and 'You' are aware of one another and intend to enter into communication, and that each is aware of O. (Macmurray 1951: 324)

> Properly understood, the transference of the locus of analysis from thought to language implies that thought is inextricably bound up with communication; that it is the individual moment in the mutual determination of a common world. So far from abolishing the 'I', it introduces the 'You' as the correlative of the 'I'. With this, the framework within which philosophical problems are discussed acquires a third dimension, a new axis of reference. (Macmurray 1951: 326)

As a result of this third dimension, Macmurray goes on to observe, the context of an utterance – who says what to whom, when and about what – is ineliminable from the meaning of communication. Consequently, to abstract language from communication, as the analytical philosophy of language that he has in his sights generally does, is to empty it of meaning.

> If I abstract completely, for purposes of analysis, from the context of a statement, what remains – we have called it the 'sentence' – has no meaning of any kind. If it seems to have a meaning, that is only because I automatically supply it with a different context of my own, possibly the barest context within which it can carry a meaning, in which case it will have the minimum of meaning for me. (Macmurray 1951: 330)

While he acknowledges that 'to some this may seem mere quibbling, to others true but unimportant', he does think that the shift from thought to language has profound implications that 'linguistic' philosophy has yet to acknowledge. One of these implications relates to its reliance on logic.

> I find it hard to believe that any mature philosopher has recourse to the principles and techniques of formal logic when he is seeking to make a contribution to philosophy, even in the field of logical theory . . . My experience as a teacher of philosophy has convinced me that formal logic . . . is an all but indispensable instrument of philosophical training . . . in the precise use of language upon which philosophy depends. But to imagine that a formal analysis of language in which a philosophical theory is communicated can determine the validity of the theory is to take logic altogether too seriously. It is indeed to fall victim to the fallacy of rationalism against which empiricism is a protest. (Macmurray 1951: 332)

It is not hard to see the philosophers he has in view here; Russell, the early Wittgenstein and A. J. Ayer spring to mind.[3] Nor is it hard to see how and why he came to be isolated by the philosophical world in which he spent the last years of his career as a professional philosopher. He was endorsing 'the linguistic turn' that philosophy had taken, but then rejecting the style of analysis that was widely assumed to go with it.

For the purposes of this chapter, however, we need not adjudicate between the two sides. It is enough to observe, first, that the radical reorientation undertaken by Macmurray in his Gifford Lectures did indeed address the Realist-Idealist controversy with which Scottish philosophy had been absorbed in the eighteenth and nineteenth centuries, and second, that this same reorientation put him at odds with most of his philosophical contemporaries. The concept of the Self as Agent brought a more satisfactory resolution to the philosophical differences between, say, Hume, Reid, Brown, Hamilton, Ferrier, Bain and Caird. At the same time, it did nothing to check the rise of 'linguistic analysis' as the dominant fashion in Scotland's expanding universities. For both these reasons, it is possible to see in John

---

[3] Macmurray protested strenuously against the suggestion of Ayer as his successor in the Grote Chair of Philosophy at UCL, but Ayer was appointed anyway, and conspicuously failed ever to make reference to his predecessor.

Macmurray another figure, a generation after Pringle-Pattison, in whom the Scottish philosophical tradition can be said to have come to a close.

This much is undoubtedly true. The year 1961 proved to be a watershed one. It was the year in which Macmurray retired, and the last plausible contributor to the debates that had animated Scottish philosophy for two centuries left the field. It was also the year in which George Davie's *The Democratic Intellect* was published, and the Scottish philosophical tradition became an object for nostalgic historical inquiry.

Bibliography

Primary Texts

Bain, Alexander (1855), *The Senses and the Intellect*, London: Longman, Roberts & Green.
Bain, Alexander (1859), *The Emotions and the Will*, London: J. W. Parker & Son.
Bain, Alexander (1872), *Mental and Moral Science*, London: Longmans, Green & Co.
Bain, Alexander (1879), *Education as a Science*, London: C. Kegan Paul & Co.
Bain, Alexander (1882), *John Stuart Mill: A Criticism with Personal Recollections*, London: Longmans, Green & Co.
Bain, Alexander (1903), *Dissertations on Leading Philosophical Topics*, London: Longmans, Green & Co.
Bain, Alexander (1904), *An Autobiography*, London: Longmans, Green & Co.
Barbour, G. F. (1933), 'Memoir of the Author', in Seth Pringle-Pattison, *The Balfour Lectures on Realism*, Edinburgh: William Blackwood and Sons.
Blair, Hugh [1783] (2005), *Lectures on Rhetoric and Belles Lettres*, ed. Linda Ferreira-Buckley and S. Michael Halloran, Carbondale: Southern Illinois University Press.
Brown, Thomas (1836), *Lectures on the Philosophy of the Human Mind*, 2 vols, Hallowell: Glazier, Masters & Smith.
Caird, Edward (1892), *Essays on Literature and Philosophy*, Glasgow: James MacLehose and Sons.
Cairns, John (1856), *The Scottish Philosophy; A Vindication and Reply*, Edinburgh: Constable & Co.
Calderwood, Henry (1854), *The Philosophy of the Infinite*, Edinburgh: Thomas Constable & Co.
Calderwood, Henry (1896), *Evolution and Man's Place in Nature*, 2nd edn, London: Macmillan and Co.
Calderwood, Henry (1898), *David Hume*, Edinburgh and London: Oliphant, Anderson & Ferrier.

Calderwood, W. L. and D. Woodside (1900), *The Life of Henry Calderwood*, London: Hodder & Stoughton.
Campbell, George [1776] (1963), *The Philosophy of Rhetoric*, ed. Lloyd F. Bitzer, Carbondale: Southern Illinois University Press.
Carlyle, Thomas [1836] (1894), *Sartor Resartus*, ed. G. T. Bettany, London and New York: Ward, Lock & Co.
Carlyle, Thomas (1970a), *The Collected Letters of Thomas and Jane Welsh Carlyle IV*, ed. Charles Richard Sanders, Kenneth J. Fielding and Clyde de L. Ryals, Durham, NC: Duke University Press.
Carlyle, Thomas (1970b), *The Collected Letters of Thomas and Jane Welsh Carlyle VII*, ed. Charles Richard Sanders, Kenneth J. Fielding and Clyde de L. Ryals, Durham, NC: Duke University Press.
Carlyle, Thomas [1881] (1997), *Reminiscences*, ed. Kenneth J. Fielding and Ian Campbell, Oxford: Oxford University Press.
Davie, George (1961), *The Democratic Intellect*, Edinburgh: Edinburgh University Press.
Ferrier, James Frederick (1856), *Scottish Philosophy: The Old and the New*, Edinburgh: Sutherland and Knox.
Ferrier, James Frederick [1875] (2001a), *Institutes of Metaphysic*, 3rd edn, vol. 1 of *Collected Works*, Bristol: Thoemmes Press.
Ferrier, James Frederick [1888] (2001b), *Lectures on Greek Philosophy*, new edn, vol. 2 of *Collected Works*, Bristol: Thoemmes Press.
Ferrier, James Frederick [1883] (2001c), *Philosophical Remains*, new edn, vol. 3 of *Collected Works*, Bristol: Thoemmes Press.
Fraser, Alexander Campbell, *Essays in Philosophy* (privately printed).
Fraser, Alexander Campbell (1898), *Thomas Reid*, Edinburgh and London: Oliphant, Anderson & Ferrier.
Fraser, Alexander Campbell (1899), *Philosophy of Theism*, 2nd edn, Edinburgh and London: William Blackwood and Sons.
Fraser, Alexander Campbell (1904), *Biographia Philosophica*, Edinburgh and London: William Blackwood and Sons.
Frost, Henry [1882] (2017), *Franz Schubert: A Biography*, introduction by William Hadow, Bendigo: A Distant Mirror.
Frye, Lowell T. (2012), '"Leaving Blair's Lectures Quite Behind": Thomas Carlyle's Rhetorical Revolution', *Carlyle Occasional Papers*, Edinburgh: Edinburgh University Press.
Greig, James A. (1948), *Francis Jeffrey of the Edinburgh Review*, Edinburgh: Oliver and Boyd.
Haldane, Elizabeth S. (1899), *James Frederick Ferrier*, Edinburgh and London: Oliphant, Anderson & Ferrier.
Haldane, R. B. (1888), 'Hegel and his Recent Critics', *Mind*, 13: 585–9.

Hamilton, W. (1853), *Discussions on Philosophy and Literature, Education and University Reform*, London: Longman, Brown, Green and Longmans.
Hamilton, W. (1872), *Notes and Supplementary Dissertations*, in *The Works of Thomas Reid*, vol. 2, Edinburgh: Maclachlan and Stewart.
Hamilton, W. [1859] (2001), *Lectures on Metaphysics and Logic*, vol. 1, ed. H. L. Mansel and J. Veitch, vol. 4 of *Collected Works*, Bristol: Thoemmes Press.
Hetherington, H. J. W. (1924), *The Life and Letters of Sir Henry Jones*, London: Hodder & Stoughton.
Hume, David (1932), *The Letters of David Hume*, 2 vols, ed. J. Y. T. Greig, Oxford: Oxford University Press.
Hume, David [1779] (1993), *Dialogues Concerning Natural Religion*, ed. J. C. A. Gaskin, Oxford: Oxford University Press.
Hume, David [1748] (1999), *An Enquiry Concerning Human Understanding*, ed. Tom L. Beauchamp, Oxford: Oxford University Press.
Hume, David [1739–40] (2007), *A Treatise of Human Nature*, ed. David Fate Norton and Mary J. Norton, Oxford: Clarendon Press.
James, William (1902), *The Varieties of Religious Experience*, London: Longmans, Green & Co.
Jones, H. (1893a), 'Idealism and Epistemology', *Mind*, NS, 2: 289–306, 457–72.
Jones, H. (1893b), 'The Nature and Aims of Philosophy', *Mind*, NS, 2: 160–73.
Jones, H. (1922), *Old Memories*, ed. Thomas Jones, London: Hodder & Stoughton.
Jones, Henry and J. H. Muirhead (1921), *The Life and Philosophy of Edward Caird*, Glasgow: MacLehose, Jackson & Co.
Knox, Thomas Malcolm (1950), 'The Philosophers', in J. B. Salmond (ed.), *Veterum Laudes*, St Andrews: Oliver and Boyd.
Laurie, Henry (1902), *Scottish Philosophy in its National Development*, Glasgow: MacLehose & Sons.
Locke, John (1975), *An Essay Concerning Human Understanding*, ed. P. H. Nidditch, Oxford: Clarendon Press.
McCosh, James (1875), *The Scottish Philosophy: Biographical, Expository, Critical, from Hutcheson to Hamilton*, London: Macmillan.
McCosh, James (1882), 'The Scottish Philosophy as Contrasted with the German', *Princeton Review*, 10: 326–44.
McCosh, James and William Milligan Sloane (1896), *The Life of James McCosh: A Record Chiefly Autobiographical*, New York: Scribner's Sons.

Macdougall, Patrick C. (1852), *Papers on Literary and Philosophical Subjects*, Edinburgh: Johnstone and Hunter.

MacMillan, Donald (1914), *The Life of Robert Flint*, London: Hodder & Stoughton.

Macmurray, John (1951), 'Some Reflections on the Analysis of Language', *The Philosophical Quarterly*, 1.4: 319–37.

Macmurray, John (1957), *The Self as Agent*, London: Faber and Faber.

Macmurray, John (1961), *Persons in Relation*, London: Faber and Faber.

Mansel, H. L. [1866] (1991), *The Philosophy of the Conditioned*, Bristol: Thoemmes Press.

Masson, David (1885), *Carlyle, Personally and in his Writings*, London: Macmillan and Co.

Masson, David (1892), *Edinburgh Sketches and Memories*, London and Edinburgh: Adam and Charles Black.

Masson, David (1911), *Memories of Two Cities*, Edinburgh and London: Oliphant, Anderson & Ferrier.

Mill, John Stuart [1873] (1971), *Autobiography*, ed. Jack Stillinger, Oxford: Oxford University Press.

Mill, John Stuart (1972), *The Later Letters of John Stuart Mill 1849–1873*, ed. Francis E. Mineka and Dwight N. Lindley, vol. 14 of *Collected Works*, Toronto: University of Toronto Press.

Mill, John Stuart [1865] (1979), *An Examination of Sir William Hamilton's Philosophy*, ed. John M. Robson, vol. 11 of *Collected Works*, Toronto: University of Toronto Press.

Murray, J. Clark (1870), *Outline of Sir William Hamilton's Philosophy*, New York: Sheldon and Co.

Oliphant, Margaret (1862), *The Life of Edward Irving*, London: Hurst and Blackett.

Oliphant, Margaret (1869a), 'The Philosopher', *Blackwood's Edinburgh Magazine*.

Oliphant, Margaret (1869b), 'The Sceptic', *Blackwood's Edinburgh Magazine*.

Oliphant, Margaret (1889), *A Memoir of the Life of John Tulloch*, Edinburgh and London: William Blackwood and Sons.

Oliphant, Margaret (1893), *Thomas Chalmers*, London: Methuen & Co.

Oliphant, Margaret (1897), *William Blackwood and his Sons: Their Magazine and Friends*, 2 vols, Edinburgh and London: William Blackwood and Sons.

Reid, Thomas [1764] (1997), *An Inquiry into the Human Mind upon the Principles of Common Sense*, ed. Derek R. Brookes, Edinburgh: Edinburgh University Press.

Reid, Thomas (2002a), *The Correspondence of Thomas Reid*, ed. Paul Wood, Edinburgh: Edinburgh University Press.

Reid, Thomas [1785] (2002b), *Essays on the Intellectual Powers of Man*, ed. Derek R. Brookes and Knud Haakonssen, Edinburgh: Edinburgh University Press.

Reid, Thomas (2005), *On Logic, Rhetoric and the Fine Arts*, ed. Alexander Broadie, Edinburgh: Edinburgh University Press.

Reid, Thomas [1788] (2010), *Essays on the Active Powers of Man*, ed. James A. Harris and Knud Haakonssen, Edinburgh: Edinburgh University Press.

Ritchie, David G. (1888a), 'Origin and Validity', *Mind*, 13: 63–79.

Ritchie, David G. (1888b), 'Review of Seth, *Hegelianism and Personality*', *Mind*, 13: 256–63.

Ritchie, David G. (1890), 'Natural Selection and the Spiritual World', *Westminster Review*, 133: 459–69.

Ritchie, David G. (1891), 'Darwin and Hegel', *Proceedings of the Aristotelian Society*, 1: 38–76.

Ritchie, David G. (1894), 'Hegelianism and its Critics', *Mind*, NS, 3: 240–1.

Ritchie, David G. (1899), 'Philosophy and the Study of Philosophers', *Mind*, NS, 8: 1–24.

Seth, James (1912), *English Philosophers and Schools of Philosophy*, London: J. M. Dent & Sons Ltd.

Seth Pringle-Pattison, Andrew (1885), *Scottish Philosophy: A Comparison of the Scottish and German Answers to Hume*, Edinburgh: William Blackwood and Sons.

Seth Pringle-Pattison, Andrew (1887), *Hegelianism and Personality*, Edinburgh: William Blackwood and Sons.

Seth Pringle-Pattison, Andrew (1894), 'Hegelianism and its Critics', *Mind*, NS, 3: 1–25.

Seth Pringle-Pattison, Andrew (1897a), *Man's Place in the Cosmos*, 2nd edition, Edinburgh: William Blackwood and Sons.

Seth Pringle-Pattison, Andrew (1897b), *Two Lectures on Theism*, Edinburgh: William Blackwood and Sons.

Seth Pringle-Pattison, Andrew (1915), 'Alexander Campbell Fraser 1819–1914', *Proceedings of the British Academy*, 6: 1–14.

Seth Pringle-Pattison, Andrew (1917), *The Idea of God in the Light of Recent Philosophy*, Oxford: Clarendon Press.

Seth Pringle-Pattison, Andrew (1933), *The Balfour Lectures on Realism*, ed. with a 'Memoir of the Author' by G. F. Barbour, Edinburgh: William Blackwood and Sons.

Seth Pringle-Pattison, Andrew and R. B. Haldane (eds) (1883), *Essays in Philosophical Criticism*, London: Longmans, Green & Co.

Stewart, Dugald (1858), 'Account of the Life and Writings of Thomas Reid D.D., F.R.S.E.', in *Collected Works of Dugald Stewart*, ed. Sir William Hamilton, vol. 10, Edinburgh: Thomas Constable & Co.

Stirling, Amelia Hutchison (1912), *James Hutchison Stirling: His Life and Work*, London: T. Fisher Unwin.
Stirling, James H. [1865] (1990), *Sir William Hamilton: Being the Philosophy of Perception – An Analysis*, Bristol: Thoemmes Antiquarian Books Ltd.
Stout, G. F. (1911), 'Philosophy', in *Votiva Tabella*, St Andrews: University of St Andrews.
Tulloch, John (1884), *Modern Theories in Philosophy and Religion*, Edinburgh: William Blackwood and Sons.
Veitch, John (1869), *Memoir of Sir William Hamilton, Bart*, Edinburgh and London: William Blackwood and Sons.
Veitch, John (1882), *Hamilton*, Edinburgh and London: William Blackwood and Sons.
Veitch, John (1883), *Sir William Hamilton: The Man and his Philosophy: Two Lectures*, Edinburgh and London: William Blackwood and Sons.
Welsh, David (1825), *Account of the Life and Writings of Thomas Brown*, Edinburgh: W. & C. Tait.

Secondary Sources

Boucher, David (ed.) (2004), *The Scottish Idealists: Selected Philosophical Writings*, Exeter: Imprint Academic.
Broadie, Alexander (2009), *A History of Scottish Philosophy*, Edinburgh: Edinburgh University Press.
Brody, Baruch A. (1971), 'Reid and Hamilton on Perception', *The Monist*, 55.3: 423–41.
Brown, Stuart (2014), 'The Professionalization of British Philosophy', in W. J. Mander (ed.), *The Oxford Handbook of British Philosophy in the Nineteenth Century*, Oxford: Oxford University Press.
Campbell, C. A. (1952), 'Philosophy', in *Fortuna Domus*, Glasgow: University of Glasgow.
Clubbe, John (ed.) (1976), *Carlyle and his Contemporaries: Essays in Honor of Charles Richard Saunders*, Durham, NC: Duke University Press.
Craig, Cairns (2007), 'Editorial', in *Journal of Scottish Thought*, 1.1: i–xix.
Craig, Cairns (2015), 'Alexander Bain, Associationism and Scottish Philosophy', in Gordon Graham (ed.), *Scottish Philosophy in the Nineteenth and Twentieth Centuries*, Oxford: Oxford University Press.
Craig, Cairns (2019), 'The Scottish Theological Diaspora: Canada', in David Fergusson and Mark W. Elliot (eds), *The History of Scottish Theology, Volume III: The Long Twentieth Century*, Oxford: Oxford University Press.
Crawford, Robert (ed.) (1998), *The Scottish Invention of English Literature*, Cambridge: Cambridge University Press.

Davie, George Elder (1991), *The Scottish Enlightenment and Other Essays*, Edinburgh: Edinburgh University Press.
Davie, George (2003), *Ferrier and the Blackout of the Scottish Enlightenment*, Edinburgh: Edinburgh Review.
Emerson, Roger L. (1994), 'The "Affair" at Edinburgh and the "Project" at Glasgow: The Politics of Hume's Attempts to Become a Professor', in M. A. Stewart and John P. Wright (eds), *Hume and Hume's Connexions*, Edinburgh: Edinburgh University Press.
Heffer, Simon (1995), *Moral Desperado: A Life of Thomas Carlyle*, London: Weidenfeld & Nicolson.
Honderich, Ted (ed.) (1995), *The Oxford Companion to Philosophy*, Oxford: Oxford University Press.
Hutton, Sarah (2015), '"Blue-Eyed Philosophers Born on Wednesdays": An Essay on Women and History of Philosophy', *The Monist*, 98.1: 7–20.
Jaki, Stanley (1995), *Lord Gifford and his Lectures: A Centenary Retrospect*, 2nd edn, Edinburgh: Scottish Academic Press.
Jessop, Ralph (1997), *Carlyle and Scottish Thought*, Basingstoke: Macmillan Press.
Keefe, Jennifer (2015), 'James Frederick Ferrier: The Return of Idealism and the Rejection of Common Sense', in Gordon Graham (ed.), *Scottish Philosophy in the Nineteenth and Twentieth Centuries*, Oxford: Oxford University Press.
McDermid, Douglas (2018), *The Rise and Fall of Scottish Common Sense Realism*, Oxford: Oxford University Press.
McIntosh, Esther (2015), 'John Macmurray as a Scottish Philosopher', in Gordon Graham (ed.), *Scottish Philosophy in the Nineteenth and Twentieth Centuries*, Oxford: Oxford University Press.
Mander, W. J. (2020), *The Unknowable*, Oxford: Oxford University Press.
Mayo, Bernard (2007), 'The Moral and Physical Order: A Reappraisal of James Frederick Ferrier', *Journal of Scottish Philosophy*, 5.2: 159–67.
Sorley, W. R. (1937), *A History of English Philosophy*, Cambridge: Cambridge University Press.
Sweet, William (2014), 'British Idealist Philosophy of Religion', in W. J. Mander (ed.), *The Oxford Handbook of British Philosophy in the Nineteenth Century*, Oxford: Oxford University Press.

Publications on Scottish Philosophy by Gordon Graham

Edited Books

Scottish Philosophy in the Nineteenth and Twentieth Centuries, Oxford: Oxford University Press, 2015.
with authored chapters:
'Scottish Philosophy after the Enlightenment' (Chapter 1)

'A Re-examination of Sir William Hamilton' (Chapter 3)
'Scottish Philosophy Abroad' (Chapter 8)
'Scottish Philosophy and the Idea of a National Tradition' (Chapter 12)
Scottish Philosophy: Selected Writings 1690–1960, Exeter: Imprint Academic, 2004.

Journal Articles

2021 'David Hume on Religion', *Humanities: Christianity and Culture*, 52.
2021 'Religion, Evolution and Scottish Philosophy', *Journal of Scottish Philosophy*, 19.1.
2020 Introduction to 'Symposium on Craig Smith's Adam Ferguson and the Idea of Civil Society', *Journal of Scottish Philosophy*, 18.3.
2019 Response to 'Symposium Essays in Honour of Gordon Graham', *Journal of Scottish Philosophy*, 17.1.
2018 'Religion and Spirituality: Adam Smith versus J-J Rousseau', *Journal of Philosophical Investigations at University of Tabriz*, 12.24.
2016 'Hume and Smith on Natural Religion', *Philosophy*, 91.3.
2014 'Aesthetics as a Normative Science: Reid contra Hume', *Philosophy*, 72, supplement.
2014 'Francis Hutcheson and Adam Ferguson on Sociability', *History of Philosophy Quarterly*, 31.4.
2013 'Adam Ferguson as a Moral Philosopher', *Philosophy*, 88.4.
2010 'Witherspoon, Reid, and Scottish Philosophy in America', *The Princeton Seminary Bulletin*, 31.
2007 'The Ambition of Scottish Philosophy', *The Monist*, 90.2.
2003 'The Decline of Common Sense and the Rise of Scottish Idealism', *Revista Neo Scholastica*, 95.1.
2001 'Morality and Feeling in the Scottish Enlightenment', *Philosophy*, 76.2.

Chapters in Books

2020 'The Nineteenth-Century Aftermath', in Alexander Broadie and Craig Smith (eds), *The Cambridge Companion to the Scottish Enlightenment*, 2nd rev. edn (1st edn 2003), Cambridge: Cambridge University Press.
2019 'David Hume and the Scottish Intellectual Tradition', in Alex Sager and Angela Coventry (eds), *The Humean Mind*, London: Routledge.
2019 'The Gifford Lectures', in David Fergusson and Mark W. Elliot (eds), *The History of Scottish Theology, Volume III: The Long Twentieth Century*, Oxford: Oxford University Press.
2019 'Scotland and Princeton', in David Fergusson and Bruce McCormack (eds), *Schools of Faith: Essays on Theology, Ethics and Education*, London: T&T Clark.

2018 'Was Reid a Moral Realist?', in C. B. Bow (ed.), *Common Sense and the Scottish Enlightenment*, Oxford: Oxford University Press.
2016 'Adam Smith and Religion', in Ryan Patrick Hanley (ed.), *Adam Smith: His Life, his Work, his Legacy*, Princeton: Princeton University Press.
2015 'Beauty, Taste, Rhetoric and Language', in Aaron Garret and James Harris (eds), *Scottish Philosophy in the Eighteenth Century: Moral Philosophy*, Oxford: Oxford University Press.
2014 'Adam Smith as a Scottish Philosopher', in Leslie Marsh (ed.), *Propriety and Prosperity: New Studies in Adam Smith*, London: Palgrave Macmillan.
2014 'Hamilton, Scottish Common Sense, and the Philosophy of the Conditioned', in W. J. Mander (ed.), *The Oxford Handbook of British Philosophy in the Nineteenth Century*, Oxford: Oxford University Press.
2010 'The Significance of Reid's Practical Ethics', in Sabine Roeser (ed.), *Reid on Ethics*, London: Palgrave Macmillan.

Book Reviews

2021 Terence Cuneo, *Thomas Reid and the Ethical Life*, Cambridge University Press, 2020, in *Review of Metaphysics*, 74.4.
2019 Jesse Norman, *Adam Smith: What He Thought and Why It Matters*, Allen Lane, 2018, in *Cosmos+Taxis*, 8.1.
2019 Simon Grote, *The Emergence of Modern Aesthetic Theory: Religion and Morality in Enlightenment Germany and Scotland*, Cambridge University Press, 2017, in *Journal of Scottish Philosophy*, 17.3.
2018 Dennis C. Rasmussen, *The Infidel and the Professor*, Princeton University Press, 2017, in *Cosmos+Taxis*, 5.3+4.
2018 Nicholas B. Miller, *John Millar and the Scottish Enlightenment: Family Life and World History*, Oxford University Studies in the Enlightenment, Voltaire Foundation, 2017, in *Journal of Scottish Philosophy*, 16.3.
2018 Raquel Lazaro and Julio Seoane (eds), *The Changing Faces of Religion in XVIIIth Century Scotland*, Georg Ohms Verlag, 2016, in *Journal of Scottish Philosophy*, 16.1.
2016 Leslie Ellen Brown, *Artful Virtue: The Interplay of the Beautiful and the Good in the Scottish Enlightenment*, Ashgate, 2015, in *Journal of Scottish Philosophy*, 14.2.
2016 Stephen Cowley, *Rational Piety and Social Reform in Glasgow*, Wipf and Stock, 2015, in *Journal of Scottish Philosophy*, 14.2.
2015 Thomas Ahnert, *The Moral Culture of the Scottish Enlightenment*, Yale University Press, 2014, in *ECSSS Newsletter*, June.

2015 Nicholas Phillipson, *Adam Smith: An Enlightened Life*, Yale University Press, 2010, in *Adam Smith Review*, 8.
2015 Ruth Savage (ed.), *Philosophy and Religion in Enlightenment Britain*, Oxford University Press, 2012, in *Journal of Scottish Philosophy*, 13.2.
2014 Jack Russell Weinstein, *Adam Smith's Pluralism*, Yale University Press, 2013, in *Eighteenth-Century Scotland*, 28, Spring.
2011 Thomas Reid, *Essays on the Active Powers*, ed. Knud Haakojnsen and James A. Harris, Edinburgh University Press, 2011, in *Journal of Scottish Philosophy*, 9.2.
2010 Eugene Heath and Vincenzo Merolle (eds), *Adam Ferguson: Philosophy, Politics and Society*, Pickering, 2008, in *Journal of Scottish Philosophy*, 8.2.
2009 Eugene Heath and Vincenzo Merolle (eds), *Adam Ferguson: History, Progress and Human Nature*, Pickering, 2009, in *Journal of Scottish Philosophy*, 7.1.
2004 Philip de Bary, *Thomas Reid and Scepticism*, Routledge, 2002, in *Philosophy*, 79.308.
2003 Paul Wood (ed.), *The Correspondence of Thomas Reid*, Edinburgh University Press, 2002, in *Hume Studies*, 29.2.

Essays and Reviews Online

Review of Jack A. Hill, *Adam Ferguson and Ethical Integrity: The Man and his Prescriptions for the Moral Life*, New York and London: Lexington Books, 2017, <https://www.gordon-graham.net/reviews.html> (last accessed 6 December 2021).
Review of James A. Harris, *Hume: An Intellectual Biography*, Cambridge: Cambridge University Press, 2015, <https://www.gordon-graham.net/reviews.html> (last accessed 6 December 2021).
Review of H. O. Mounce, *Hume's Naturalism*, London: Routledge, 1999, <https://www.gordon-graham.net/reviews.html> (last accessed 6 December 2021).
'Scottish Philosophy in the Nineteenth Century', in *Stanford Encyclopedia of Philosophy* (most recent revision 2020), <http://plato.stanford.edu/entries/scottish-19th/> (last accessed 6 December 2021).
'Thomas Carlyle and Scottish Philosophy', *Carlyle Society Occasional Papers*.

Index

Aberdeen Philosophical Society, 103
Absolute, 28, 32–3, 119, 122, 145, 146, 198, 200
Act of Union 1707, 100
action
   and agency, 223
   and feelings, 89
   and reason, 221
   and thought, 218, 223–4
aesthetic education 92–3
agency, 124, 186
   and action, 223
   77and causality, 215
   and freedom, 215
   and existence, 198
   and humans, 223
   and Hume, 220
   and reflection, 223
   and self-consciousness, 177
   and spiritual, 199
   and thought, 223–4
   divine, 165
   moral, 183
   rational, 156
agnosticism, 168, 176, 183, 199
   and faith, 182
   methodology, 182
Analogy of Religion, Natural and Revealed, 169
angels, 183
Annals of a Publishing House: William Blackwood and his Sons, xii-xiii
Appearance and Reality, 198
Aristotle, 2, 23, 155, 200, 224, 225
Aristotlelian Society, The, 138, 142

Arnold, Matthew, 168
astronomy, 182
atomism, 170
Austin, J. L., 2, 11
Ayer, A. J., 2, 8, 229

Bach, J.S., 143
Bain, Alexander, 10, 15, 16, 21–2, 54, 63–4, 75–94, 104, 118, 121, 171, 204, 207, 229
   An Autobiography, 93
   and Bentham, 90, 91
   and common sense, 86
   and empiricism, 87
   and Hume, 86–7, 88–92, 94
   and McCosh, 136–7
   and Macmurray, 209, 212n
   and materialism, 85, 136–7
   and Mill, 84, 90, 94
   and natural science, 86
   and philosophy of mind, 88
   and poetry, 93
   and positivism, 168
   and psychology, 136, 145
   and Reid, 86
   and religion, 93–4
   and school education, 89
   and Scottish Philosophy, 82–8
   and science of mind, 136
   and Stirling, 135–6
   and teleology, 145
   and truth, 92
   biography of 82–3
Beattie, James, 78
beauty, 165
behaviour, 159, 160

belle lettres, 103–4
Bentham, Jeremy
  and Bain, 90, 91
Berkeley, George, xi, 71, 81, 130, 200
Bible, The, 156
  and evolution, 161
Biographica Philosophica, 17, 174
Biographical History of Philosophy,
  xi, 10
biology, 153–66, 199
  and causes, 153–4
  and morality, 162–63
  and teleology, 154
  evolutionary, 158–60, 224
  see also evolution
Blackwood, John, x, xii, 73
Blackwood, William, x, xii, 167, 207
Blackwood's Edinburgh Magazine, x,
  xi, xii, 52, 53, 60
*Blackwood's Philosophical Classics
  for English Readers*, 175
Blackwood's Philosophical Classics,
  134
Blair, Hugh, 103–5, 112
*Blue-eyed Philosophers Born on
  Wednesdays*, 12
Body, 218–19
Bowman, A.A., 204
Boyle, Deborah, ix
British Idealists, 3
British Quarterly Review, 34, 136
Broadie, Alexander, 18, 188, 189,
  206–7
Brown, Thomas, 10, 15, 21, 23,
  30, 51, 53, 79–80, 107–8, 114,
  132–33, 141, 142, 229
  and Descartes, 133
  and Hamilton, 134–35
  and Hume, 133–34
  and Reid, 133–34
  and Scottish Philosophy, 132–34;
  and Veitch, 134–35
Butler, Bishop, 169

Caird, Edward, 10, 15, 16, 54, 68–9,
  117, 118–19, 137, 142, 146, 184,
  187, 207, 208, 209, 211, 229
  and Carlyle, 109–11

Caird, John, xii, 68
Cairns, Craig, 82, 86, 189, 208
Cairns, John, 55, 60, 175
  and Ferrier, 57, 59
Calderwood, H., 9, 15, 17, 21, 54,
  78, 114, 155, 159–63, 164, 165,
  166, 204, 207
  biography of, 150
  and Hamilton, 32–4
Calvinism, 167
*Cambridge Companion to the
  Scottish Enlightenment*, 15
Cambridge Platonists, 171
Campbell, George, 20, 103, 112
Carlyle and Scottish Thought, 98
Carlyle, Jane Welsh, 95
Carlyle, Thomas, 16, 69, 95–112, 117
  biography of, 96, 107–8
  and Caird, 109–11
  and Goethe, 108–9
  and Hamilton, 108
  and Hume, 108
  and metaphysics, 108, 110
  and Reid, 108
  and Shakespeare, 110–11
  categorising, 97–9
Categorical Imperative, 218
causality, 153, 158
  and reason, 180, 181, 215
  and science, 153
Chalmers, Thomas, xiii, 111–12
Church of Scotland, The, 107, 167
  the Disruption, 9, 10, 167
Collected Works of Dugald Stewart,
  25
Collected Works of Thomas Carlyle,
  96
Collected Works of Thomas Reid,
  24–5
College of New Jersey see Princeton
  University
Collingwood, R.G., 3, 11
Common sense, principles of, 20–1,
  22, 23, 27, 29, 36–9, 42–4, 51–3,
  59, 63, 65, 69, 78, 114, 117,
  124, 131, 157, 171, 172, 175
  and atheism, 193
  and Bain, 86

and Ferrier, 52, 56, 64
and God, 185
and Hamilton, 37–8
and Reid, 10
and Seth Pringle-Pattison, 194–5
and scepticism, 193
and Scottish Philosophy, 79
and Stewart, 185
and theism, 187
and universal power, 177
Comte, Auguste, 167, 140–1, 169–70
Concept of Mind, 2
consciousness, 37–45, 85, 121–2, 124, 219
and existence, 196
and Ferrier, 74
and Hamilton, 39–40
and materialism, 178
as matter in motion, 177
and Mill, 39–40
and observation, 60
and perception, 29–31
divine, 196–7
human, 177, 196–7
nature of, 40–1
see also self-consciousness
Copernican Revolution, 116
Course de Philosophie, 27
Course on Positive Philosophy, 167
Cousin, Victor, 27, 39, 57, 63, 175, 185
Crisis of Modern Speculation, The, 60
Critical Philosophy of Kant, 117
criticism, 100, 141
Critique of Pure Reason, 27, 114
Custom, 181–82; and psychology, 186

Darwin, Charles, 148–9, 155, 158, 159, 160–6, 168
and Hume, 149
and metaphysics, 149
and religion, 168
and Scottish Philosophy, 149–50
and theism, 150
as dogma, 156
Darwinism, 146, 199
Davie, George, xiii, 2, 6, 9, 48–57, 60, 64–5, 71, 73, 230

deduction, 77, 80
and Ferrier, 60
Democratic Intellect, The, xiii, 6, 9, 48–57, 65, 230
Democritus, 170
Descartes, René, 2, 77, 106, 215, 216, 223, 226
Descent of Man, and Selection in Relation to Sex, 168
design argument *see* teleological argument
determinism, 89, 150
Dialogues Concerning Natural Religion, 146, 147–8, 151–3, 155, 177
Discussions on Philosophy and Literature, Education and University Reform, 25
divine, nature of, 165, 196–7, 198
dog training, 161–2
dualism, 122, 155–7, 195, 214, 215
and supernaturalism, 156

Edinburgh Philosophical Institution, 108
Edinburgh Review, 24, 25, 53, 114, 134
education, 89, 90, 93, 94
Elements of Rhetoric, 103
Eliot, George, 97
eloquence *see* rhetoric
Emerson, Ralph Waldo, 105
emotion 85–6
and aesthetic education, 92–3
and religion, 93
and rhetoric, 102
Emotions and the Will, 81–4, 86, 94
empiricism, 42, 51, 67, 79–81, 123, 136, 139
and Bain, 87
and Hume, 152, 153
and idealism, 204
and philosophy, 176
and metaphysics, 201
and Seth Pringle-Pattison, 152
and teleology, 199
Lockean, 157

end, the, 145
English Utilitarians, 79
Enquiry Concerning Human Understanding, 186
Epicurus, 163
epistemology 2, 120-1
  and metaphysics, 121
  and psychology, 121
  and science, 170
  reformed, 126
Essay Concerning Human Understanding, An, 102, 126
Essay upon the Relation of Cause and Effect, An, ix
Essays in Philosophical Criticism, 118, 122, 127
Essays on Literature and Philosophy, 69
Essays on the Active Powers of Man, 83, 221, 222
Essays on the Intellectual Powers of Man, 59, 185
ethics, 158-9
  practical, 222
Evolution and Man's Place in Nature, 150, 155, 159
evolution, 153-66
  and beauty, 165
  and the Bible, 161
  and ethics, 158-9
  and intuitionism, 163
  and metaphysics, 149
  and reason, 161
  and teleology, 153-4
  and theory, 160
  and truth, 165
Examination of Professor Ferrier's Theory of Knowing and Being, 57
Examination of Sir William Hamilton's Philosophy, An, 16, 39, 46, 81, 135, 188
existence
  and agency, 198
  and self-consciousness, 196
  understanding of, 198
Experience and its Modes, 3

Experience
  and absolute idealism, 196
  and association, 81
  and emotion, 199
  and logic, 196
  and observation, 201
  and perception, 199
  and philosophy, 144, 197
  explanation of, 202
  understanding of, 198
eyes,
  and knowledge, 41-2
  and perception, 41-2

Ferguson, Adam, 8, 10, 200
Ferrier and the Blackout of the Scottish Enlightenment, 64
Ferrier, James F., xii, 2, 5, 8, 9, 10, 15, 48-74, 88, 115-16, 142, 174-5, 198, 200, 201, 204, 207, 210-12, 216, 229
  and Cairns, 57
  and common sense, 52, 56, 64
  and consciousness, 73-4
  and deduction, 60, 72
  and dualism, 214
  and experience, 214
  and Hamilton, 50-2, 56, 61, 66, 67
  and Hegel, 61, 69-70
  and human mind, 215
  and Hume, 55, 63
  and idealism, 71
  and Kant, 61
  and Macmurray, 209, 210, 213
  and materialism, 171
  and methodology, 60, 72
  and perception, 214
  and rationalism, 60
  and Reid, 51, 55, 56, 59, 78, 193-4
  Collected Works, 71
  contribution of, 70-4
  metaphysics, 71, 184
  'renovation', 52
Fichte, Johann G., 116, 136
Flint, Robert, xii, 17, 54

Fraser, Alexander Campbell, xii, 5, 9, 17, 18, 24, 56–7, 78, 95n, 116, 126–7, 142, 150–1, 174–87, 188, 198, 207
  and Hamilton, 174
  and Hume, 176–7
  and Reid, 175–6, 184–5, 187
  and religion, 94
  biography of, 174–5
Free Church, 52
French Revolution, 96
Frye, Lowell T., 98

Gaskell, Elizabeth, x
Gifford Lectures, The, 172–6
  and truth, 173
Gifford, Lord Adam, 172–76
Glennie, George, 83
God, 155, 172, 179
  and common sense principles, 185
  and experience, 179–80
  and natural law, 185
  and Reid, 185
  as perfect, 180
  existence of, 147–66
  idea of, 200
  knowledge of, 34
  revelation of, 180
Gorgias, 102
Graham, Gordon, 1–19
Green, T.H., 69, 109, 118
Grote, John, 81–2, 86, 136

Haldane, Elizabeth, 73, 193–4
Haldane, R.B., 113, 117, 119, 120, 121–2, 124
Hamilton, Elizabeth, ix
Hamilton, Sir William, xii, 4, 9, 10, 13, 15, 16, 18, 20–47, 53, 117, 134, 141, 142, 172, 185, 188, 200, 204
  and Brown, 134–5
  and Calderwood, 32–4
  and Carlyle, 108
  and common sense, 37–8
  and consciousness, 39–40
  contribution of, 46–7
  and Ferrier, 50–2, 56, 61, 66, 67

  and Fraser, 174
  and Kant, 114
  and methodology, 61
  and perception, 34–7
  and Reid, 115, 192–3
  and scepticism, 37–8
  and Stirling, 34–9, 116–17
  biography of, 22–5
  influence of, 27–32
Handel, George F., 143
Hare, R. M., 2, 11, 74
Hegel, Georg W. F., 3, 9–10, 13, 23, 35, 65, 67, 109, 111, 116, 136, 142, 200
  and Ferrier, 61, 69–70
Hegelianism and Personality, 119, 151
Hegelianism, 113–27, 135, 166, 172, 184, 187
  and philosophy of history, 157
  and Seth Pringle-Pattison, 151, 195–8
History of Scottish Philosophy, A, 15, 18, 188, 206–7
Hobbes, Thomas, 2
human nature, 155–57
  and custom, 181–2
  and knowledge, 183
  science of, 100, 128
humans
  as agents, 222–3
  as doers, 225
  as organisms, 224–5, 226
  as perceivers, 225
  as persons, 224–5, 226
  as spectators, 222–3
Hume, David, ix, xi, 2, 10, 11,14, 16, 18, 19, 21, 27, 28–32, 42, 47, 69, 98, 99–100, 106, 107, 114, 128–35, 137, 141, 142, 146, 147–8, 154, 158–61, 186, 200, 205
  and agnosticism, 180–1
  and Bain, 86–7, 88–92, 94
  and Brown, 184
  and Carlyle, 99
  and Darwin, 149
  and empiricism, 8, 152, 153
  and Ferrier, 55

Hume, David *(cont.)*
　and Fraser, 176–7, 180
　and Kant, 121–2, 195
　and Masson, 112
　and materialism, 171
　and methodology, 77
　and naturalism, 152, 165, 199
　and nature, 153
　and psychology, 182, 184, 186
　and reality, 37
　and reason, 182
　and Reid, 51, 63, 75–8, 80, 153, 195
　and rhetoric, 102
　and Scottish Philosophy, 51, 75–80, 149
　and Seth Pringle-Pattison, 151–2
　dualism, 195
Hutcheson, Francis, 2, 5, 20, 22, 47, 131, 200
Hutton, Sarah, 12–13
Huxley, Thomas, 168

'I think therefore I am', 216, 223
Idea of God in the Light of Recent Philosophy, 151–2, 200, 201, 205
idealism, 27, 31, 42, 52, 54, 65, 66, 67, 70, 74, 200, 207, 209, 226, 227, 229
　Absolute, 192, 196
　and empiricism, 204
　and experience, 214
　and Kant, 191, 199
　and pantheism, 179
　and personalism, 189
　and psychology, 202
　and realism, 60, 109, 113–27, 164, 165, 171, 172
　and Scottish Philosophy, 35, 113–27
　German, 212
ideas, 87, 94
immortality, 172
impressions, 87, 94
India, 179
Infinite, 28, 32–3

Inquiry into the Human Mind upon the Principles of Common Sense, 20, 21, 27, 42, 59, 75, 130–1, 176, 185
instinct, 161
　and intelligence, 163
Institutes of Metaphysics, 56, 57, 60, 61, 65, 67, 71, 73, 116, 175
intelligence, 157, 160–1
　animal, 160–2
　and instinct, 163
Introduction to the Philosophy of Consciousness, xii
intuition, 36–9, 51–2
　and experience, 81
　and evolution, 164
　and morality, 165
　and Reid, 80

James Hutchison Stirling: His Life and Work, xiv
James, William, 25–6
Jardine, George, 22
Jeffrey, Francis, 53
Jessop, Ralph, 98, 99
Jessop, T.E., 10
Jesus, 180
Jones, Henry, 5, 11, 15, 16, 69, 113, 117, 123, 125, 137–38, 142–44
　and Seth Pringle-Pattison, 120–1
Jouffrey, Théodore, 30

Kames, Lord (Henry Home), 200
Kant, Immanuel, 8, 19, 21, 23, 26, 27, 35, 43, 66, 67, 73–4, 78, 109, 111, 113–16, 119, 124, 136, 152
　and Ferrier, 61, 62
　and Hamilton, 114
　and Hume, 121–2
　and idealism, 171
　and morality, 172
　and psychology, 63
　and Reid, 172
　and religion, 172
　and scepticism, 152
　translation of, 113–14

Keefe, Jennifer; and Ferrier, 66
Kemp Smith, Norman, 114, 151, 204
Knight, William, xii, 226
knowledge, 90, 92
   and eyes, 41–2
   and realism, 120
   and the soul, 157
   and truth 124
   nature of, 125–6
   theory of, 120
Knox, Sir Malcolm, 67–8, 227

La Philosophie écossaise, 57
Lady Literate in Arts Diploma (LLA), ix
Lang, Andrew, 173
language
   and communication, 228
   and logic, 229
   and MacMurray, 227
   and thought, 227–29
   nature of, 228
   philosophy of, 227
   see also rhetoric
Laurie, Henry, 10, 62
Lectures on Greek Philosophy, 72
Lectures on Metaphysics and Logic, xii
Lectures on Realism, 120
Lectures on Rhetoric and Belles Lettres, 103, 105
Lectures on the Philosophy of the Human Mind, 79, 133, 134
Leibniz, G.W., 114, 180
Leviathan, 3
Lewes, G. H., xi, 169
libertarianism, 149
Life of Edward Irving, Minister of the National Scotch Church London, xiii
Life of Henry Calderwood, The, 14
Limits of Religious Thought, The, 25
Lindsay, A.D., 204
linguistic analysis, 229
Literature and Dogma, 168
Locke, John, 2, 40, 41, 66, 81, 102, 107, 126–27, 155, 200
   and empiricism, 157

logic
   and experience, 196
   and rhetoric, 99
Logic, Truth and Language, 8

McCosh, James, 5, 7, 10, 22, 24, 54, 56, 60, 62, 75, 175, 201, 202, 207
McDermid, Douglas, 60, 70, 71
   and Ferrier, 65–6
Macdougall, Patrick Campbell, 54
MacIntosh, James, 114
MacIntyre, Alasdair, 2
Macmurray, John, 18, 206–230
   and Bain, 209, 212n
   and Brown, 209
   and empiricism, 213
   and Ferrier, 209, 210, 213
   and Hume, 209, 219
   and Kant, 213–15
   and language, 227
   and Smith, 209
   and Veitch, 212n
   biography of, 208
   personalism, 209
Mair, John, 206-07
Man's Place in the Cosmos, 151
Mander, W. J., 26, 40, 71
   and Ferrier, 66–7
Mansel, Henry, 25, 40-2, 57
Masson, David, xiii, 46, 97n, 111–12
   and Carlyle, 95, 111
   and Hume 112
materialism, 31, 42, 71, 150, 179, 198
   and Bain, 85, 136-7
   and consciousness, 178
   and Ferrier, 171
   and Hume, 171
   and observation, 178
   and pantheism, 179
   and self-destruction, 178
   anti-, 171–2
   scientific, 170, 183
   spiritual, 163
   universal, 177–8

mathematics
  and evolutionary biology, 163
matter, 216, 219, 227
  in motion, 199
Mayo, Bernard, 2, 71, 73–4
meaning of life, the, 183
Meiklejohn, J.M.D., 114
Memoir of the Life of John Tulloch, xiii
Memoirs of Modern Philosophers, ix
Memories of Two Cities, xiii, 46
Mental and Moral Science, 83, 86
Metaphysics of Ethics, 114
metaphysics, 51, 58, 60, 63, 69, 139, 141, 155–7
  and Comte, 140–1
  and evolutionary biology, 163
  and Ferrier, 41
  and morality, 170
  and psychology, 63, 88
  as verbalism, 169
  inductive, 169–70
  theistic, 186
methodology, 61, 121–2
  agnostic, 182
  and Ferrier, 60, 72
  and Hume, 77
  and natural world, 182
Mill, J.S., 10, 11, 16, 19, 39–46, 73, 81, 93, 96n, 123, 135, 167–8, 171, 188, 200
  and Bain, 84, 90, 94
  and consciousness, 39–40
  and Hamilton, 39–41
mind, 10–11, 28, 30, 136, 181–2
  and Bain, 136
  and evolution, 160
  and inductive science, 175
  and matter, 177–9
  and nature, 170, 199
  and scepticism, 186
  as belief forming, 186
  as consciousness, 169
  as fundamental, 199
  as truth seeking, 186
  conception of, 20–47
  theory of, 2, 40, 80–2, 83
  see also science of mind

Mind, 63, 113, 118, 120, 207
Minto, William, 104
miracles, 170
Modern Theories of Philosophy and Religion, xii, 168, 170
monism, 183
Moore, G. E., 2, 3
moral education, 90–1
moral ideals, 91
moral philosophy, concept of, 3
  and psychology, 75–94
  as science, 77
  see also philosophy
morality, 158
  and biology, 158–9, 163
  and duty, 221
  and feeling, 220–1, 222
  and human mind, 221
  and intuition, 165
  and metaphysics, 170
  and pantheism, 180
  and remorse, 180
  and survival, 158–69
  judgement, 222
  theory of, 222
Müller, Max, 173
Murray, John Clark, 25
music
  and evolutionary biology, 163
  and progress, 143
Mylne, James, 22
mysticism, 27

Natural History of Religion, 177, 222
Natural Law and Enlightenment Classics, 6
natural selection, 163
  and rationality, 164
  see also evolution; Darwinism
naturalism, 106-07, 149, 155–57
  higher, 157
  and Hume, 152, 165
  and Seth Pringle-Pattison, 152, 157
nature, 170
  and experience, 181
  and God, 185
  and human mind, 170, 199

and materialism, 199
and reality, 179
and systems, 163-4, 169
see also supernaturalism
Newtonianism, 154
non-contradiction, law of, 201
North British Review, 175
Notes and Supplementary Dissertations, 35

Oakeshott, Michael, 3
observation, 77, 80, 153
　and consciousness, 60
　and experience, 201
　and reason, 152
　and teleological argument, 152
Oliphant, Margaret, ix-xiv
omniscience, 183
On the Origin of Species by Means of Natural Selection, 168
ontology, 122;
　see also metaphysics
organisms, 153-4
　and teleology, 154
Oswald, James, 78
Outline of Sir William Hamilton's Philosophy, 25
Oxford Companion to Philosophy, 207
Oxford Handbook of British Philosophy in the Nineteenth Century, 15, 189
Oxford Realists, 11

pan-psychism, 199
panegoism, 178-9
　as absurdity, 178
　and human mind, 177
pantheism, 179
　and God, 177
　and idealism, 179
　and materialism, 179
　and morality, 180
　and nature, 179
　elasticity of, 179
perception, 34-7, 153
　and consciousness, 29-31
　and eyes, 41-2

and Hamilton, 34-7
and Reid, 38
and scepticism, 36
and sensation, 36
personalism, 189
　and idealism, 189
　and materialist psychology, 189
　and naturalism, 189
　and rationalism, 189
Persons in Relation, 224
persons, 224-25
　and reality, 189
　and the body, 219
　as fundamental, 219
　individuality of, 119
persuasion
　and rhetoric, 102
pessimism, 170
phenomenalism, 35, 41-2
Philo, 162
Philosophical Investigations, 3
Philosophical Remains, 55, 72, 73
Philosophical Review, 113, 120, 151
Philosophy of Consciousness, 175
Philosophy of Kant, 117
Philosophy of Perception, 134
Philosophy of Rhetoric, The, 103
Philosophy of the Conditioned, The, 40
Philosophy of the Infinite with special reference to the theories of Sir William Hamilton and M Cousin, 32, 34
Philosophy of Theism, The, xii, 126, 127, 174, 175, 176, 183
philosophy
　and empiricism, 176
　and experience, 144, 197
　and history, 141-2
　and life, 194-5
　as perennial, 201
　and rationality, 102
　and reality, 196
　and science, 129-30, 141, 144
　and Scottish Philosophy, 58-9
　and teleology, 198
　and women, ix-xiv, 12-13
　as activity, 143

philosophy *(cont.)*
  history of, 3, 14
  nature of, 42
  of mind, 2, 80–2, 83
  principles of 58–9
  purpose of, 196
  study of, 2–19
  vs science, 42
  see also moral philosophy; Scottish philosophy
Plantinga, Alvin, 126
Plato, 2, 47, 116, 155, 171
  and rhetoric, 102
pleasures, 93
Porter, Noah, 25
positivism, 140, 169–70, 199
  and Bain, 168
  and theism, 167
  logical, 11
power, 177
practicality, 216
presentationism, 35, 41–2
Priestley, Joseph, 57
Princeton Review, 60
Princeton University, 7, 10, 202
Principles of Biology, 168
Pringle-Pattison *see* Seth Pringle-Pattison
Problem of Knowledge in Scottish Philosophy, The, 6, 48
Proceedings of the British Academy, 127
psychology, 16, 39–47, 121–25, 158
  and Bain, 136, 145
  and custom, 186
  and epistemology, 121
  and Hume, 182, 184, 185–6
  and Kant, 63
  and metaphysics, 62–3, 88
  and moral philosophy, 75–94, 139–42
  phenomena, 86
  and Reid, 176, 186
  and science, 139
  and Seth Pringle-Pattison, 139–40
  and teleology, 148
  and the senses, 182
  empirical, 139

Queen's University Belfast, 10

Rational Philosophy in History and in System, 175
Rational Theology and Christian Philosophy, 171
rationalism, 51–2, 77, 229
  and Ferrier, 60
  and personalism, 189
  and Reid, 78
rationality, 161
  and behaviour, 159, 160
  and natural selection, 164
  and theology, 167
realism, 119, 127, 149
  and idealism, 60
  and knowledge, 120
  and Seth Pringle-Pattison, 151
  hypothetical, 31–2, 36, 38, 41, 115
  natural, 27–40, 115, 152
reality
  and human mind, 195
  and nature, 179
  and person, 189
  and philosophy, 196
  and thought 122
  and truth, 122, 124
  infinite, 179
reason, 29, 60, 77, 92
  and action, 221, 223
  and agency, 215
  and belief, 221
  and causality, 180
  and dualism, 215
  and evolution, 161
  and experience, 29
  and God, 162
  and Hume, 182
  as motivation, 102
  and nature, 220, 223
  and observation, 152
  and reflection, 216
  and scepticism, 180
  and senses, 186
  and theism, 187
  and thought, 114
  practical, 215, 218, 221, 222, 226
  pure, 215
  theoretical, 221, 222, 226

reductionism, 54, 197, 198, 200
Reformation, The, 207
Reid, Thomas, ix, 2, 4, 5, 8, 9, 10, 19, 20–3, 25–7, 28–32, 35, 40, 42, 47, 56–7, 65, 66, 75, 77, 83, 98, 101, 112, 114, 117, 119, 123, 124–5, 127, 132–4, 138, 141, 142, 152, 184
  and Bain, 86
  and Carlyle, 99
  and common sense, 10, 171
  and Ferrier, 51, 55, 56, 59, 78
  and Fraser, 175–6, 184–5, 187
  and God, 185
  and Hamilton, 115
  and human mind, 30, 153
  and Hume, 51, 63, 75–8, 80, 128–32, 153
  and intuition, 80
  and Kant, 172
  and perception, 38
  and psychology, 63, 176, 184, 185–6
  and rationalism, 78
  and religion, 94
  and rhetoric, 102–3
  and scepticism, 152
  and Stewart, 131–2
  and teleology, 186
  and theism, 166
Reid's Collected Works, 6, 30
Religion 93–4, 146–66
  and emotion, 93
  and supernaturalism, 170
  see also theism
remorse, 180
representationalism, 195
Republic, The, 102
rhetoric, 95–112
  and emotion, 102
  and logic, 99
  and persuasion, 102
  and Plato, 102
  and practicalities, 100–1
  as intellectual cultivation, 101–2
  constituents of, 101
  new conception of, 101–4
Rise and Fall of Scottish Common Sense Realism, 65

Ritchie, David G., 9, 10, 113, 117, 119–20, 121–2, 138, 142, 144, 163–5, 187
Romanes, George, 160
Rousseau, Jean-Jacques, 2, 106
Royer-Collard, Pierre, 30
Russell, Bertrand, 2, 229
Ryle, Gilbert, 2, 11

Sartor Resartus, 105–7, 109–11
scepticism, 28–32, 51, 58, 75, 77, 86, 115, 150, 170, 183
  and common sense, 193
  and Hamilton, 37–8
  and human mind, 186
  and perception, 36
  and reason, 180
  Hume on, 181
Schelling, F.W.J, 23, 116
Schiller, Friedrich, 97
Schleiermacher, Friedrich, 170
science of mind, 80–2, 94
  and philosophy of mind, 88
  and psychology, 88
science
  and causality, 153
  and epistemology, 170
  and human mind, 175
  and philosophy, 129–30, 141, 144
  and progress, 143
  vs philosophy, 42
Scots Philosophical Club, 226
Scottish Philosophical: Biographical, Expository, Critical, from Hutcheson to Hamilton, 10
Scottish Philosophy as Contrasted with the German, The, 136
Scottish Philosophy in its National Development, 10, 62
Scottish Philosophy in the Nineteenth and Twentieth Centuries, 15
Scottish Philosophy, 128–46
  and Bain, 82–8
  and Brown, 132–4
  and common sense, 79, 206–7
  and Darwin, 149–50
  and the Disruption, 50
  and evolution, 147–66
  and Hume, 51, 75–80, 149

Scottish Philosophy *(cont.)*
  and idealism 9, 35, 113–27
  and induction, 201
  and Macmurray, 206–30
  and Reid, 132–34, 138
  and religion, 147–66
  and theism, 183–4
  Chronology of, xv-xvii
  conception of, 11–19
  culmination of, 188–205
  development of, 48–74
  methodology 14, 60
  old and new, 55–62, 64, 115–16
  revitalisation of, 20–47, 79
  trajectory of 13–14, 183–4
  University of Edinburgh, 50–5
Scottish Philosophy, Journal of, 2, 7
Scottish Philosophy: A Comparison of the Scottish and German Answers to Hume, xii, 114, 119, 151, 152, 172
Scottish Philosophy: A Vindication and Reply, 57
Scottish Philosophy: Biographical, Expository, Critical, from Hutcheson to Hamilton, The, 62, 75
Scottish Philosophy: The Old and the New, 55, 57–8, 59
Scottish Universities, development of, 203–4
Secret of Hegel, The, 15, 34, 54, 67, 68, 116, 117, 136, 184
Segerstedt, Torgny, 6, 48
self-consciousness, 201
  and existence, 196
  divine, 196–7
  human, 196–7
  see also consciousness
self, 124, 165
  and knowledge, 216
  and other, 217–18
  and scepticism, 226
  and solipsism, 226
  as agent, 210–30
  as reflective being, 215, 216
Sellers, Wilfred, 125–6
Semple, J.W., 114

sensationalism, 41, 42, 107, 116
sensations, 41
  and perception, 36
  and reality, 41
Sense and Sensibilia, 2
Senses and the Intellect, The, 81, 83, 84–5, 94
senses, 183
  and reason, 186
  perception of, 217
  touch, 217
Seth Pringle-Pattison, Andrew, xii, 8, 10, 11, 12, 15, 18, 65, 73, 103, 113, 117, 121–4, 127, 150–1, 153, 155–7, 165, 166, 172, 175, 188–205, 207, 230
  and categories, 119
  and empiricism, 152
  and Hegelianism, 151–52, 192, 195–8
  and Hume, 151–2
  as idealist, 189, 192
  and Jones, 120–1
  and Kant, 191
  and naturalism, 152, 157
  and personalism, 189–91
  and realism, 151
  and Reid, 192, 194
  and Scottish idealists, 151
  biography of, 190
Seth, James, 26, 45–6, 69, 78, 86, 204
Shakespeare, William, 110–11
Shepherd, Mary, ix
Shooting Niagara, 95
Sidgwick, H., 204
Sir William Hamilton: Being the Philosophy of Perception – An Analysis, 34
Smith, Adam, 2, 4, 10, 19, 100, 112, 200
Smith, John, 57, 61
Smith, William, 169
sociability, 90–1
Socrates, 47, 180
solipsism, 226
Sorley, W.R., 70, 117, 204
Spectator, The, 96

Speeches on Religion, 170
Spencer, Herbert, 168, 168n
Spinoza, 77, 177, 180
    as atheist, 179
Stanford Encyclopedia of Philosophy, 15, 189
Stephen, Leslie, ix, 79
Stevenson, John, 104
Stewart, Dugald, 4, 10, 21, 23, 53, 59, 79, 112, 114
    and common sense principles, 184
    and methodology, 61
Stirling, Amelia Hutchison, xiv
Stirling, James Hutchison, 9–10, 15–16, 17, 34–9, 42, 54, 61, 67, 68, 108, 116, 135–6, 137, 172, 173–4, 184, 187, 207
    and Bain, 135–6
    and German philosophy, 136
    and Hamilton, 116–17
Stout, G. F., 49, 72–3
Strawson, P.F., 74
supernaturalism, 155, 199
    dualistic, 156
    natural, 107, 109
    and religion, 170
Swift, Jonathan, 110
System of Logic, 16, 84, 167

teleological argument, 144–5, 147, 149, 162, 165, 198
    and Bain, 145
    and biology, 154
    and empiricism, 199
    and evolution, 153–4
    and psychology, 148
    and Reid, 186
    and Seth Pringle-Pattison, 145
    natural, 155
Textbook to Kant, A, 136, 172
theism, 71, 149, 145–6, 155–7, 161–6, 175–6
    and common sense, 187
    and Darwinism, 150
    and India, 179
    and metaphysics, 125–7
    and positivism, 167
    and reason, 187
    and Scottish Philosophy, 183–4
    and universe, 183
    Calvinism, 167
    conceptions of universe, 183
    re-affirmation of 167–87
    see also pantheism; panegoism; materialism
Theism: the Witness of Reason and Nature to an All-Wise and Beneficient Creator, 167
thought, 114, 122, 218
Treatise of Human Nature, A, xi, 75, 77, 87, 89–90, 92, 94, 99–100, 102, 111, 128–35, 137, 158, 180, 181, 219–22
Treatise on Sociology, Instituting the Religion of Humanity, 167
truth, 44–5, 58, 90, 92
    and evolution, 165
    and knowledge, 124
    and motivation, 102
    and nature, 143
    and reality, 122, 124
Tulloch, John, xii, 16, 48–9, 73, 167–72, 204
Turnbull, George, 20, 101
Tylor, E.B., 173
Tyndall, John, 169

understanding, 29, 142
Universities Scotland Act, ix
University College London, 108
University of Aberdeen, 20, 81, 104
    Marischal College, 103
University of Edinburgh, 2, 18, 20, 23, 103, 104, 107
    and Hume, 53
    and Scottish Philosophy, 50–5
University of Glasgow, 20, 117
University of St Andrews, 1–2, 4, 20, 104, 108, 112, 167
Ussher, Archbishop, 148
utilitarianism, 16, 93
Utility of Religion, The, 168

Veitch, John, 9, 10, 15, 18, 24, 25, 27, 43–5, 104, 174, 204, 207, 212

Veterum Laudes, 67
Votiva Tabella, 49, 72

Wallace, A.R., 163
Watt Smith, G., 93
Welsh, David, 133–4
Whateley, Richard, 103
Whigs, 53
will, 198, 199
Wilson, John, 53–4
Wilson, Margaret *see* Oliphant
Witherspoon, John, 7, 10
Wittgenstein, Ludwig, 3, 125, 229
Wolterstorff, Nicholas, 126
women, and education, ix
   and philosophy, ix–xiv, 12–13
world, explanation of the, 151–5

Zeitgeist, 169